THE SOCIAL WORK CAREER GUIDEBOOK

HOW TO **Land Your Ideal Job** AND **Build a Legacy**

Jennifer Luna, Cindy Snell, and Michelle Woods

NASW PRESS

National Association of Social Workers
Washington, DC

Yvonne Elder Chase, PhD, LCSW, ACSW, *President*
Anthony Estreet, PhD, MBA, LCSW-C, *Chief Executive Officer*

Cheryl Y. Bradley, *Publisher*
Rachel Meyers, *Acquisitions Editor*
Julie Gutin, *Project Manager*

First impression: September 2024

© 2024 by the NASW Press

All rights reserved. No part of this book may be reproduced or transmitted in any form or by any means, electronic or mechanical, including photocopying, recording, or by any information storage and retrieval system, without permission in writing from the publisher.

Library of Congress Cataloging-in-Publication Data

Names: Luna, Jennifer, 1966- author. | Snell, Cindy, 1965- author. | Woods, Michelle, 1968- author.
Title: The social work career guidebook : how to land your ideal job and build a legacy / by Jennifer Luna, Cindy Snell, and Michelle Woods.
Description: Washington, DC : NASW Press, [2024] | Includes bibliographical references and index. | Summary: "This book offers social workers an intentional, inspired, and visionary approach to job searching. Using the career trajectory model of the professional development cycle of social workers, the authors will set you on a path toward your dream job. Hands-on exercises will prepare you for your job search, including self-assessment tools that identify your skills, career-defining moments, and target areas for growth. You will learn to give an 'elevator pitch' at social events, seek out and conduct informational interviews, and grow your network of mentors and like-minded professionals. The authors will guide you through applying for jobs, interviewing, evaluating offers, negotiating salary and benefits, and successfully onboarding at your new job"—Provided by publisher.
Identifiers: LCCN 2024023042 (print) | LCCN 2024023043 (ebook) | ISBN 9780871016034 (paperback) | ISBN 9780871016041 (ebook)
Subjects: LCSH: Vocational guidance. | Social workers.
Classification: LCC HF5381 .L7825 2024 (print) | LCC HF5381 (ebook) | DDC 361.3023—dc23/eng/20240819
LC record available at https://lccn.loc.gov/2024023042
LC ebook record available at https://lccn.loc.gov/2024023043

Printed in the United States of America

Table of Contents

Preface: Why We Wrote This Book v
Introduction vii
Chapter 1   A Road Map to the Profession of Social Work 1
Chapter 2   Social Work Career Planning for Advancement and Fulfillment 21
Chapter 3   Assessing Need and Building Relationships: Determine Your Career Direction 33
Chapter 4   Creating Your Brand Identity as a Social Work Agent of Change 51
Chapter 5   Your Resume, Cover Letters, LinkedIn Profile, and Other Job Search Materials 63
Chapter 6   Implementing Your Job Search Plan 91
Chapter 7   Evaluating and Negotiating Job Offers 119
Chapter 8   Mapping Your Legacy as a Social Work Agent of Change 133
Appendix A   Comprehensive List of Social Work Skills 155
Appendix B   Assess Your Career Stage with the PDCSW Assessment Tool 169
Appendix C   Sample Informational Interview Questions 177
Appendix D   Career-Defining Moments, Patterns, and Professional Themes 179
Appendix E   Sample Resumes and Curriculum Vitae 181
Appendix F   Sample Cover Letters and Other Job Search Correspondence 207
Appendix G   Sample Questions to Evaluate Organizational Fit 225
Appendix H   Determine Your Budget 227
Appendix I   Evaluate Job Offers 231
References 233
Index 235
Acknowledgments 241
About the Authors 245

Preface: Why We Wrote This Book

As directors of career services at top schools of social work in Texas (Jennifer Luna), Massachusetts (Cindy Snell), and Michigan (Michelle Woods), the three of us have been coaching and advising generations of social workers over many decades. We each bring our unique life story and professional background to help inform our work with social workers throughout their careers.

The social work students and alumni in our respective schools have had access to career professionals who provided resources, advice, and support through their career advancement. Unfortunately, this is not the case for most social workers. Some observations we have made in our work:

- Social workers are good at and comfortable with advocating for others but not themselves.
- Social work is a broad field, and social workers contribute in many different roles and settings. While this allows for a multitude of career options, creativity, and flexibility, it can be challenging to find your direction.
- There are a lot of career development books geared toward the for-profit world, and there is a need for those more focused on careers in nonprofit or governmental organizations, where most social workers are employed.

We wrote this book to share the wisdom and experience we have gathered over the years and allow you, the reader, to feel informed, supported, and in charge of your career progression, throughout your career journey. With knowledge in hand, you, as a job searcher, can feel more confident and better able to be an agent of change in your own career advancement.

Introduction

Are you new to the field of social work? Or are you an experienced social worker thinking about changing your specialization? Are you hoping to take that next step into leadership? Or perhaps you are returning to work after a long absence? Wherever you are in your journey, let this book be your guide to a rewarding social work career.

You are reading this book because you want to have a job that is fulfilling and meaningful to you. You are reading this book to find direction and practical tips for your job search. You are reading this book because you want to be strategic about your career journey. You are reading this book because you want to maximize your impact on the clients and communities you serve. You are reading this book because you are an *agent of change*, both personally and professionally. So, jump in, read, and explore!

Social workers are often referred to as agents of change because they join the social work profession with the intention of making the world a better place, to effect change in improving the lives of vulnerable people at the individual, community, and systems levels. Social workers are committed to social justice and to challenging social injustice. Agents of change identify the need for change, advocate for change, and are the catalysts of change.

We think the following definition captures the essence of an agent of change that describes both a social worker and a successful job searcher.

> An agent of change is someone who sees a problem in their community, large or small, and does something to take action for substantial change. This person is someone who listens to the people in the community where the issue exists and makes sure that they truly understand the root of the problem before implementing a new idea. This person is someone who is willing to take risks and doesn't always claim to know the answer. They are willing to ask hard questions and help find creative solutions. An agent of change has the courage to think outside the box and makes an impact that is greater than themself. (Jennifer Ciok, Education Pioneers, quoted in Escalante, 2023, para. 3)

As seasoned career advisors, we are firm believers that everyone should be actively engaged in the management of their careers. Throughout this book, you will find many parallels between an agent of change and a successful job seeker. In fact, the characteristics of agents of change—assessment, informed decision making, taking action, relationship building, risk-taking, and creativity—are critical in managing your career so that it is rewarding, impactful, and sustaining over a lifetime. This book is written to give you the tools to be a successful agent of change in your career. We encourage you to embrace change and self-advocacy and use this book as a road map to building your legacy.

Why is considering your legacy important? As a social worker, you are committed to making an impact that will be remembered long after you are gone. This impact could be made up of a multitude of "career moments" throughout your life, both modest and significant achievements. A strong legacy can demonstrate the impact of social work to the broader community, including policymakers, funders, and the public. Finally, leaving a legacy can provide a sense of personal fulfillment and satisfaction, knowing that your work has had a positive impact on others and will continue to do so for years to come. We are fortunate to have chosen a career in which we can make a lasting impact nearly every single day. Imagine if we were more intentional about this journey. Imagine what your legacy could be if you mapped it out. For this reason, we have incorporated legacy as part of the career management process throughout the book.

We will start this career journey together by orienting you to the broad field of social work, providing examples of career trajectories and offering practical tips on how to manage your career in social work with intention. We then provide self-assessment tools that will help you determine your best fit in the field based on your current interests and experience. This information will, in turn, help you determine the career direction that will play to your strengths and interests and provide professional fulfillment along the way.

After you identify the next steps in your career path, this book will help you create the tools and strategies to reach your destination through effective branding and networking, including writing your resume and making online and in-person connections. We will provide guidance on your job search, including the application and interview process. We will help you effectively negotiate and evaluate job offers to ensure they meet your needs both personally and professionally. Finally, we will discuss strategies for mid- to late-stage social work career development and provide a framework for maximizing opportunities.

CHAPTER 1: A ROAD MAP TO THE PROFESSION OF SOCIAL WORK

Social work is a broad field with diverse career paths. In this chapter, we will discuss the depth and breadth of this profession including the roles and settings that social workers can pursue and the populations they can work with. We will define and give examples of micro, mezzo, and macro social work careers both domestically and internationally. We will include examples of job postings, key skills, and various case studies spanning different stages of a social work career from entry level through seasoned professional.

CHAPTER 2: SOCIAL WORK CAREER PLANNING FOR ADVANCEMENT AND FULFILLMENT

This chapter will present a career trajectory model of the Professional Development Cycle of Social Workers (PDCSW), which will provide you with insight into the typical career path of a social worker. From there, we will provide strategic tips on how to advance your career, by either moving forward on your current path or stepping back to gain additional skills. This process also identifies crucial opportunities to enhance your expertise, increase your visibility, and maximize your career prospects. By applying suggested tips and tailoring them to your career trajectory, you will set a path toward your dream job, career fulfillment, and, ultimately, your legacy.

CHAPTER 3: ASSESSING NEED AND BUILDING RELATIONSHIPS: DETERMINE YOUR CAREER DIRECTION

In this chapter, self-assessment is discussed as a critical component of informed career decision making. We will provide definitions, samples, and strategies for gathering information about your skills, qualities, priorities, and knowledge based on self-awareness and reflection on past experiences. Through several exercises, you will gain a better sense of what you would like to do, what skills you have, and what type of organization you find most rewarding. Using this information as a framework, we will share tips on how to identify career opportunities through research and informational interviewing.

CHAPTER 4: CREATING YOUR BRAND IDENTITY AS A SOCIAL WORK AGENT OF CHANGE

Building on the information you have gained through assessments and research discussed in chapters 2 and 3, chapter 4 will help you identify career-defining moments, themes of your work, and "power words" to create an appealing professional brand. You will learn how to create a persuasive bio statement, professional summary, and "elevator pitch" through exercises and samples.

CHAPTER 5: YOUR RESUME, COVER LETTERS, LINKEDIN PROFILE, AND OTHER JOB SEARCH MATERIALS

Creating winning applications—including customized resumes, cover letters, and your LinkedIn profile—is critical to your successful job search. This chapter will outline the essential items you will need to showcase your skills and experience through your application materials. We will show you how to create a resume and cover letter that stand out in a variety of job search scenarios. We also guide the reader on creating an engaging and welcoming online presence.

CHAPTER 6: IMPLEMENTING YOUR JOB SEARCH PLAN

This chapter will take you through the major steps of the job search, including identifying job opportunities, effectively networking, and creating a winning job application. We provide extensive information on how to prepare for and deliver a successful job interview, including sample responses and interviewer questions that will impress any potential employer.

CHAPTER 7: EVALUATING AND NEGOTIATING JOB OFFERS

You got an offer! Now is the time when all your hard work and strategizing will pay off. This chapter will help you to evaluate employment opportunities, such as deciding whether the job offer aligns with your career goals, assessing the organizational culture of your potential new employer, and reviewing the compensation package. Once you accept your job offer, a smooth transition to your new position is key. We will discuss the process of onboarding and strategies for early success in your new position.

CHAPTER 8: MAPPING YOUR LEGACY AS A SOCIAL WORK AGENT OF CHANGE

Career development does not end when you get the job. Rather, social work is a career of lifelong learning and development. Successful social workers make a commitment to maximize impact or create legacy by sharing their expertise, continuing their education, seeking professional advancement opportunities, and professional networking. This chapter will cover the career management challenges and opportunities that arise over the course of a typical social work career. As we embark on our journey in social work, we must remember that our career is not confined to a single role but is a lifelong dedication to growth and service. Our commitment to making a difference will ripple through the lives we touch, carving out a legacy that extends far beyond ourselves. As we navigate the challenges and opportunities of our careers, we strive to build a legacy that inspires future generations of social workers to continue the pursuit of positive change and empowerment in the individuals, organizations, and communities we serve.

Throughout the book are useful tools for every stage of your career journey, including action plans, takeaways, case studies, and exercises. Appendices provide useful references, including inventories of skills by function, sample resumes and branding statements, and a guide to creating a personal budget to assist with salary negotiations. This book is not intended to be read from cover to cover and then put back on the shelf. It is meant to be an interactive reference that social workers can employ at any time in their career. We encourage you to take notes in the margins, highlight tips that speak to you, flag inspiring pages, and underline thought-provoking advice. Let us begin this exciting journey!

CHAPTER 1

A Road Map to the Profession of Social Work

What You Will Learn

- ❏ The definitions of the three scopes of practice: micro, mezzo, and macro
- ❏ An overview of the five major areas of social work practice: generalist, clinical, macro, international, and nontraditional
- ❏ Sample skill sets, job titles, positions, descriptions, and case studies for each area of practice

Action Plan

- ❏ Acquaint yourself with the different practice options in the field of social work
- ❏ Consider how the work you have done or want to do fits into these categories
- ❏ Use this information to start thinking about next steps in your career advancement

---

This book offers a lifelong road map to your social work career, providing guideposts as you find your career path, change directions, or chart a new course. Social work is broad and offers myriad opportunities to contribute to the field you find rewarding. While this broad array of choices brings many people into this profession, it can be overwhelming to new graduates or seasoned social workers making a career change. The purpose of this chapter is to orient you so you can best maneuver your way to your destination. We will define and give examples of micro, mezzo, and macro social work careers both domestically and internationally. We will describe five scopes of social work practice: generalist, clinical, macro, international, and nontraditional. Under each scope of practice, we will explore a variety of job titles and skills, required degrees, professional licensure and certification information, and sample job descriptions. Case studies of clients we have worked with over the years will illustrate social work's vast career options. For those of you who are mid-career or thinking of seeking a PhD or DSW, we have included this information in chapter 8, which provides an overview of advanced careers in social work.

As we look at the profession from a career planning perspective, let us begin with the foundations on which the profession is built. Social work is unique in that it is grounded in the National Association of Social Workers' (NASW; 2021) *Code of Ethics*. Let us begin with the mission of social work according to the code:

> The primary mission of the social work profession is to enhance human well-being and help meet the basic human needs of all people, with particular attention to the needs and empowerment of people who are vulnerable, oppressed, and living in poverty. A historic and defining feature of social work is the profession's dual focus on individual well-being in a social context and the well-being of society. Fundamental to social work is attention to the environmental forces that create, contribute to, and address problems in living. (NASW, 2021, p. 1)

While the mission of social work as defined by the *Code of Ethics* is broad in its scope, encompassing various aspects of human well-being and societal issues, it can be challenging to apply it to the multifaceted nature of the work required to fulfill this mission. Breaking it down into layers can be helpful. In order to understand the depth and breadth of the social work profession, it is important to know that

> the practice of social work is divided into three systems, which are like layers, one building off the next. At the center is the "person-in-environment" (PIE) theory, which is central to and connects all three systems: micro, mezzo and macro social work. (Conrad-Amlicke, n.d., para. 4)

In the *Social Workers' Desk Reference*, researchers James M. Karls and Maura E. O'Keefe (2009) defined *person in environment* as the way to reference the complex problems that people face related to their social functioning and "in terms of societal constructs." The person-in-environment framework is based on the belief that individuals can best be understood in the context of their environment, which includes their family, health, spiritual beliefs, social identity, and political views. This is why social work is different from other similar helping professions and why it offers a broad scope of career opportunities. Micro, mezzo, and macro practice all focus on improving well-being but differ in method, scope of impact, and how closely you work with the benefitting population. Many social work positions have a combination of micro, mezzo, and macro focused practice.

- **Micro Practice:** Micro social work focuses on helping individuals, families, and groups with emotional, financial, or basic needs, and is often referred to as "direct practice" or "clinical work." The focus of this work is to provide one-on-one assistance to help clients meet challenges through social services, counseling, or healthcare. An example of this type of work would be a domestic violence advocate for a client seeking assistance in a family violence center.
- **Mezzo Practice:** Mezzo practice provides direct work but in small communities, such as schools, churches, and neighborhoods. The focus of this work is to assist small groups of people through advocacy, community organizing, or program development; for example, creating a food pantry. Another example of mezzo work would be a school social worker who assists parents by organizing a community health fair to provide vaccinations and resources for general wellness.
- **Macro Practice:** Macro practice addresses social problems, with a broader view of impacting systematic injustice or change. This type of work includes policy, research, and evaluation. An example of this type of work would be a social worker who works at a public policy think tank to research and write policy related to children and Medicaid.

Social workers are increasingly working at more than one level of practice in one job. This is one of the great advantages of the social work profession! Many jobs allow you to create a niche for yourself by gaining skills in different areas depending on the needs of the clients. For example, a school social worker often helps individual students one-on-one (micro) and also creates and facilitates social skills groups (mezzo). Next, we will discuss the different types of social work that fall within micro, mezzo, and macro practice, including the five areas: generalist, clinical, macro, international, and nontraditional. Appendix A: Comprehensive List of Social Work Skills shows you which skills you will need to develop, depending on which area of practice speaks to you.

GENERALIST SOCIAL WORK

Generalist social work is commonly practiced at the BSW level but can also be practiced at the MSW level. Generalist social workers know the basic concepts of social work at the micro, mezzo, and macro levels, including the ability to apply preventative care and intervention to individuals, families, groups, organizations, and communities while following ethical principles defined by NASW and social work licensure. Common skills include screening, assessment, problem solving, identification of resources and referrals, and using a strengths-based, systems theory approach. Generalists are trained to integrate direct practice, social policy, and research into their chosen career paths. Many social workers who follow a generalist career path choose positions in casework, community organizing, policy development, or nonprofit coordination. They are trained to facilitate groups; conduct research; and broker between clients, agencies, and other sources to help clients. These social workers also possess relevant communication skills, including empathetic listening, case documentation, and advocacy.

Licensure for Generalist Social Work

Each state currently determines the levels and requirements for social work licensure. In some states, a person with a BSWs is eligible to be licensed as a social worker at the bachelor's level. The bachelor's-level social work license may be required in some states for certain roles as case managers, volunteer coordinators, community outreach workers, and child or adult protective services workers.

Sample Job Titles

Some of the job titles that you may encounter as a generalist social worker include:

- Intake specialist
- Case worker/manager
- Entry-level social worker
- Family service specialist
- Volunteer coordinator
- Community engagement coordinator
- Group facilitator
- Human services coordinator

Sample Skills

Some of the knowledge areas and skills that a generalist social worker needs to know include:

- Assessment skills
- Case management
- Client-centered approaches
- Community outreach
- Development and implementation of service plans
- Knowledge of human behavior and theory
- Verbal, oral, and written communication skills
- Understanding of group dynamics
- Interpretation of laws and policies
- Designing, planning, and leading programs

For a more comprehensive list of generalist social work skills, see Appendix A. Box 1.1 features a generalist job description, demonstrating how generalist skills and knowledge can help define the role of a particular job title.

> **Box 1.1**
>
> **Sample Generalist Job Description: Medical Social Worker, BSW**
>
> **Job Description**
>
> Under the supervision of a clinical social worker, support patients and families dealing with medically related problems by connecting with appropriate resources.
>
> **Responsibilities**
>
> - Assess patients and their families to determine their needs and eligibility for services
> - Develop and implement a service plan and provide services to patients and families, including resolution of practical problems of daily living
> - Connect with outside agencies and coordinate referrals
> - Maintain appropriate documentation
> - Generate and maintain current list of hospital and community services and resources
> - Support families and social work team with patient discharge planning
> - Maintain contact with insurance companies to secure authorizations for admission and ongoing care
>
> **Qualifications**
>
> - BSW and one year of professional experience working in healthcare setting or human service agency preferred
> - Knowledge of healthcare and healthcare delivery systems
> - Problem-solving skills to evaluate a patient's concrete needs and create and implement a treatment plan
> - Interpersonal skills to effectively interact with patients, families, medical staff, and outside agencies

CASE STUDY

Dakota

While Dakota was completing her BSW, she applied for and completed the Title IV-E program, a federally funded program that is designed to prepare social work students to work in the child welfare system. After graduation, Dakota pursued her licensure as an LBSW and was hired as an investigator for Child Protective Services. In this position, she investigated cases of child abuse and neglect. This role involved interviewing people including teachers, doctors, and nurses; conducting forensic investigations and assessments; and documenting all relevant information. She was required to maintain objectivity and empathy for the families that were in these crisis situations. Although this was difficult work, she implemented a good self-care plan including daily journaling and exercise. In the process of investigating her cases, she became interested in offering resources to the families she was working with. This experience inspired her to pursue a case management certification, which she completed in one year. After two years of working with Child Protective Services, she realized that her passion was working for children entering the foster care system. With the experience she gained in her role of investigator, including engaging with children and families, addressing the trauma of removing children and documentation, she applied for and was hired as a case manager for the Helping Hand foster care program. Here she was able to apply the skills she had learned, such as crisis intervention, assessment, and documentation, and integrate her knowledge of case management.

CLINICAL SOCIAL WORK

Clinical social work involves doing therapy directly with clients and requires an MSW degree. Clinical social workers offer services in a wide variety of settings, including community mental health, primary care, hospitals, nonprofit organizations, and private practice. This specialty practice area of social work focuses on the mental health and well-being of individuals, couples, groups, and families through assessment, diagnosis, treatment, and prevention. Social workers who provide these services must be licensed or certified at the master's or clinical level in their state of practice.

Some of the job titles you may encounter as a clinical social worker include:

- Clinical social worker
- Behavioral health clinician
- Counselor
- Clinical director
- Clinician/therapist
- Family violence counselor
- Hospice social worker
- Health career social worker
- Addictions counselor
- Mitigation specialist

Some of the knowledge areas and skills that a clinical social worker needs to know include:

- Knowledge of cognitive conditions, mental health issues, and the revised fifth edition of the *Diagnostic and Statistical Manual of Mental Disorders* (DSM-5-TR; American Psychiatric Association, 2022)
- Assessment and diagnosis

- Treatment planning
- Group facilitation
- Crisis intervention
- Grief and loss theory
- Discharge planning
- Conducting individual and group therapy
- Documentation
- Supervisory experience and training

For a more comprehensive list of clinical social work skills, see Appendix A. Box 1.2 features a clinical job description, demonstrating how clinical skills and knowledge can help define the role of a particular job title.

Box 1.2

Sample Clinical Job Description: Clinical Social Worker

Job Description

As the licensed clinical social worker, you will be responsible for comprehensive assessment and treatment of persons whose lives are impacted by cognitive conditions, mental health issues (depression, anxiety, adjustment disorder, Alzheimer's, dementia), or a declining capacity to function independently.

Your duties will include, but are not limited to, completing cognitive and mental health evaluations; delivering cognitive and emotional therapies; completing timely and accurate charting; and providing therapy in individual and group settings.

Responsibilities

- Function as part of a multidisciplinary team that provides care for seniors and their families in nursing homes and assisted living facilities
- Assist in training of new psychotherapists
- Be available to answer questions of clinical nature
- Lead or develop nursing home in-service training
- Attend behavioral rounds at nursing home facilities

Qualifications

- Master's degree in social work and active clinical social work license
- Geriatric experience a plus
- Electronic medical records experience a plus
- Testing experience a plus

Licensure for Clinical Social Work

If you want to practice as a clinical social worker, looking into the requirements and process for licensing in the state you want to practice in should be a top priority. First and foremost, as stated earlier, you must have an MSW degree to do clinical social work and advance to a clinical social work license. This licensing process also requires you to have a clinical supervisor and a supervision plan. Familiarize yourself with the requirements in your state of practice and seek opportunities that will give you the required experience (usually assessment, treatment, and diagnosis) and provide a means for supervision in the process. If supervision is not provided, you may certainly negotiate for it when you accept the position (see chapter 7). In most instances, you will be able to apply for job opportunities that require a clinical license if you have passed the test; however, you may not be able to practice until you obtain the license.

CASE STUDY

Emmett

Emmett became a licensed clinical social worker at a local medical care facility with a passion for person-centered care. He worked as part of an interprofessional healthcare team that provided care to patients experiencing medical issues. He primarily assisted residents in attaining or maintaining the highest physical, mental, and psychosocial well-being possible, given their diagnosis. Emmett provided triages and assessments and developed treatment plans that sometimes included brief interventions. He utilized evidence-based practices in his approach to working with clients, managed his case load, and completed case notes regularly. He worked with the patients' families to connect them with outside supports. In addition to gaining field experience in a healthcare setting, he completed both BSW and MSW degrees. Through his coursework he learned about the field of gerontology and gained knowledge of interpersonal and family/system dynamics.

MACRO SOCIAL WORK

Macro social work is an intervention designed to bring about change at the organizational, community, and policy levels, and can be done with a BSW or an MSW. Macro social work practice can involve work in management/administration, community organization, policy, evaluation and research, and development/fundraising work. Macro social workers are employed in many settings, including nonprofit organizations, government agencies, universities/colleges, businesses, think tanks, foundations, and consulting firms.

The following are examples of common macro-focused roles, including some job titles and skills needed for each line of work. Keep in mind that positions are fluid and may require skills that cut across several macro areas.

Administration/Development

Administration/development are usually leadership roles that involve the management of human service agencies and nonprofit organizations. Macro social workers in development create funding revenue and funding streams for organizations.

Some of the job titles you may encounter when researching macro-related jobs in administration/development include:

- Assistant director/director/executive director
- Manager/supervisor
- Program officer
- Project coordinator
- Fund/grant manager
- Development officer
- Engagement specialist

Some of the skills and knowledge one needs to be successful in administration/development positions include:

- Interpersonal (e.g., communication and engagement)
- Strategic planning
- Finance
- Organization
- Problem solving and decision making
- Training and talent management
- Search engine optimization
- Event planning
- Grant writing/fundraising

Community Organizing

Community organizing focuses on the process of mobilizing people to address community issues within systems. Community organizing involves advocacy work and creates change at a grassroots level. Some of the job titles you may encounter when researching macro-related jobs in community organizing include:

- Community outreach coordinator
- Project coordinator
- Community organizer
- Community liaison
- Engagement coordinator

Some of the skills and knowledge one needs to be successful in community organization include:

- Consensus building
- Group facilitation
- Creating community partnerships
- Advocacy
- Negotiation/conflict resolution
- Event planning
- Grant writing/fundraising
- Search engine optimization

Policy/Evaluation/Research

Policy involves addressing social issues in policies and procedures that govern organizations and locales. Macro social workers in evaluation and research analyze programs and policies using qualitative and quantitative modalities.

Some of the job titles you may encounter when researching jobs in policy, research, and/or evaluation include:

- Policy/data analyst
- Legislative aid
- Professor
- Elected official
- Policy and strategy specialist
- Public policy manager
- Data and evaluation consultant/specialist
- Researcher
- Data manager/specialist

Some of the skills and knowledge one needs to be successful in policy/evaluation/research jobs include:

- Synthesizing and analyzing information
- Data collection and analysis
- Communication (writing, presenting, persuading)
- Budgeting
- Negotiation
- Team building
- Project management
- Survey design
- Needs assessment
- Project/program design
- Technology

For a more comprehensive list of macro social work skills, see Appendix A. Box 1.3 features a macro social work job description, demonstrating how macro skills and knowledge can help define the role of a particular job title.

Box 1.3

Sample Macro Social Work Job Description: Community Engagement Officer, Homes for Families

Homes for Families is a nonprofit community development organization dedicated to strengthening families and their communities through the development of housing and neighborhoods. We look to empower individuals and ensure economic justice through strengthening financial knowledge of our community members and encouraging advocacy and grassroots community organizing. Supporting and fostering diverse and inclusive communities is a priority of Housing Families and is demonstrated through our staffing, programs, and approach to community building.

Job Description

We are looking to hire a collaborative, solution-oriented community engagement officer committed to Homes for Families' priorities of maximizing housing stability, health, and wellness and increasing economic resiliency of our families and community members. We do this through leadership and advocacy training, financial stability training and coaching, and working in partnership with other human service agencies that provide support services such as elder services, workforce development, domestic violence prevention, and after-school programs. The community engagement officer focuses on connecting residents to social service providers, increasing the income of families, and supporting neighborhood-led activities and initiatives. The community engagement officer works closely with a variety of stakeholders, including residents, neighborhood organizations, and local government agencies.

Responsibilities

- **Resident Leadership Development:** Refine and lead our resident leadership program, which encourages active resident involvement in our efforts around housing stability and community development. Create a system for identifying and engaging future leaders. Identify and lead community advocacy efforts that address the needs of our community and encourage resident involvement.
- **Community Partnerships:** Cultivate relationships with community partners that focus on housing, workforce development, and supporting families experiencing housing instability. Represent agency at local and state-wide meetings and initiatives.
- **Resident Training:** Create and execute resident trainings to promote economic responsibility and success focusing on topics such as budgeting, education, and home ownership.

(continued)

> **Evaluation and Needs Assessment:** Ensure an effective and regular needs assessment and evaluation plan to continually meet the needs of our clients and ensure the effectiveness of our efforts. Analyze and synthesize the data into both internal reports and external communication pieces.
>
> **Qualifications**
>
> - A bachelor's degree and at least two to three years of experience in community organizing, housing, and/or resident support services or a related master's degree
> - Strong facilitation, communication, and customer service skills
> - Strong client management skills
> - Strong organizational and decision-making skills along with the ability and desire to work independently and collaboratively
> - A demonstrated commitment to working with a diverse population in a way that demonstrates respect and understanding and encourages the opportunity for clients to thrive
> - Bilingual (e.g., English plus Spanish, Mandarin, Haitian Creole) a plus

Licensure for Macro Social Work

Job positions in the macro social work area often do not require social work licensure. There are only a handful of states that have a nonclinical or macro license category. Getting a social work master's-level license as a macro practicing social worker might be valuable in a variety of different circumstances: if you work in a setting with many other social workers and you want to indicate your commitment to the field, if you might supervise social work interns or BSW-level social workers, or if you work in a setting with many degreed or professionally licensed individuals.

CASE STUDY

Dwayne

After earning his MSW, Dwayne completed a two-year post-degree Presidential Management Fellowship and was hired as a program analyst for the U.S. Department of Housing and Urban Development. He oversees projects and programs to address housing needs in an urban city and evaluates fair housing issues. To be effective at his job, Dwayne uses interpersonal skills to engage with the community and his coworkers when working on team projects. This job also requires Dwayne to research and analyze data, interpret policies, and manage large projects, requiring excellent organizational skills. He must provide guidance on complex, sensitive, and sometimes controversial issues. His fellowship experience, along with a field placement at a local city council, helped him understand how to work within larger systems and realize that social workers contribute a people-centered and empowering approach to organizations.

Growing up, Dwayne wondered about the history of his town and its people, and about the issues they faced every day—especially the lack of adequate, safe, and affordable housing. Dwayne has the goal of advocating for and creating equitable policies while also hoping to create spaces for people who experience systematic oppression to have their voices heard and their challenges resolved on a macro level.

INTERNATIONAL SOCIAL WORK

International social work is similar in focus to domestic social work in that it can be done with any level of social work degree. International social workers contribute to program development, policy, practice, and research that improve the lives and well-being of individuals, families, and communities around the world. These social workers help those dealing with issues such as poverty, health and mental health issues, trauma, displacement, and housing, most often in developing countries. Examples of international social work practice include human rights, social development, advocacy, poverty, and social justice, as well as responding to conflict, disasters, and the needs of displaced populations such as immigrants and refugees.

International social work is informed by a clinical understanding of the impact that violence, displacement, and other such events have on a group or individual. However, international social workers do not provide group/individual clinical interventions. This work is done by local staff. International social work is more macro in focus, including training, community assessment and organizing, program design, implementation and evaluation, promoting humanitarian assistance, postdisaster development and reconstruction, and social and economic development. International social work can be done in settings like nongovernmental organizations, higher education, research centers, domestic agencies that help with refugee and immigrant resettlement, international relief organizations, human rights organizations, refugee relief organizations, and intergovernmental organizations.

Some of the job titles you may encounter when researching international social work jobs include:

- Psychosocial coordinator
- Gender-based violence coordinator
- Child protection specialist
- Monitoring and evaluation manager
- Refugee resettlement manager
- Technical advisor
- Program coordinator for anti-trafficking
- Humanitarian assistant officer
- Case worker

Some of the knowledge areas and skills that are necessary to be successful in international social worker include:

- Capacity building
- Building community partnerships
- Training
- Program management
- Language other than English
- Resourcefulness
- Adaptability
- Cultural awareness, humility
- Evaluation

For a more comprehensive list of international social work skills, see Appendix A.

Licensure for International Social Work

There is currently no international social work license. You can choose to obtain and maintain your license in a particular U.S. state, but this does not give you permission to work clinically internationally nor allow you to obtain the clinical hours needed for an advanced clinical social work license in the United States.

Box 1.4 features an international social work job description, demonstrating how skills and knowledge can help define the role of a particular job title.

CASE STUDY

Erica

As a gender-based violence specialist for the International Refugee Service, Erica worked in East Africa in a large refugee settlement. In her role, she applied her knowledge of gender-based violence and child protection to provide advocacy and raise awareness of violence for children and women refugees. Erica worked with, oversaw, and helped train community-based volunteers and workers and created collaborative relationships with community partners and other local nongovernmental organizations. Being successful in this role required excellent case management, training, and communication skills and the ability to remain effective in difficult and often unpredictable circumstances. Erica had previous experience domestically working in the Department for Children and Families as a protective case manager and did a semester-long field placement in South Africa working with victims of trafficking.

> **Box 1.4**
>
> **Sample International Job Description: Education and Youth Employment Project Officer, Catholic Refugee Services, Central America**
>
> **Job Description**
>
> The Youth Employment Project is a new initiative focused on increasing equitable access to formal educational opportunities for potential migrants and returnees. The goal is to engender hope, prosperity, and positive self-worth in their lives and reduce the need to migrate from their home country.
>
> **Responsibilities**
>
> - Conduct outreach with potential youth trainees, community businesses, and local governments to conduct needs assessment, create synergy, and articulate the mutual benefit of this new program
> - Collaborate with local education centers to develop and improve education and workforce development programs that result in skills development, job training, and placement in the local community
> - Facilitate groups of youth participants to support their well-being as they participate in this new initiative
>
> **Qualifications**
>
> - Bachelor's degree in education, international relations, the social sciences, or related field from an accredited academic institution with two years of relevant professional experience or a master's degree in the previously mentioned fields
> - Working experience in technical vocational training, job creation, and placement that addresses gender- and social inclusion–related education constraints
> - Experience in working with migrants, refugees, internally displaced persons, victims of trafficking, and other vulnerable groups
> - Prior work experience with international humanitarian organizations, nongovernmental, or government institutions/organizations in a multicultural setting is an advantage
> - Fluency in Spanish
> - Familiarity with and commitment to youth development with attention to addressing gender equality and social inclusion

NONTRADITIONAL SOCIAL WORK

Social workers have many transferable skills that play valuable roles in other disciplines and industries considered nontraditional social work. These areas include politics, technology, corporate, and education. Social workers bring unique strengths, skills, and perspectives to this work, including systems theory, a strengths-based perspective, and advocacy, all viewed through a social justice lens. Additionally, social workers possess valuable transferable skills, including the ability to build consensus with multiple constituents, community organizing, and group facilitation. These skills foster productive conversations between various work groups and organizations to achieve common goals and improve engagement among stakeholders. Organizations and industries also recognize social workers as innovators, organizers, implementers, and leaders. They are trained to work on a micro level while also being able to see the "whole picture" of social problems from a macro level. They learn to work with a multitude of populations in various types of organizations, including private, nonprofit, and public sectors (such as international, federal, state, and municipal governments). The common thread that ties their work to multiple populations is grounded in a strong foundation of equity, justice, and inclusion.

Some of the job titles you may encounter when researching nontraditional social work jobs include:

- Community outreach coordinator in a bank
- Community engagement specialist in a philanthropic organization/foundation
- Sports social worker for a professional basketball team
- Dean of diversity and inclusion in higher education
- Director of corporate responsibility for a high-tech corporation
- Corporate social worker
- Learning enhancement specialist
- Employee assistant program (or EAP) counselor
- Community outreach specialist
- Conflict mediator
- Military social worker in the U.S. Navy
- Career coach at a consulting firm

Some of the knowledge areas and skills that a social worker in a nontraditional role needs to know include:

- Clinical social work
- Communication, counseling, problem solving, goal setting
- Community outreach
- Diversity, equity, and inclusion
- Familiarity with employee assistance programs
- Entrepreneurship
- Evaluation
- Financial literacy
- Mediation/dispute resolution
- Mental health counseling
- Mitigation
- Negotiation
- Research/assessment
- Social enterprise

- Social responsibility
- Training and education
- Wellness

For a more comprehensive list of nontraditional social work skills, see Appendix A. Box 1.5 features a nontraditional social work job description, demonstrating how skills and knowledge help define a job title.

Box 1.5

Sample Nontraditional Social Work Job Description: Assistant Dean of Students, Adeline University

Job Description

Under the direction of the dean of students, serves as an impartial facilitator in supporting, and in some cases resolving, undergraduate student academic, personal welfare, and financial matters. These concerns are often of a sensitive nature and may not have a formal avenue of redress through official university channels. The assistant dean of students interacts with various campus departments and community-based agencies, as well as with faculty, staff, and student guardian/family members.

Responsibilities

- Supervise due process procedures and assist the dean of students with the resolution of student conduct concerns, Title IX investigations, and disciplinary processes
- Manage and resolve crisis situations involving undergraduate and graduate students, including student care and high-level conduct/Title IX cases
- Serve as a member of university committees related to student welfare, enrollment management, academic affairs, and other aspects related to student status
- Work collaboratively in the development and execution of new student orientation programs, including creating training modules around sexual assault and academic honesty
- Participate as a resource in the decisions and enforcement of academic probation/dismissal regulations as well as extension of academic deadlines on unfinished coursework and the rescheduling of final exams
- Interview and counsel students contemplating withdrawal, leave of absence, or readmission from the university in collaboration with deans of schools/colleges
- Assist students in understanding their rights and responsibilities as community members and the university conduct system
- Stay current with changes in rules, regulations, and policies as they relate to the student experience
- Serve as a resource to the university community regarding status of students and make presentations to groups

(continued)

- Supervise administrative support staff and graduate assistants working in the dean of students' office

Qualifications, Required

- Master's degree in college student affairs, higher education administration, guidance and counseling, or related
- At least three years postsecondary experience in professional student affairs/student development work
- Excellent communication, interpersonal, and counseling skills, including conflict resolution and the ability to establish strong working relationships with faculty, staff, and others
- Demonstrated ability to exercise independent and sound analytical/diagnostic judgments
- Flexibility to manage complex roles, requiring a broad base of knowledge

Qualifications, Preferred

- Experience working with students who have experienced personal crisis and crime-related trauma, including sexual assault, domestic violence, and intimate partner violence
- Experience developing and presenting educational programming for students

Licensure for Nontraditional Clinical Social Work

While licensure for nontraditional social workers may not be necessary, it is a credential that protects the social worker and the client. Moreover, in some cases, it may be necessary depending on the funding of the position or organizational oversight.

CASE STUDY

Jing

Jing graduated with a MSW degree in macro social work with a focus on public health. Upon graduation, she was committed to working on improving the health outcomes of marginalized populations in the Seattle area. At a statewide public health organization, she worked on a variety of public health issues including obesity, substance use, and chronic disease management. In each position she utilized her macro social work skills in conducting needs assessments, creating effective programs, developing community partnerships, managing data, and creating relationships with state legislators to influence policy and legislation. With the onset of the COVID-19 pandemic, Jing took advantage of the many new opportunities for macro social workers to make their contributions in nontraditional settings. Joining a biotech company specializing in the coordination of COVID testing, Jing's role as a strategy and innovation developer allowed her to use her social justice lens to help ensure that these new systems, policies, and procedures were benefitting all individuals and communities. Drawing upon the community partnerships she had created previously, she was able to help the for-profit company understand how different systems interact and how individuals might work across or fall between different systems like schools, hospitals, and daycare centers. This knowledge helped allow for more effective testing. Jing shared her understanding of marginalized communities to create effective communication, outreach, and interventions to help individuals stay healthy.

CONCLUSION

In this chapter, we have provided a landscape for you to explore your career path in the field of social work. We have discussed the three scopes of practice (macro, mezzo, and micro) and the five major areas of practice (generalist, clinical, macro, international, and nontraditional). We have provided sample skill sets and job titles, job descriptions, and case studies to help you better understand different career roles. As we continue our journey in the coming chapters, you will further explore your career options and assess your unique experiences, values, and skills to help you feel empowered to make informed career decisions.

CHAPTER TAKEAWAYS

- With a commitment to social justice, social workers work to improve the lives of the most vulnerable.
- The skills and knowledge gained through a social work job/education can be applied to many different work opportunities.
- Reflecting on your own interests and skills will help you determine the role in social work you want to play. Refer to Appendix A: Comprehensive List of Social Work Skills for a more in-depth review of the skills necessary for various areas of practice.

CHAPTER

2

Social Work Career Planning for Advancement and Fulfillment

What You Will Learn

- ❐ The six stages of the Professional Development Cycle of Social Workers and how the PDCSW can help you to strategically plan your career advancement
- ❐ How to balance your skills, knowledge, and interests for maximum career fulfillment
- ❐ The strategic steps in your career that will define your legacy, setting an example for others to follow

Action Plan

- ❐ Use the PDCSW Assessment Tool to gauge your career trajectory
- ❐ Identify skills, tasks, and knowledge areas from previous PDCSW stages that you may have skipped
- ❐ Apply strategic career tips to each stage of the PDCSW
- ❐ Consider your legacy through each stage of the PDCSW process

Congratulations! As a social worker you have chosen a meaningful career that will lead to a remarkable legacy. You are committed to building human capacity by solving complex social problems, advocating for historical policy change, and building authentic connections with the clients you serve to create a more just and equitable society. Some may ask, "What does a legacy in social work entail?" As you embark on your career, your legacy will be measured by every life you touch. This may seem like a tall order, but social workers bring positive change and hope to our society every day—one person, one system, and one policy at a time. It is important to embrace your role as an agent of change. This chapter will apply the following characteristics of an agent of change: awareness, continuous learning, and courage.

Your social work career journey is about being intentional and informed. It is about being open to new challenges and ready for unexpected pivots that happen when working with people impacted by societal changes. This book is not just for those starting their career in social work. The strategies, exercises, and tips are also for those thinking about next career moves, re-entering the workforce after an absence, or thinking about their five- or 10-year plan. While social work can be a demanding profession, it is also a very meaningful career.

As a social worker, you are trained to assess the person and their environment to create goals that lead to strategic change and growth. Strategic career planning involves a similar process: assess where you are in your career, determine how you can prepare for future career changes, and develop core skills that will ultimately lead to career fulfillment. Each time you make a career transition, it is important to make sure it is intentional and will contribute to a clear and logical career trajectory. This also includes goal setting for each stage of your career to enhance your skills, increase your visibility, and maximize your career opportunities. Along the way you will find opportunities to network with experts and advance your knowledge. By taking the following steps, you will set a path toward your dream job.

THE PROFESSIONAL DEVELOPMENT CYCLE OF SOCIAL WORKERS

The PDCSW is a model of career development based on six stages of career advancement in the profession of social work (see Figure 2.1). This model was created by colleagues Professor Andrew T. Marks of Texas State University and Jennifer Luna of the University of Texas, who observed and assessed the careers of thousands of social workers through their work with NASW, the licensing board, continuing education, and social work education. Marks and Luna began to observe specific benchmarks that social workers could use to propel their career to the next level, yet these benchmarks were rarely talked about in social work education or published in trade literature. From this gap, the PDCSW model was born and used as a career management tool to gauge an individual's readiness and prepare them for career advancement.

While there are a variety of different avenues a social worker can take throughout their career, the PDCSW framework can be used to help social workers assess where they are and help them determine concrete action steps to advance in their career (Luna & Marks, 2014). Because career advancement demands changes in knowledge areas and/or skills that require remediation, PDCSW uses a step-by-step approach. As with career advancement in most industries, advancing in social work may mean familiarizing yourself with a new subject area, learning new industry lingo, or brushing up on previously learned skills. It may sometimes feel like taking two steps forward and one step back. Furthermore, since social work often attracts career changers, some may find themselves negotiating changes more rapidly because their combined experience, practical wisdom, and technical knowledge obtained

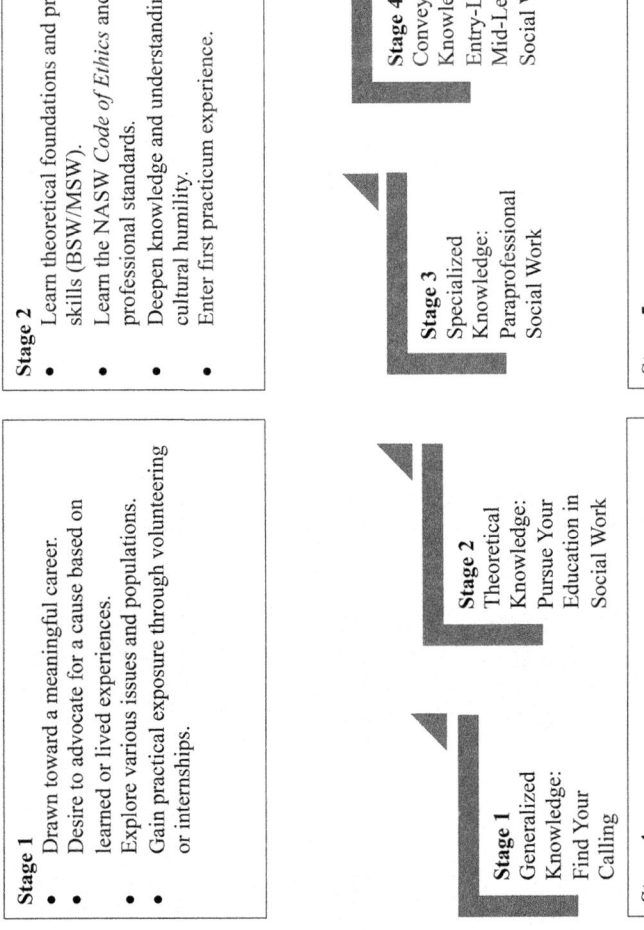

Figure 2.1: The Professional Development Cycle of Social Workers

through previous work takes them in new and exciting directions. Finally, learning and advancing is required to continue our engagement in the profession. Our social work licensure requires us to engage in continuing education to keep abreast of recent research, and our *Code of Ethics* keeps us accountable to our clients, to the profession, and to ourselves through self-care that prevents burnout. As an agent of change, you are your most trusted advocate. Lean into it, embrace it, and use the PDCSW as a road map to your legacy.

Stage 1: Generalized Knowledge: Find Your Calling

The first stage in the professional development cycle is recognizing that your natural aspiration to make a difference can translate into a meaningful and fulfilling career. At some point in your lifetime, you may have had a sense of wanting to help people, communities, or society. Some may say this is a calling. For others, it may be a desire to change to a more meaningful career or advocate for a cause. Regardless of the reason, you likely knew you wanted to work with others, and you did not shy away from situations in which you were responsible for their well-being. If this describes you, you are in the right place! Some of the concrete actions of this first stage might look like:

- You recognize that you enjoy helping people and facilitating positive change, which leads you to pursue an education in social work.
- You identify and develop transferable skills such as communication, customer service, conflict resolution, or project management, and learn how these skills can apply to multiple levels of your career path.
- You have a strong interest in seeking leadership roles, working on teams, or participating in group projects.
- You recognize that you are drawn toward advocacy or participation in civic activities.
- You acknowledge that your experience (professional and/or lived) sets you up for a natural transition to the social work profession.
- You seek volunteer opportunities to get experience helping others.
- You have begun to gather information on social work graduate programs or dual degree programs that will set you up for a successful career in social work.

CASE STUDY

Luis

As Luis was deciding what to major in, his college advisor asked him about his greatest interests and attributes. Luis told her that he had not realized how much he enjoyed helping people until he began community service to strengthen his college application when he was a senior in high school. He also stated that he had always been deemed a good listener by friends and family and he thrived on problem solving, especially when it came to working with complex assistance programs. As the son of immigrants, the oldest child, and a first-generation college student, he helped his parents fill out documents and translated for them. He recognized that someday he would like to advocate for families similar to his, to make it easier for those families that came after him. You can imagine his excitement when he realized he could make a career out of this type of work! With help from his advisor, Luis began his search for a BSW program by researching the accredited programs on the Council on Social Work Education (CSWE) website and applied for college at a nearby university with an accredited social work program.

Stage 2: Theoretical Knowledge: Pursue Your Education in Social Work

The next stage in the career development process is formal education. As a social work student, you are learning the knowledge, skills, and cognitive and affective processes that require the social worker's critical thinking, affective reactions, and exercise of judgment regarding unique practice situations (CSWE, 2022). Additionally, one of the most important components of your social work education will be the NASW (2021) *Code of Ethics*, which will be critical to your role and obligations as a licensed social worker throughout your entire career. While there are many avenues of employment for a BSW, the options for licensure and employment increase for those with a graduate degree. While some social workers complete their BSW before moving on to an advanced degree, others may pursue an undergraduate degree in another field such as psychology and find social work as a graduate school option. The advantage of completing a BSW first from an accredited program is that many graduate programs will allow BSWs to do an accelerated MSW and finish the program in 12 to 15 months. Regardless of how you arrive, the MSW is said to be the "terminal degree" required to pursue most clinical opportunities. While a PhD or DSW in social work will advance you in careers such as research and academia, you do not need them to excel as a practitioner.

As a student, you can enhance your skill set to prepare for your professional career. If you have a BSW or you are considering an MSW, ask yourself these questions:

- What opportunities are available to add to your career toolbox? These could be career development workshops, lectures, advocacy opportunities, specialized fellowship programs, or certificates.
- Are there employment, volunteer experiences, or service-learning experiences that you might like to try to expand your skill set or experience with a particular population?
- What organizations are you affiliated with? What causes are you interested in? Have you pursued a leadership position? Why or why not? What skills could you gain from these opportunities?
- What types of certifications, licenses, or specialized training should you pursue after you get your degree?

- As a social worker, are you willing to learn and take responsibility for the moral, ethical, and legal obligations that may arise from your religious or cultural affiliations, NASW professional standards, or civil and criminal laws?
- Do your personal and professional values fall in line with the CSWE Core Values?
- What are the things that you *do not* want to do?

At this point, you should know or have some understanding about the career and education options you would like to see in your future. This would be the time to build out your resume and find career areas that might interest you by increasing your knowledge of and skills in various types of social work jobs. If you are considering applying for your MSW, it is wise to get a year of professional experience in the field beforehand to strengthen your application to graduate school and improve your classroom learning experience when you begin your academic program.

CASE STUDY

Chloe

Chloe finished her BSW and decided to work for a year to get experience before applying to graduate school. She knew that she wanted to be a clinical social worker, and someday perhaps open her own practice. Since she had completed her BSW field placement at an elementary school, she pursued her first job after college in an organization serving children and families. In this position, she did case management and started a parenting group to get experience working with adults. She also began attending her state's NASW chapter conference, even joining the chapter's conference planning committee. This experience, coupled with excellent reference letters and strong narrative statements, helped her gain entrance to her first choice of social work graduate programs.

Stage 3: Specialized Knowledge: Paraprofessional Social Work

The next stage in the cycle is gaining practical and/or technical knowledge from formal experience, including your field placements. The field placement is what sets social work apart from all other helping professions, and many say it is the heart of social work education. Under supervision, you will have the opportunity to apply what you have learned with individuals, groups, and communities. Make the most of these opportunities by focusing on skill building and making valuable connections in the field, even if you do not get placed in the field placement you wanted. In fact, many times in social work we learn what we do not want to do before we find our true calling. If you find yourself in a field situation that is not a perfect fit, articulate your experience strategically to your advisor and potential future employers. Focus on the skills that you learned, the knowledge areas that you gained, the connections that you made, and what you learned from the experience. This is all part of the learning process for social workers. At this point in your career, you should learn and utilize the NASW *Code of Ethics* for professional decision making. Remember, many social work skills, knowledge areas, and theories are transferable, regardless of the area of practice you are in.

During this time, you should also join the "corps" of professional associations, such as NASW, American Association of School Social Workers, or Network of Social Work Management. Almost all associations have a student membership for a reduced rate. This is also the time to know what learning, leadership, and supervision styles work best for you. For example, are you more of a visual learner or an auditory learner? Is your leadership style more laissez-faire or strategic? Do you prefer hands-on supervision, or would you prefer autonomy? (See chapter 3 for Exercise 3.5: Defining Your Ideal Supervisor.)

As you cycle through this stage of your career, consider the following:

- What opportunities will you ask for to make the most of your social work field placement?
- How will you set yourself up for the types of opportunities you will seek postgraduation?
- What certifications, licenses, and/or registrations should you pursue? What can you do now to prepare for these?
- How will you demonstrate leadership in your field placement, student organization, advocacy activities, or group projects?
- Are you willing to assume supervisory roles and take responsibility for others?
- How will you incorporate your own values and beliefs into your professional practice?
- Have you grown a sense of confidence in your work, and do you hold yourself accountable for your values and beliefs?
- Have you identified your niche or what qualities set you apart from others?
- Have you identified professional opportunities and challenged yourself to attempt new things?

CASE STUDY

Sidney

Sidney entered an MSW program in pursuit of a career in macro social work. They had an undergraduate degree in education and had worked as an elementary school teacher for seven years. Through this experience, they became interested in systemic racism, educational disparities, and public policy. As a graduate student, they sought out opportunities to gain public speaking experience and enhance their writing skills, and led efforts to advocate against discriminatory policies for transgender athletes in public schools. They utilized social media including Instagram and Twitter to bring attention to these issues and gain a following among other college students from across campus. These experiences of campus advocacy and networking helped them to land their dream internship with the ACLU in Washington, DC.

Stage 4: Conveyed Knowledge: Entry-Level to Mid-Level Social Work

After two to five years as a professional social worker, you should begin to increase your expertise in your field of practice or with the population you are working with. As this expertise grows, so will your reputation. It is important to recognize that this expertise could be related to your practice area; your target population; or a subject matter knowledge such as the utilization of a specialized clinical framework, leadership style, or advocacy issue. During this season of your career, it is imperative to develop a strong elevator pitch about your professional value and your brand (see chapter 4). You will need to be intentional and invest time in networking, adding value to your professional organization, and growing your circle of colleagues. Remember, expanding your expertise and your network can be a tall order, and while the importance of self-care cannot be overstated throughout a social worker's career, you may overlook it as you undertake additional responsibilities. It is crucial to have a good self-care plan in place. As we have a career toolbox, we also need a self-care toolbox. Remember to give your clients the best of you, not the rest of you.

During this stage, many social workers begin to feel boredom, burnout, or both. You may find that your opportunities are limited. You may feel understimulated in your workplace. Conversely, you may find that your workload is overwhelming, impacting your personal life, professional life, or both. You may realize that change is inevitable. Rather than despair, consider these warning signs indicators that it may be time to carve out a new path!

The good news is that with some years of experience under your belt, you will be looked upon as a leader in your field. Rather than get stuck or burned out, consider the many ways you can grow your knowledge and your career opportunities, such as:

- Lead a committee—either internal in your organization or external such as an interagency collaboration—to refine your expertise and build strong connections
- Share your expertise with others through LinkedIn, organizational newsletters, discussion groups, or trade magazines
- Serve as a reviewer for conference proposals
- Teach or facilitate workshops or serve as a guest presenter
- Serve on a board or commission appointment
- Supervise a social work student and/or mentor an incoming professional
- Share knowledge and expertise with others in supervision or professional peer consultation
- Actively seek strategic continuing education to grow new skills
- Consider two-for-one career opportunities; for example, negotiate an additional certification at your current job to have it in your career toolbox for your next job

- Continue to develop formalized leadership skills through associations and other leadership activities

CASE STUDY

Sam

Immediately after passing his licensure exam, Sam began clinical supervision with the goal of working as a therapist in a wellness program. To this end, he utilized LinkedIn to make connections with other therapists working in specialized programs including smoking cessation, weight loss education, and fitness challenges. He also connected with like-minded professionals from insurance programs, human resources departments, and corporations to learn industry language and about opportunities in this specialized area. His employer allowed him to serve as a field instructor and create the first field placement focusing on the utilization of health and wellness techniques with families.

Stage 5: Imparted Knowledge: Demonstrated Expertise

As your career progresses, your path may include opportunities to impart knowledge to others both in and outside of social work. In this stage of your social worker career, you may be asked to become a field instructor for BSW or MSW students. This is a natural progression that will often build leadership and supervision experience in a social worker's career. You may be asked to guest lecture, serve on a panel, or participate in the formal training of others. During this stage, it is vital to build communication skills by giving presentations, speaking in virtual classrooms, and creating learning activities for a variety of audiences. If there are limited opportunities to share your knowledge, consider writing a proposal for a conference presentation or training workshop. You may also consider writing a journal article, a book chapter, or an entire book of your own. This stage requires that you have a well-articulated professional brand; that your credentials are up to date; and that you have an updated resume, biographical statement, and professional headshot (see chapters 4 and 5). These are all materials that will be asked of you when you are invited to speak. The following are a few examples that demonstrate opportunities at this stage of your career:

- Your expertise is widely noticed in the field
- You share your expertise at workshops or presentations at professional meetings
- You actively seek opportunities as an adjunct instructor in formal education programs
- You are sought out as an expert witness or for consultation
- You write articles, letters to editor, technical pieces, blogs, and posts on social media

- You author or coauthor journal articles, book chapters, or entire books
- You serve on editorial boards of journals
- You are invited to participate at regional or national meetings
- You serve on a board of directors or hold a commissioned appointment
- You consider applying for a PhD or DSW program to expand your knowledge and credibility
- You recognize and cultivate the talents of others through supervision or mentoring

CASE STUDY

Case Study: Julie

With over 10 years of experience working with university athletes, Julie began presenting her work at the state NASW conference. She created a model of utilizing mindfulness with athletes that could be applied to many different types of sports and coaching. She partnered with the Department of Kinesiology to survey the college athletes and determine the effectiveness of mindfulness on stress reduction, academic performance, and overall well-being. Her research became of interest to a popular athletic brand, which funded her project for five years. Throughout this work, she also became involved in the Alliance for Social Workers in Sports. After writing about her research in a couple of trade magazines, she was invited to speak at the national conference. These presentations led to consultation work for the local school district, teaching coaches how to utilize mindfulness with high school athletes.

Stage 6: Explored/Examined Knowledge: Subject Matter Expert

The final stage of many social work careers is to become a recognized expert in the profession and/or a thought leader. At this point, you will be recognized as *the* expert in your field and be naturally driven to share your knowledge on a larger scale. This might include naming a theory or an intervention, developing a course at the university level, or creating a certification program. Other platforms may include writing a memoir, running for public office, working directly with elected officials, and contributing to the research on policy or theory. At this point, you are establishing your legacy. You could even be considered for one of social work's greatest honors, recognition as an NASW Social Work Pioneer (NASW Foundation, n.d.). As you read through this book, it is our hope that you will begin to think about your legacy as you progress through the stages of professional development. Consider the following items as you contemplate your legacy:

- What might you like to be known or recognized for as *the* expert?
- What do you want to share on a larger scale (not necessarily a larger audience)?

- Is there a policy or theory of intervention that you would like to name?
- Do you want to hold public office or be connected with an elected leader?
- Is there someone who might consider nominating you to be an NASW Social Work Pioneer?

CASE STUDY

Andrea

Andrea has her PhD and has worked in academia for nearly 20 years. Her focus has been maintaining leadership of a grant-funded program for first generation Latinx students who are seeking to go to college. Andrea had several years of clinical and macro experience in this field before landing her tenure track position at a Tier 1 university. During her career, Andrea coordinated two federal grants focusing on the national landscape of disparities for Latinx families and their communities. She presented at the national and international levels on her work and was sought out as an expert witness and keynote speaker. In her home state of Texas, her work is viewed as highly significant because it focuses on the connection between Latinx students, community resources, and educational outcome measures. Recently, Andrea was selected to receive a lifetime achievement award through the NASW Texas Chapter.

PROFESSIONAL DEVELOPMENT CYCLE OF SOCIAL WORKERS ASSESSMENT TOOL

Now that you have learned the six stages of the PDCSW, you can assess your career and rate your proficiency level for each stage in Appendix B. This chart will help you to gauge where you are in your career and set goals for the next level. Use the blank fields to add notes on your individualized career trajectory, goals, and milestones that will set you in your desired career direction. Remember, while the PDCSW model is a step-by-step model, there is a small slope between each stage. As you progress through your career, there will always be small steps backward; for example, skills, knowledge areas, and other competencies that you must learn. While you may not have mastered every indicator in each stage, do not let that hold you back from progressing; you can always go back and learn it.

CONCLUSION

At each career stage in the PDCSW, there are opportunities to make your journey more meaningful and interesting while helping to solve the most difficult problems of humankind. While everyone's path will look different, these stages can serve as a framework for moving forward with intention while seeking career fulfillment. It is important to remember that in all these stages, there are critical skills that are necessary to move from one step to the next:

- Communication skills, such as writing, presenting, listening, and training
- Leadership skills, including building relationships with others, holding yourself and others accountable, and having integrity
- Lifelong learning, such as attending continuing education workshops; pursuing certifications; or gaining knowledge of information technology, social media, or productivity tools

If you follow the steps of your career path with good planning, intention, and strategic thinking, you will gain the skills needed to move forward and, eventually, create your legacy.

CHAPTER TAKEAWAYS

- Use the PDCSW to determine what cycle of your career you are currently in.
- Use the PDCSW Assessment Tool and always look at the next stage of career advancement to be aware of the skills, knowledge, and experience you will need to get to the next opportunity and maximize your career fulfillment.
- Consider your legacy, even when thinking about short- or mid-range career plans. Ask yourself, "What do I need to do next to make a larger impact on my career, the profession, and society?"

CHAPTER
3

Assessing Need and Building Relationships: Determine Your Career Direction

---

What You Will Learn

- ❐ How to conduct a self-assessment that will help you with your career decision making
- ❐ How to find career opportunities that are a good fit for you
- ❐ The importance of informational interviews

Action Plan

- ❐ Complete at least two self-assessment exercises
- ❐ Create a list of skills, knowledge, and values that are important to you
- ❐ Describe your ideal supervisor
- ❐ List three job titles that align with your self-assessment
- ❐ Contact two people for informational interviews

To make informed decisions about the direction of your career, you need to know what you are looking for in your next job and what opportunities would allow you to do this work. In this chapter, we will discuss self-assessment as a critical first step of strategic career decision making. We will offer strategies for gathering information about your skills, qualities, priorities, and knowledge based on your self-awareness and reflection on your past experiences. Through this process, you will gain a better sense of what you would like to do, what skills you enjoy using, and what type of social work you may find most rewarding. Using this information as a framework, we will share tips on how to research career opportunities.

SELF-ASSESSMENT: START WITH YOU

Being aware of your strengths, motivations, and priorities is an important component of successful career decision making and job search:

- Knowing your strengths will inform your decisions about what area of social work you can best contribute to
- Knowing what you have to offer and what you are looking for allows for a more efficient and effective job search
- Being able to articulate your skills, abilities, and knowledge allows for the creation of strong application materials and professional branding (see chapters 4 and 5)

Creating a self-inventory can be done through creative writing, reflective exercises, and simple worksheets. In this chapter, we provide several exercises to get you started.

Reflecting on Previous Experiences

The self-assessment process requires reflecting on past experiences in both social work and other fields. Looking back on volunteer, internship, and work experiences can help you gather information about your skills and experience, the type of work culture you like, colleagues and supervisors you are most compatible with, and the work that you enjoy doing.

In Exercise 3.1, reflect on one past work experience and answer the questions as specifically as possible. Repeat the activity for several work experiences.

Skills and Abilities

Many skills are universal across positions and careers, such as writing or time management. People use the term "transferable skills" to refer to skills that are valuable in many different work environments. Consider what you have learned from previous jobs that will help you move forward. What will help you "transfer" into new environments, even if they seem vastly different from anything you have done before? These transferable skills will also allow you to create a niche for yourself in your job. For example, if you have excellent leadership skills, you may be sought out by your employer for management positions or to lead a committee or strategic partnership. Here are a few examples of transferable skills to get you started:

- Communication skills, including public speaking, running meetings, liaising between agencies, and knowledge of a foreign language

Exercise 3.1
Reflecting on Past Experiences

Organization Name: _____

Job Title: _____

Employment Dates : _____

Supervisor(s) Name(s): _____

Awards/Promotions: _____

Training Received: _____

My roles and responsibilities:

_____

My accomplishments (problems solved, efficiency improved, extra projects taken on, etc.):

_____

What I liked about this job/organization (people, environment, mission, etc.):

_____

What I disliked about this job/organization (people, environment, mission, etc.):

_____

What aspects of your supervisor's management style, personality, and interactions did you feel were effective for you (communication style, availability, level of oversight)? Provide specific examples.

_____

_____

_____

- Written skills, including creating newsletters, letters to the editor, fundraising letters, journal or book authorship, and clinical documentation
- Social media skills, including blogging and web page design
- Research skills, including survey instrument development, proposal writing, and presentation development
- Leadership expertise, including direct management, supervisory skills, and evaluation experience
- People skills, including volunteer recruitment and coordination, facilitation, and conflict resolution

- Project management, including development, coordination, and evaluation
- Outward facing skills, including community outreach, marketing, and public relations

There are also skills specific to the field:

- Micro social work skills, including conducting assessments, creating treatment plans, and building rapport for clinical social work
- Macro social work skills, including advocacy, community development, and policy skills
- Contextual skills, involving knowledge about a specific population; for example, hospice social work requires a knowledge of hospice philosophy and interventions (specific skills), as well as clinical skills in working with patients and families (broad skills)

A comprehensive list of social work–specific skills is provided in Appendix A.

Next, in Exercise 3.2, consider which skills you already have and which skills you hope to acquire. This list of skill words can also be helpful when writing resumes and cover letters.

Knowledge

Important knowledge about the issues you are hoping to improve, the population you want to work with, and the context of the identified problems can be gained through classes, field placement, and work experience. For example, if you are interested in working in domestic violence, you might learn about trauma-informed care through a class, gain experience understanding programs to prevent domestic violence through your field placement, and learn how to provide individual therapy to victims through your job. It is also important to remember that while theoretical knowledge is the foundation of social work practice, practical knowledge is essential in every job. For example, if you have worked with older adults and you are familiar with the Medicare system, this knowledge would be invaluable to a supervisor. It demonstrates that you can negotiate complex systems with little hand-holding. Gather the courses you have taken related to social work and create an inventory of the important bodies of knowledge you have gained. Pay special attention to the knowledge that is relevant to the work you want to do. Contextual knowledge specific to social work might look like the following:

- Clinical frameworks or treatment modalities including play therapy, solution-focused therapy, brief therapy, motivational interviewing, and psychodynamic theory
- Developmental theories, stages of grief and loss, child development theories, logic models, leadership theories, and organizational theories
- Public assistance programs including housing, the Supplemental Nutrition Assistance Program (SNAP), Social Security, Medicaid, Medicare, veterans' benefits, and Section 504

Exercise 3.2
Social Work Skills

Put a check next to each skill you have acquired or demonstrated. Circle those you hope to acquire.

adapting	goal setting	program evaluation
administration	grant writing	program management
advocacy	hiring	public relations
analyzing	home visiting	public speaking
assessing	implementing	recruiting
board development/management	information system management	referral
budgeting	initiating projects	reframing
capacity building	innovating	reinforcing
case management	interagency liaison	research
clinical work with x population	job designing	strategic planning
coaching	leading others	structuring
collaborating	limit setting	summarizing
community building	listening (active)	supervising
community organizing	lobbying	synthesizing
coordinating	marketing	teaching
crisis intervention	mediating	therapy
diagnosing	mentoring	training
discharge planning	modeling	treatment planning
documenting	motivating	volunteer management
educating	negotiating	writing
empathizing	organizing	
evaluation	personnel recruitment and selection	Add your own:
event planning	persuading	
facilitating	policy development	
fundraising	presenting	
gatekeeping	program design/development	

- Community resources, social services systems, funding streams, and legislative processes
- Policy issues concerning child welfare, immigration rights, or health access

Work Qualities

Work qualities or characteristics allow someone to be more successful in specific roles or environments. Indeed, work qualities are often indicated in job postings; for instance: "Looking for someone who demonstrates flexibility, a growth mindset, and willingness to learn new skills." What are your work qualities and how have you demonstrated them in your previous work? For example:

- Have you demonstrated your adaptability in the face of an agency undergoing leadership change?
- Have coworkers commented on your calm demeanor in times of crisis?
- Have you shown your resourcefulness in creating innovative programs on a limited budget?

Consider these questions and use Exercise 3.3 to assess your work qualities.

Values and Priorities

Career values represent your beliefs about what is important in your work and what makes it meaningful to you. These are important factors that determine whether you find your work motivating, rewarding, and impactful, and, ultimately, influence whether you will live the life you want. For this discussion, it is helpful to think in terms of intrinsic and extrinsic values.

Intrinsic values are intangible rewards that keep you motivated and engaged at your job and can include your work style and your relationship with your supervisor. Intrinsic values include how you view your work and whether it is challenging, has variety, allows for autonomy, helps make the world a better place for a certain population, or helps improve a societal problem. Some questions to ask yourself about your intrinsic values are:

- Do you prefer to work independently or collaboratively?
- Is it important that your day is predictable or can your responsibilities change as the day progresses?
- Do you prefer a fast- or slower-paced environment?
- Are you looking for mission- or role-driven positions?
- Do you want to work in a big organization with a distinct set of tasks or do you want to do a little bit of everything at a smaller organization?

Extrinsic values are tangible rewards acquired at work, including salary, benefits, and advancement opportunities. Thinking of your priorities over the next two years,

Exercise 3.3
Work Qualities

Put a checkmark next to each quality that describes you. Remember, authenticity is key. Be honest and indicate who you really are rather than who you would like to be. Then, circle your top five strengths and give an example of when you have demonstrated each characteristic successfully.

able to concentrate	confident	good-natured	outgoing
able to manage stress	conscientious	helpful	patient
accountable	consistent	honest	perceptive
accurate	cooperative	humorous	persevering
adaptable	creative	imaginative	persuasive
adventurous	curious	independent	poised
ambitious	decisive	inventive	practical
analytical	dependable	kind	precise
approachable	determined	learns quickly	proactive
articulate	diplomatic	likeable	problem solver
assertive	discreet	logical	progressive
attention to detail	easygoing	loyal	punctual
calm	efficient	mature	quick
careful	eloquent	meets deadlines	quiet
caring	empathetic	methodical	rational
cautious	enthusiastic	meticulous	realistic
charismatic	ethical	motivated	reflective
cheerful	even-keeled	open-minded	relaxed
clear-thinking	flexible	open to feedback	reliable
collaborative	focused	opinionated	reserved
competent	friendly	optimistic	resilient
competitive	genuine	organized	resourceful

(continued)

respectful	sincere	tech savvy	understanding
responsible	sociable	tenacious	versatile
risk-taker	strong work ethic	thorough	willingness to learn
self-aware	supportive	thoughtful	
self-confident	tactful	tolerant	
self-starter	teachable	trusting	
sensitive	team player	trustworthy	

Next, indicate each of your top five qualities and give an example of when you have demonstrated them. For example:

Top Quality: able to concentrate

Description: My first-year field placement was in an after-school program. It was noisy, chaotic, and unpredictable. My coworkers commented on my ability to tune all of that out when talking to a student who needed my attention. I knew to find a quiet space and use my nonverbal communication skills to indicate to the student that they had my undivided attention.

determine what is most important to you in your next job. That type of thinking also puts you in a good place for your next career move and allows you to best balance work and life. Some questions to ask yourself about your extrinsic values are:

- Is salary a significant factor in accepting a position?
- Are certain benefits a deciding factor in accepting a job?
- Is the ability to balance your responsibilities both at work and outside work an important thing to consider when accepting a job?
- Is the prestige of the agency you work at important to you?
- Is it important to accept a job in a field of social work that is well established and has job security or are you willing to take a risk at something new?
- Is the ability to move up in the same organization important to you?
- Is there a certain set of skills that you want to acquire to get you to the next stage in your career?
- Is having a designated office space important to you?

Values to Consider Specific to Social Work

People interested in social work careers share the common values of promoting social justice, helping vulnerable populations, and following the NASW (2021) *Code of Ethics* in their work. Social workers also feel that the intrinsic values of helping people and making the world a better place outweigh the extrinsic value of making a lot of money. But within the scope of work, there are a few considerations to make:

- How closely to a population do you need to work to feel you are making a difference? If you are a macro social worker and creating policy around refugee resettlement, do you want to see the population you are serving, or is it sufficient to know that the work you are doing has an impact?
- What kind of clinical relationship do you want with your clients? Is it therapeutic, educational, or about connecting them with resources? Is it short-term or longer term? Is it at an agency or within a context like a school, a client's home, or a long-term care facility?
- Is the type of agency important to you, such as nonprofit, for-profit, or government?
- Is it important that your clinical supervisor shares the same therapeutic approach, or can you learn from someone with a different approach?
- Does this position give you the required clinical hours and supervision to get or maintain your social work license?
- Are you willing to work for an organization outside the scope of a traditional social work organization in which the NASW *Code of Ethics* is not recognized?

Most jobs will not have everything on your wish list, but it is important to list the things that you are looking for in your next job or two and then spend some time prioritizing. Ask yourself, which are preferences and which are priorities? What concessions am I willing to make? Are some of these items longer-term needs or wants and others more immediate? Use Exercise 3.4 to take an inventory of your values.

Defining Your Ideal Supervisor

Your supervisor can have a huge impact on your experience at work, from how comfortable you feel, to how long you stay, to your career advancement. It is an important part of self-assessment to be able to define your ideal supervisor. What you want and need from a supervisor will change over time as you develop professionally and personally, so just like other parts of self-assessment, defining what you are looking for in a supervisor is something you should evaluate periodically throughout your career lifetime, and particularly when looking for a change. The definition of an ideal supervisor can be made up of qualities, roles, and styles and often relates to communication style, accessibility, and level of oversight. Your own needs may depend on your personality, work style, or stage of your career.

When interviewing for jobs and internships keep this "ideal supervisor" definition in mind when responding to questions about what you are looking for in a supervisor as well as asking questions to determine if this job will meet your career needs (chapter 6 discusses interviewing in more detail). Remember we are talking about *ideal*, so make sure you remember that being adaptable and demonstrating an ability to get along with coworkers are important traits for you to demonstrate as well. Exercise 3.5 can help get you started in defining your ideal supervisor right now.

Exercise 3.4
Values Inventory

What are your core values that you prefer/require at your next job to be able to do your best work?

achievement	honesty	power
autonomy	independence	respect
balance	influence	status
fairness	integrity	

What kind of work environment and interactions with coworkers do you prefer/require?

Work Environment	Personal Interactions
at home/hybrid/remote	collaborative
fast-paced	competitive
flexible	friendly
learning	open communication
open schedule	recognition
predictable	social
quiet	strong management
relaxed	supportive
structured	transparent
	trust

What are the preferred/required characteristics of the work you do?

analytical	innovative	research
challenging	interacting with public	risk-taking
creative	physical	variety

Which extrinsic values do you prefer/require in your next job?

certain geographic location	high earnings	rewarding
commitment to professional development	licensure supervision	stability
	mentoring	work/life balance
gaining certain skill set	opportunity for advancement	

Exercise 3.5
Defining Your Ideal Supervisor

Work Qualities: Use the work qualities in Exercise 3.3 to identify the top five qualities you are looking for in a supervisor that will allow you to do your best work.

Work Values: Review the values you identified for yourself in Exercise 3.4 and consider the role your supervisor could play in helping you attain those values and priorities. For example, if you prefer to work independently more than collaboratively, what do you need from your supervisor to be successful? Is it someone who allows you to work autonomously and lets you prioritize what needs to get done? Someone who advocates for you or is a good sounding board? Or perhaps rapid advancement through an organization is important and you want your supervisor to be an advocate, mentor, or someone who challenges you?

Roles: What kind of relationship is important to have with your supervisor at this point in your career and life? What type of supervisor do you want them to be? The following are some common supervisor types:

advocate	connector	leader
challenger	defender	manager
cheerleader	delegator	problem solver
coach	friend	role model
collaborator	goal setter	teacher
colleague	guide	

Behaviors: Using examples articulated in Exercise 3.1, write down some specific examples of supervisor behaviors that you have experienced that demonstrate the traits, qualities, and roles you are seeking in a supervisor. For example, perhaps a previous supervisor encouraged collaborative work by setting aside time at each biweekly staff meeting for someone to present a challenge or issue, and then opened up the space for everyone to brainstorm solutions. Or, perhaps your previous supervisor was a strong advocate, which she demonstrated through her request for a monthly report that captured your work, accomplishments, challenges, and new ideas. In doing this, your supervisor was able to regularly document important information to include in your annual performance review and have immediate information to share with her supervisor to advocate for you and those who reported to her. Identifying specific examples will help you to further develop what you are looking for in an ideal supervisor.

NEXT STEPS

Now that you have created a gold mine of information about your skills, attributes, and values, use the data collected through your self-assessment exercises to do the following:

- Create a plan to research job opportunities
- Identify gaps in your credentials that you can then fill in with activities such as courses, continuing education units (CEUs), volunteering, class projects, and internships
- Write strong application materials, a LinkedIn profile, and other professional branding materials
- Talk about yourself in informational interviews, job interviews, and networking events
- Determine what questions to ask in an interview or informational interview to determine if the role, agency, and supervisor are consistent with what you learned about yourself through your self-assessment
- Evaluate a job offer, negotiate salary, and be clear and confident about what you are bringing to the position in terms of skills, knowledge, abilities, and commitment

Self-assessment is a lifelong process, and the data acquired during self-assessment can be used throughout the Professional Development Cycle of Social Workers (see chapter 2). We encourage you to periodically reflect and update your self-assessment data to ensure your job is satisfying, determine your next career move, rebalance your work and life, and keep growing professionally.

Finally, it is important that you periodically update your self-assessment because over a lifetime:

- You learn more about yourself
- Life stages and situations change
- Career opportunities evolve
- Priorities change
- Skills evolve

The following case study illustrates how self-assessment can be valuable to someone undergoing a career change.

CASE STUDY

Clarissa

Clarissa is a 50-year-old, final year, clinically focused MSW student with an interest in mental health issues of adolescents and young adults. She has a prior master's degree in nonprofit management, and over the past 20 years, has offered nonprofit consulting on a part-time basis. She has also co-raised her children and volunteered extensively in her town and public schools with a focus on prevention and awareness of mental health issues. She feels confident in her macro skills but less so with her newly acquired clinical skills, although this is the direction she wants to pursue in her next career move. She also worries about how her age will affect her chances in the job market.

Clarissa would benefit from a self-assessment to understand her "new" professional self as a clinical social worker. She needs to inventory her new clinical skills (e.g., assessment, counseling, case management) and decide which of her previous macro skills (e.g., budgeting, program design, fundraising) she wants to apply in her new job without feeling like she is going backward in her career development. She needs to explore her new values around work/life balance, work environment, and the ability for her to feel both appreciated as a seasoned professional and supported as a new clinical social worker. She should be aware of what she needs from her supervisor as she embarks on her new career.

IDENTIFYING AND RESEARCHING CAREER OPTIONS

With the inventory of information gained through a self-assessment, you now have a framework and key words to use when researching career opportunities. Your goal is to explore and identify roles, settings, and agencies that allow you to apply the skills you have, contribute to improving the lives of the populations you want to work with, and operate in a work culture that is consistent with your values. Here, we offer several strategies to research career opportunities that may be consistent with your self-assessment inventory.

Review Job Postings

Job postings give you an idea of the job responsibilities and required qualifications for specific positions and alert you to the job titles that match what you are looking for so you can find similar opportunities elsewhere. Collect the postings that most interest you and identify the parts of the descriptions that excite you. With two highlighters of different colors, highlight those skills and experiences you already have with one color, and those you still need to gain to be qualified with another color. Do this with several job postings and you may start to see a pattern of similar words that can provide you with insight into why you are attracted to a particular job. Maybe it is the way the agency describes the culture of the organization, or the population you would be working with, or the openness to creativity. Whatever it is, write down your ideas and keep them organized.

Reviewing job postings shows you what skills, knowledge, and experience you are missing from the qualifications and provides a road map to filling those gaps. If you are still in school, maybe you can take a class or write a research paper to become more familiar with a topic. You could volunteer to gain experience or offer to get involved with something new at your field placement. For postgraduates, CEUs are a great way to add to or sharpen your social work qualifications. CEU accredited activities can be easily found at schools of social work, professional conferences, or through NASW national or state chapters. Perhaps the job you are interested in is something you are shooting for in a couple of years. Again, you might not be qualified for the job now, but knowing what skills, experience, and knowledge are required helps you to create a plan of action for the future.

Conduct Informational Interviews

We highly recommend that, whatever stage of the PDCSW you are in, you conduct informational interviews to inform and guide you in your next steps. Whether you know exactly what you want to do or are still determining, getting information directly from the people who do the work is invaluable. Information about trends in the field (e.g., impact of policy, laws, funding), salaries, career trajectories, a typical day, qualifications, and which agencies are better suited for your career stage is important in helping you determine your career direction. You can take this information and start to match it with the information you found out about yourself in the self-assessments. You will then begin to identify settings, roles, and agencies that are a good fit for you. Consider this quote from a job seeker:

> With the insightful help of my job coach, I found the informational interview process to provide realistic and invaluable descriptions of working with different client populations from an expert's perspective. Through my coach's expertise in matching the experts in the field with my career goals, I had a distinct advantage and was able to learn about relevant trainings; connect with a variety of social work professionals; ask authentic questions regarding my concerns; and even had some job offers! I highly recommend the informational interview process especially when guided by an experienced job coach who takes the time to recommend expert professionals while assessing and identifying your personal strengths and talent! (Judy Green, LCSW, MSEd, personal communication, January 18, 2023)

Contacting someone you do not know well (or at all!) to have a conversation can seem daunting. You might think, "Why would someone be willing to talk to me? What am I supposed to say? Whom should I reach out to?" Remember, people generally love talking about themselves, especially about their career. Look at this as an opportunity to listen and learn from an expert. Let us get your questions answered and put your mind at ease—you can do this!

Contact Your Network

Call or email (see sample email in Appendix F) people to set up a 30-minute meeting. You can also send a request to connect on LinkedIn or other professional networking sites. Make it clear you are looking for information and not a job. Explain why you selected them to meet with; for example, you were referred by a mutual acquaintance, they have a job you are interested in learning about, they work for an agency you are interested in, or you are exploring a number of career fields and want to get a real-world sense of what it is like to work in that field.

Prepare for the Informational Interview

This is an opportunity for you to make a good impression professionally, so dress the part, come prepared, and be respectful of the person's time. You are responsible for conducting the informational interview, not the interviewee. You must prepare ahead of time what information you are seeking and what open-ended questions you want to ask (see Appendix C for sample questions). Write questions around these themes:

- What is your job like?
- What do you like and dislike about your work?
- How did you prepare to work in this field?
- What job search advice do you have for someone entering this field?

Make sure to do your research beforehand so you are not seeking information easily accessible on an agency's web page.

Bring Your Resume

Bring copies of your resume for your contact to review. They might have some useful tips for improving it from an employer's perspective. Getting feedback on your resume will allow you to sell yourself better in future cover letters and interviews.

Expand Your List of Contacts

One of the goals of the informational interview is to obtain additional names of people to talk with. Always end the interview by asking if they can suggest additional people you should speak to. Try to connect with those people on LinkedIn or by email, making sure to include the subject line, "Referred to you by . . ." and insert the name of the person who referred you.

Thank-You and Follow-Up

It is important to send your contact a thank-you email within a day or two. Keep them updated on your job search and let them know that you followed up on their referrals. Make sure to keep a record of the people you have contacted, how you were connected with them, and when and how you last connected (see chapter 6). Let us take a look at the case study of Alex to see how this career research plays out for him.

CASE STUDY

Alex

Alex is a macro-focused social worker with an interest in criminal justice reform. His previous job experience working with youth in the juvenile justice system inspired him to find ways to improve the system. Although he has two years of program management experience and solid management and policy skills gained through his MSW coursework, he is not sure what career options are available that fit his interests. What should he do to learn more?

The data that Alex has collected through self-assessment—the skills he has, the skills he wants to develop, the social issues he wants to work on, the populations he wants to work with, and the preferred geographic location—provides information and key words to begin researching opportunities.

Alex can use his MSW program field database to identify agencies that work on these issues, or search the internet for agencies in his geographical area of preference using industry language such as "criminal justice," "criminal reform," or "restorative justice." He can identify agencies, professional associations, and funding streams involved in this work. Alex should continue researching until he has a list of people to talk to, agencies to explore, careers identified, and jobs to apply for.

CONCLUSION

Self-assessment is critical to knowing both what you have to offer and what you are looking for, in both the short and long term. This information helps you make informed decisions about what area of social work you can best contribute to. This inventory of skills, qualities, knowledge, and values creates a framework that you can use in researching and evaluating job opportunities. You will have the key words to be able to research career opportunities. It is important to connect with people through informational interviews to learn more about their job's responsibilities, expectations, and qualifications so you know the steps to pursue this type of career. The work you have done in this chapter sets you up to create your professional brand and marketing package in chapters 4 and 5, as well as identifying and applying for job opportunities in chapter 6. You are well on your way to creating the career change you desire!

CHAPTER TAKEAWAYS

- Self-assessment is gathering information about your skills, qualities, priorities, and knowledge, based on self-awareness and reflection on past experiences.

- Self-assessment is important because it
  - allows you to make informed career choices based on who you are, what you value, and what you have to offer.
  - provides information that is critical in researching opportunities.
  - provides the personal information used to effectively interview, create application materials, and evaluate job offers.
- Connecting with professionals through informational interviews is an important activity to obtain firsthand knowledge about a career field that can help you chart your path.

CHAPTER
4

Creating Your Brand Identity as a Social Work Agent of Change

---

What You Will Learn

- ❒ What a professional brand is and why it is important
- ❒ How to create and use a strong professional brand
- ❒ How to write a bio statement, craft your elevator pitch, identify power words, and prepare for a professional headshot

Action Plan

- ❒ Form your professional brand by identifying career-defining moments and themes of your work
- ❒ Write a bio statement, develop your elevator pitch, and identify power words
- ❒ Schedule a professional headshot

Your professional brand is how you present yourself to the world. When well designed, it is a strategic career development tool that encompasses your image, work style, personality, values, knowledge areas, and professional reputation. Branding is a journey, and eventually, your brand becomes your legacy.

As an agent of change, it is critical for you to have a professional brand because it conveys your unique value. Creating a professional brand means creating a strong image of what you, and only you, will bring to the job. All social workers learn similar theories and skills through their education, but your brand is what sets you apart. To create trust, credibility, and influence in social work, authenticity is key. If you remain authentic, your brand will be consistent and genuine. In this section, we will focus on strategies to identify your expertise, unique qualities, and professional experience to create the foundation for an intentional branding message.

To get to the heart of your reputation and the image that you would like to portray through your professional brand, you will utilize the self-assessments that you completed in chapter 3. As with many of the elements in your career advancement journey, this is a process. It is very unlikely that you got to your current position by happenstance. You may have had professional or life experience that brought you to the place you are now, or perhaps you had one task at a previous job that you really enjoyed and you felt as if you were in your element. By reviewing your career journey through multiple lenses, including the assessment tools in chapter 3 and what others have said about your work, you can identify themes that will eventually become the foundation of your professional brand.

CRAFTING YOUR PROFESSIONAL BRAND

Create an Inventory and Identify Themes

In chapter 2, you identified where you are in the Professional Development Cycle of Social Work. In chapter 3, you identified your skills, knowledge areas, values, and experience. Now it is time to review this information and discover professional themes that have been consistent throughout your career. To begin this process, identify (a) consistent patterns of your performance that you have applied in all your professional interactions; (b) personal characteristics you incorporate into your professional and personal lives; (c) feedback you have received from others about your work, including recognition from your colleagues, clients, and supervisors; and (d) what makes you stand out among your peers.

There are other factors to consider for your brand besides your knowledge and experience. Your brand includes your style of dress, your personal characteristics, and your manner of communication. To begin this process, review your career-defining moments. These comprise the career roles listed on your resume and those that arose in the career development exercises you have done thus far. A career-defining moment is a significant experience or career event that may cause you to think more deeply about your work and make decisions that change the course of your career trajectory.

CASE STUDY

Darius

Table 4.1 shows career-defining moments, patterns, and professional characteristics for Darius, an entry-level social worker who is preparing for his job search by identifying themes for his professional brand.

Table 4.1 Career-Defining Moments, Patterns, and Sample Professional Themes Inventory

Career-Defining Moments	Patterns	Personal Characteristics	What Others Said	What Made You Stand Out
Showed early interest in working with children	Worked as a nanny and in childcare for day care center; volunteered as a mentor	Compassion and patience	Commented on my patience and ability to lead children's activities and create a fun learning environment	My ability to confidently communicate with teachers, parents, and children
Student member of NASW	Attended every meeting and introduced myself to colleagues	Dressed professionally in all meetings	Commented on my professionalism	Made a point to introduce myself to all speakers
Social work intern at elementary school	Made a point to learn the various roles of teachers, administrators, and counselors, and familiarize myself with in-school settings	Always took notes and used a paper calendar with color coding	Commented on my organizational skills	Every morning, stood at the front of the school and greeted the children
Social work student participating in group exercises for social work class	Volunteered to create presentation materials	Passion for working as a team	Peers commented on my flexibility	Positivity and leadership throughout the process
Entry-level professional job	Proactive about taking the lead on team projects	Utilized professional sense of humor to engage coworkers	Staff commented that I "created a sense of community in every project"	Celebrated team successes

Common Professional Themes:
Communication, leadership, group work, experience working with children, positivity, humor, and organization

In this example, you can see that Darius has experience working with children. He possesses strong communication skills including the ability to engage multiple audiences, facilitate groups, and create presentations. He also demonstrates excellent leadership skills, including supervision of teams, professional communication, and organizational skills. Finally, he approaches his work with positivity, flexibility, and a strong sense of community building among team members, all with confidence and a good sense of humor.

Now, it is your turn! Go to Appendix D for a blank Career-Defining Moments, Patterns, and Sample Professional Themes Inventory form. As you complete the form, consider your professional brand. Think about what you would like your primary message to be and include at least three of your strongest supporting themes.

In social work, a strong professional brand is crucial. As the field evolves into new industries and nontraditional jobs, we must be able to articulate and demonstrate the depth and breadth of our profession. It is no secret that some people have misconceptions about the profession. For years, social workers have faced preconceived notions about what their role is in the workplace. For this reason and others, it is important to develop your professional brand. Your brand should be intentional and inspiring, and you should actively curate and maintain the way that others perceive your work.

Apply Your Professional Brand

Now that you have identified and embraced the essence of your professional brand, it is time to apply it to your other materials. Begin by working on a bio statement, an elevator pitch, and power words that create a compelling narrative to grab the attention of your audience. Table 4.2 describes each of these elements, how to use them, and why they are important. Next, we will go into detail about each of these aspects of your brand.

YOUR BIO STATEMENT

A bio statement tells the reader who you are in two to three paragraphs and is a vehicle for conveying your experience, value, and unique qualities. For inspiration, think about a book's "about the author" section, or how a speaker is introduced at a

Table 4.2 The Story of You: Applying Your Brand to Your Narrative

	What Is It?	How Do You Use It?	Why Is It Important?
Bio Statement	A brief statement that tells the reader who you are in two to three paragraphs	Used for personal/professional websites, LinkedIn, and introduction purposes	Allows your audience to learn more about the scope of your career, credibility, and expertise
Elevator Pitch	A 30- to 60-second verbal statement that captures your background, experience, and purpose	When introducing yourself in professional networking opportunities	By articulating your experience verbally in a concise statement, you will become more confident networking and interviewing
Power Words	Unique and powerful words that you use to describe your own experience	During an interview, while networking, or in composing your materials such as resumes and cover letters	These words help you to make a compelling and memorable impression on your audience

conference or on a podcast. If you were that author or speaker, what details would tell the reader or audience who you are, what you do, and why you were invited to speak?

The bio statement should be written in the third person and you should use your desired pronouns throughout the statement. Begin the statement with your first and last name, credentials, job title, and organization. To create a strong bio statement, begin by identifying the following three elements: context, audience, and purpose. Please see Exercise 4.1 to learn how to create your own bio statement.

Exercise 4.1

Biographical Statement

Now it is time to write your own bio statement! Remember, your bio statement should be no longer than two to three paragraphs.

Step 1: Write a topic sentence. In one sentence, state your name, your title, your position, and where you are in your career. Sample topic sentence: *Alexis Jones is an LMSW and currently works as a program director at the Salvation Army.*

Step 2: Identify three primary themes. In three to five sentences, describe three primary themes. These could be your years of experience, education, training, expertise, the type of clients you have worked with, clinical frameworks with which you are familiar, or your leadership style. For example:

> **Sample Primary Theme 1:** Alexis has over four years of experience working in nonprofit organizations primarily with people experiencing homelessness.
>
> **Sample Primary Theme 2:** She became passionate about client advocacy after identifying a lack of social services available to people experiencing homelessness.
>
> **Sample Primary Theme 3:** She uses a collaborative leadership style to gain community consensus regarding issues of persons experiencing homelessness and applies these skills to community engagement and fundraising.

Step 3: Identify secondary themes. Secondary themes are job related, but may reflect your personal characteristics, passions, values, and transferable skills.

> **Sample Secondary Theme 1:** In her field placement Alexis discovered a knack for community organizing to address the lack of resources available to the homeless population. Under the supervision of a clinical social worker, she became knowledgeable regarding the connections between homelessness, mental health, and stigma.
>
> **Sample Secondary Theme 2:** Alexis has developed excellent communication skills, including public speaking and writing, leadership development, and a natural ability to build consensus among stakeholders.

(continued)

Step 4: Write a closing statement. Depending on your audience, there are various ways to close your statement. For example, if you are making a presentation, tell your attendees what impact you wish to make. If your audience is a potential employer, tell them how your experience will make an impact in the field or where you see your career going. Reinforce key points and highlight your passion. You may also use personal information to connect with your audience if appropriate. Always finish the statement with your education and the institutions from which you earned your degrees.

> **Sample Closing Statement:** Her primary mission is to alleviate homelessness in her community through program development, community organizing, and consensus building. Alexis believes that homelessness is a community issue, and that as a community we should help our neighbors. Alexis holds an undergraduate degree in psychology from State University and an MSW with a concentration in social service administration from the University of Illinois.

A bio statement that follows these guidelines will provide a clear focus of what skills you have and what you would like to do with them, not only for you, but for anyone reading it. Pulling it all together, Alexis's bio statement looks like this:

Alexis Jones' Bio Statement

> Alexis Jones is an LMSW and currently works as program director at the Salvation Army. Alexis has over four years of experience working in social services, primarily with people experiencing homelessness, including as a case manager, coordinator, and program director. She became passionate about client advocacy after identifying a lack of social services available to people experiencing homelessness. Following her experience of working directly with clients, she sought to further her education and gain more knowledge about community organizing, advocacy, and the stigma associated with homelessness. She uses a collaborative leadership style to gain community consensus regarding issues of persons experiencing homelessness and applies these skills to community engagement and fundraising.
>
> While in graduate school, Alexis had her first field placement at Refugee Services. She began to discover a knack for community organizing to address the lack of resources available to the homeless population. Under the supervision of a clinical social worker, she became knowledgeable regarding the connections between homelessness, mental health, and stigma.
>
> Following graduation with her MSW, Alexis took a position with the Salvation Army, working as a program director with the executive director on projects related to community engagement and fundraising. She has been recognized for her advanced communications skills in writing and public speaking, for her leadership development, and for her natural ability to build consensus among stakeholders. Her primary mission is to alleviate homelessness in her community through program development, community organizing, and consensus building. Alexis believes that homelessness is a community issue, and that as a community we should help our neighbors. Alexis holds an undergraduate degree in psychology from State University and an MSW with a concentration in social service administration from the University of Illinois.

Context

The context is the type of situation or setting in which your bio statement is being used. Common contexts include formal email introductions, job search activities, conference proposals and proceedings, funding applications, personal and professional websites and blogs, institutional websites, and social/professional networking websites such as LinkedIn and X (formerly Twitter).

Audience

Who is the bio statement written for? Your audience may include future employers, networking connections, colleagues in and outside of your discipline, and your clients. Considering who your audience is will help you adjust your language and tone for the reader. For example, if your audience is colleagues at a presentation, you should make sure you address your role or title, career background, and number of years of experience in the field, all using industry language and a collegial tone. If you are writing for a layperson, you should adjust your language so your points are clearly understood by all audience members.

Purpose

As evidenced by the wide array of context and audiences, the purpose of the bio statement can vary. The following are some common purposes of a bio statement:

- Tells your colleagues who you are and what you are about
- Acquaints others with your work history
- Provides clients with a sense of whom they are working with
- Gives readers of an article or conference proceeding a sense of who is providing the information
- Contributes to an institutional, departmental, or programmatic identity (remember, you are an ambassador for your place of employment, your current field placement, and the profession of social work)
- Gives potential collaborators or potential employers a sense of the work you do along with your professional and leadership identity

Regardless of the purpose of your bio statement, it should be well thought-out, intentional, and strategic.

YOUR ELEVATOR PITCH

While the bio statement is a written expression of your marketing package, the elevator pitch is your verbal expression. Simply stated, the elevator pitch is a way to introduce yourself during professional networking opportunities. The name comes from this scenario: Imagine being in an elevator with a potential employer. What would you say in those 30 to 60 seconds between floors to make a good impression?

Now that you have a strong sense of your professional brand and a bio statement, your elevator pitch will flow naturally. While it may seem awkward at first, if you put effort into developing and practicing your elevator pitch, you will be able to articulate it more confidently. The keys to a great elevator pitch are:

- Create an authentic, persuasive, and memorable connection
- Consider your audience and customize your pitch; pay special attention to acronyms and jargon that your audience may or may not be familiar with (for example, if you are in an elevator with an HR person, they may not know what NASW is, but a social worker would)
- Focus on your current professional situation and what makes you unique to the audience
- End with a call to action

As you become more comfortable with embracing your brand and articulating it to different audiences, here is what *not* to include in your elevator pitch.

- Do not mention your age, marital status, children, or other irrelevant personal information
- Do not use too much jargon or too many clichés
- Do not be disingenuous
- Do not ramble; remember, it is called an elevator pitch for a reason; keep your pitch at 30 to 60 seconds max
- Do not sound over-rehearsed; paradoxically, the more you practice, the more naturally the pitch will come to you and the more natural it will sound to the listener

Here is an example of a bad elevator pitch:

> Hey, my name is Gina! I was born in Dallas, went to college at State, and now I'm looking for a clinical supervisor and a job that pays more money. I have good experience and skills. I like working with people and I hope I can get into graduate school someday.

Instead, how about the following pitch:

> Hello! My name is Gina and I have an LBSW and over two years of experience working with substance use disorders. During my field placement in an inpatient treatment center for individuals with substance use issues, I developed strong skills in conducting screening, assessment, and intake in both English and Spanish. I also had the opportunity to run a group for Spanish-speaking adults transitioning out of the center. For my macro project, I wrote a culturally competent relapse prevention curriculum which was implemented with Spanish-speaking clients who were being discharged from the center. I am very interested in continuing this work while pursuing my MSW. My

long-term goal is to pursue my LCSW and to find a clinical supervisor who can guide me in applying culturally competent approaches and support my passion for working with the Latinx community.

As you can see in the first example, Gina has been nonspecific about her skills, provided too much irrelevant personal information, and has not ended with a call to action. In the second example, Gina has drawn attention to her specific and unique skills, avoided jargon, and ended with a call to action.

YOUR POWER WORDS

Have you ever heard someone describe a photo or a piece of art with words like "breathtaking," "stunning," or "brilliant"? *Power words* evoke emotion and leave people with a desire to learn more. These words have been used for years in the marketing industry to influence the reader's feelings about the information that is presented. From a career advancement perspective, these verbs and adjectives will help you to articulate your skills and knowledge in a way that is interesting, compelling, and memorable. When you pair these power words with attention to detail, your professional brand will stand out from the others. Details may include more specific information about the skill you are describing, the scope of your work, or even more descriptive verbs. These are the statements that will pop out and will be repeated in your application materials and professional branding. When considering these statements, make sure they include industry language.

As we discussed in chapter 2, key words are used to describe areas of interest, skills, populations, settings, qualifications, knowledge, or industry language related to the jobs you are interested in pursuing. These key words are used to conduct your search or find resources that will help you to identify people, job titles, professional membership organizations, or agencies that you would like to apply for. Power words, however, are used to describe *your own experience*. These words can be used during an interview, in your pitch, or in your materials such as resumes and cover letters. While it is crucial to know key words to identify your career opportunities, they can become dull and overused in application materials. This is where power words come in.

Table 4.3 provides some examples of how power words and attention to detail can make a significant difference in describing your abilities.

As you can see, power words make your experience more interesting, compelling, and thoughtful. If power words are a new concept for you, there are many simple ways to develop this vocabulary. Appendix A can help you get started. Keep abreast of industry-specific language through relevant articles, posts, podcasts, and other social work sources. For example, if you are applying for jobs in a nontraditional field such as corporate social work, you might use terms like "partner development manager," "community engagement," or "change management consultant." All of these words have similar meanings in social work, but will be more familiar in a corporate setting. Consider subscribing to a "word of the day" website to increase your vocabulary. A dictionary or thesaurus can give you alternatives to overused words. Spending a

Table 4.3 Using Power Words and Attention to Detail—Before and After

Before	After
Led efforts to create a new program	*Orchestrated* efforts to *design* and *implement* an *innovative* program to address substance use in middle school
Assisted with group	*Co-facilitated* psychoeducational group with adults in substance use recovery program
Won volunteer of the month	*Awarded* volunteer of the month *recognition* for Big Brothers Big Sisters program
Found resources for families	*Identified* and *connected* resources for unsheltered families including the explanation and assistance with complex federal programs such as Medicaid and SNAP
Reviewed and recorded survey results	*Analyzed* survey data using SPSS and *examined* data points for statewide study focusing on childcare need for low-income families
Set up meetings to discuss diversity and inclusion issues	*Founded* ad hoc committee to address diversity and inclusion efforts for faculty and staff in a large university setting
Helped plan a fundraiser and made several calls to donors	*Co-coordinated* fundraising *gala* for over 200 attendees and demonstrated *tenacity* in securing donations to successfully raise over $5,000
Worked with client to get basic public assistance	*Collaborated* with client and community agencies to *navigate complex public assistance systems* and secure housing, food, and transportation
Spoke with government officials to fight for public housing	*Demonstrated* persuasive communication skills to *advocate* for public housing within small rural community
Scheduled meetings with several agencies to recommend policy changes for clients with mental health needs	*Revolutionized* local mental health system by *building consensus* among multiple mental health organizations to *streamline* services for clients facing physical and behavioral health challenges

few minutes each day to expand your vocabulary can make a significant difference in your professional brand.

YOUR PROFESSIONAL HEADSHOT

As you launch your career and your online professional presence, it is worth investing in a professional headshot. Professionals may delay building their online presence because they do not have a good professional headshot. Make your headshot a priority so that you can create your LinkedIn profile and marketing package.

If you can afford to do so, use a professional photographer. They will coach you through the process of preparing for and taking the headshot. After your photo session, they will crop and edit the best ones and provide you with many photos to choose from. Ask your friends and colleagues for input about which photo they like best.

If a professional photographer is not in your budget, you can use your smartphone to take your own headshot. Here are a few simple tips to get you started:

- Take a current photo in which your face fills the frame
- Use portrait mode and adjust the light settings
- Have someone else take the picture, or use a smartphone stand to steady the camera; never use an "arm out" selfie
- Edit the photo to your liking, but do not overdo it—it should look natural
- Do not crop yourself out of another photo, and do not pose with your colleagues, partner, children, or pets
- Choose a clean, neutral, or blurry background
- Ideally, use natural light either indoors or outdoors; check for shadows and brightness
- Wear light or muted-color clothing (grey, white, navy); do not wear flashy jewelry and avoid large patterns or multicolored tops
- Present yourself as you would with a job interview; if you wear glasses regularly, wear them in your photo; wear your hair and makeup as you normally would for an interview or work
- Keep your body language open; pose at an angle with your shoulders back and chin forward
- Relax your jaw and smile naturally

If you still struggle with your professional headshot, do not be afraid to do online research! LinkedIn is a great place to look for step-by-step instructions on professional headshots, along with the size dimensions recommended for your profile photo. There are also many apps you could use to help you freshen up your headshots such as Facetune or Snapbar. You can use an app such as Canva to help you adjust the shape or background of your headshot. Additionally, several artificial intelligence (AI) applications are available, some that are low cost or even free. Just make sure you do your research and that your headshot is true to life and not overly touched up with filters and such. Last but not least, remember to stay true to your professional brand. If you are known for eyeglasses that stand out, such as cat-eye frames or large circular frames, wear these in your headshot. If it is not in your nature to wear a coat and tie, wear a nice dress shirt. This is the employer's first professional impression of you, but it is also to help people to recognize you and connect with you. Always stay true to yourself.

CONCLUSION

While the exercises we have discussed may seem like a lot of effort to create your professional brand, think of them as the building blocks of your legacy. Each of these components will help you to feel more confident and strategic with your application materials, networking, and overall career advancement. When you build a strong branding foundation, it will be easier to make career changes on your terms and timeline, identify the jobs you want and the people you want to work with, and build a fulfilling career and lasting legacy.

CHAPTER TAKEAWAYS

- Your professional brand is how you represent yourself to the world and conveys your unique value.
- Identify your audience, identify themes, and use power words to create a positive image.
- Reevaluate your brand annually and be consistent across all materials including your bio statement, elevator pitch, and headshot.
- Though it may change over the years, investing time in your professional brand will be foundational to your career and eventually your legacy.

CHAPTER
5

Your Resume, Cover Letters, LinkedIn Profile, and Other Job Search Materials

What You Will Learn

- ❒ What a job search marketing package is and why it is important
- ❒ How to write an engaging, powerful, and well-organized resume that will grab the attention of hiring managers
- ❒ How to complement your job search with a strong marketing package, including a resume, customized cover letters, references, business cards, social media presence, LinkedIn profile, and writing samples

Action Plan

- ❒ Prepare your materials for the job search in advance
- ❒ Apply your professional brand to all aspects of your job search marketing package, including your resume, cover letter, business cards, and LinkedIn profile
- ❒ Identify and reach out to three to five people who can be your references

A job search marketing package contains the materials you will need to apply for jobs, including, but not limited to:

- Resume
- Cover letter

- Personal or professional business cards
- References
- Social media and LinkedIn profiles
- Writing samples

Your professional brand will be the foundation for all of these materials. As with your professional brand, these materials should be consistent across all platforms, both online and offline. Consider the job search marketing package your toolbox for career advancement. While it may seem like it would be easier to create these materials as you go rather than preparing them ahead of time, we highly recommend creating these materials before you apply for a job. As you review unique job postings, you will want to customize some materials, such as your resume, in response to what each prospective employer wants to see in applicants. Making changes to a boilerplate document is easier than starting from scratch each time. Furthermore, you want to be prepared rather than scramble in response to a hiring manager's request. If you are prepared, you will be able to quickly pull these materials from your job search toolbox and be ready to apply.

PREPARATION IS KEY TO SUCCESS

CASE STUDY

Myra

As Myra entered the last semester of her MSW program, she began to think about her job search. She knew she needed to update her resume, but put it off due to all the other demands entailed in finishing up her final semester. Since she did not have an updated resume, she procrastinated looking for jobs. She thought that it would not do any good to look for a job unless she had her resume ready. Three weeks later, after she found the perfect job to apply for, she began to update her resume. When she finished her resume, she realized that the job called for a cover letter. Until that moment, Myra had not even considered writing a cover letter. She asked for guidance from her career center advisor, who read through the job posting with her. Her advisor pointed out that she would also need three references for the job. Myra forgot to ask her supervisor for a reference, and she was too worried about the cover letter to even consider who her other two references would be. Myra's career advisor also mentioned that the agency she was applying for had a good LinkedIn presence. Myra realized that she had not kept up with her LinkedIn profile since her undergraduate days. By the time Myra considered all of the marketing materials that were needed for her search, she realized that she did not have time to get these materials together before the closing date of the job listing. This was a huge letdown for Myra, and she felt overwhelmed and disappointed in herself.

Myra's example demonstrates how being unprepared can set your job search back weeks. In addition to saving time, preparing early for your job search can help you by

- crystalizing your thinking about your career history, present, and future, which will have a positive impact on your interviews
- providing you with a better understanding of your skills so you will be better prepared to articulate them to the hiring manager
- building confidence in your experience and articulating it with poise
- finding your flow and becoming more excited about the opportunities ahead of you

As the Roman philosopher Seneca said, "Luck is when preparation meets opportunity." Yes, your job search will involve some luck, but preparation is essential if you want to seize opportunities.

USING ARTIFICIAL INTELLIGENCE TO CREATE YOUR MATERIALS

Before we go further, let us discuss the utilization of AI to create your job search materials. One potential benefit of using AI is the ability to save time and streamline the job search process. AI-powered tools can help social workers craft resumes, cover letters, and other job search materials quickly and efficiently, using data-driven insights and language models to ensure that the materials are tailored to the specific job requirements and industry standards. AI can be a great tool to help you get started and add structure to your materials, especially if you are starting with a blank page.

However, crafting these materials is only one component of the job search process. The purpose of these materials is to get your foot in the door for an interview, and by writing these materials yourself, you will gain confidence in your knowledge, skills, and abilities. If you decide to use AI in your materials, think of it as a career coach or consultant: a tool that supports you, but does not do all the work for you.

How to Use AI

When using AI, it is critical that you give the AI tool the right prompts to generate accurate information. A quick search on the internet can help you to identify prompts for this technology. You will note that you can prompt the AI tool several different times and in different ways to generate the information you need to create your own materials. For example, you might say, "Write a cover letter for a medical social work position," which would generate a broad response. However, you can make further requests to customize the response into a more specific, intentional answer. For example, you can direct the AI tool to "Write a cover letter for a medical social work position from a licensed social worker with three years of experience working in school settings and with minimum healthcare experience." This more specific prompting will generate a more specific response. Another strategy is to paste your resume in the chat box and ask the AI tool to "Write a cover letter for a position based on the experience of this resume." The technology will generate the letter utilizing the information that you provide and even help you to translate your skills into the skills required for the job. If you choose to engage with AI in this way, do not cut, paste, and send. Employers are already using AI-detecting software to reveal AI-generated text, and you do not want to be perceived as lazy in your application. You must tailor the text with your own writing and voice.

Pitfalls to Using AI

As we alluded to, there are many pitfalls to using AI in your job search materials. One concern is that AI-generated materials may lack the human touch and personalization that can make a job application stand out. AI tools may reduce the authenticity of your materials. You want to be genuine and true to yourself throughout the job search process, including presenting yourself honestly and transparently to potential employers, rather than trying to present a certain image or persona that may not align with your true self.

Another potential pitfall is the risk of errors or inaccuracies in the AI-generated materials. While AI is a powerful resource, it is not infallible, and there is always the risk that an AI tool may misinterpret information or produce incorrect results. This could result in job search materials that are inaccurate or misleading, which could harm your chances of securing a job.

While AI can save time, it may also lack the personalization and accuracy that are crucial to job search success. Social workers should use a hybrid approach that combines AI-generated materials with personalized touches to ensure that their job applications stand out and accurately represent their qualifications and experiences.

Finally, be wary of using AI to generate your professional headshot. While you may be able to create a good look or the perfect background, you do not want to accidentally give yourself three hands, an extra arm, or a fake appearance.

RESUME CONTENT AND FORMATTING

The most important element of your marketing package is an outstanding resume. A resume is a strategically designed marketing tool that intentionally highlights those aspects of your background you wish to draw the reader's attention to. Resumes are personalized documents that include the content of your experience written and formatted in a way that maximizes your opportunities and highlights the relevance of your experiences to the positions you are applying for. In this chapter, we will provide resume writing guidance, in terms of both content and format. Social work entails a unique blend of transferable skills, education, accreditation, and training, and it is important to get writing and reviewing help from experienced colleagues who are familiar with the profession, whether that is your adviser, your field instructor, or the authors of this book.

Your resume should be concise, easy to read, and revised for each job or purpose. The resume is often the initial contact an employer has with you, and will be the basis upon which hiring managers decide whom to interview.

Make 30 Seconds Count

Did you know that many employers spend as little as 30 seconds skimming your resume? The reality is that employers are usually inundated with resumes, so they are trying to weed out as many resumes as possible as quickly as possible. In your mind, the purpose of the resume should be to avoid being passed over and to get your foot in the door for an interview. Make those 30 seconds count by following these tips:

- **Be Concise:** Use phrases, not sentences. Use the minimum words necessary to accurately convey what you wish to say. Highlight experiences most relevant to the position you are applying for.
- **Use "First Person Implied":** Remove first person pronouns and determiners such as "I," "my," and "our." Instead, make statements that are in the first person but leave out the pronoun. For example, "Manage a weekly group for pregnant teenagers for this community health agency."
- **Think in Terms of the Reader:** Using the job description of the position to which you are applying and your research in the field, identify what skills, experiences, and qualities employers are looking for in a candidate. Demonstrate that you know your own strengths and skills.
- **Make Your Resume Easy to Read:** Choose a layout that allows the information to be read easily and quickly. Use bold, underline, and italics to highlight what is important. Make sure there are no errors and be consistent with your formatting.
- **Minimize Pages by Using Strategic Headers:** Rather than listing everything you have done in your career, be intentional by using terms like Experience Highlights or Selected Presentations. These terms will allow you to focus on the most important information while conveying to the reader that the information you are providing is not meant to be complete, but relevant to the job you are applying to.

Creating Great Content: Resume Formats and Suggested Headings

There are as many formats for resumes as there are unique areas of practice in social work. As with most of the tips shared in this book, intentionality is key. While there are very few hard and fast rules regarding resume formats for job seekers in general, in the profession of social work there are ways to highlight your experience that will speak to your audience. For that reason, it is better to compose your own resume than to use a template, an online resume generator, AI, or even a professional resume writer. Ideally, it makes sense to determine a format based on the experience you have, your education level, and your stage in the Professional Development Cycle of Social Workers from chapter 2. As your career advances, you may find it necessary to have more than one resume for different purposes, such as a very targeted job opportunity, different jobs in the same field, public relations (such as speaking engagements), or funding opportunities. Let us discuss the different types of resumes. Examples for all can be found in Appendix E.

Reverse Chronological Resume

The reverse chronological resume—the most common type—organizes your experience section by job title with the most recent position listed first. This format emphasizes career progression. The experience section in a chronological resume must concisely emphasize your most important duties with an employer, skills that apply to your career goals, awards or achievements, and specific benefits that you brought to the employer. Dates are key in the chronological resume and should be placed in the right-hand margin so that they are easy to follow. For job seekers with solid experience and a logical job history, the chronological resume is the most effective.

Functional Resume

The functional resume uses a format that is skill-based rather than position-based. Based on the jobs you are applying for, you would select three to four skills areas (e.g., fundraising, organization, youth development, leadership) and then place bullet points under each that would describe the best examples of when you have demonstrated these skills. The next section on your resume would be Employment Highlights and include only the job title, agency name, city, state, and dates of each work experience. Rather than describing each experience in full, this section is a simple list of the places you have worked or volunteered. The idea is that you have already elaborated upon your most important accomplishments and abilities in the Skills section, and now you are backing it up with where you obtained these skills. This type of resume might be thought of as a "problem-solving" format. It gives you the opportunity to make sense of your work history and match up accomplishments and abilities that might not be obvious to the employer. The functional resume is useful if you are a recent graduate, if you have a nonlinear work history or one that has large gaps, or if you are making a career change—either changing fields (from macro to clinical) or changing occupation (from business to social work). If you are choosing this style to make a career change or if you have gaps in your resume, you might make this resume transition by clustering your experience into similar groups and then identifying various skill sets. While this resume style might be the best fit for your personal circumstances, it is important to get feedback from a career advisor, friend, or trusted reader on the final product to make sure that it makes sense and presents the best overview of your experience while highlighting your skills.

Combination or Targeted Resume

The combination (or targeted) resume is a cross between the functional and chronological resume styles. You can use the combination resume when you have relevant work experience that is of short duration, your education is an important part of your overall experience, your background reflects a range of unrelated skills, or your work history reflects more time in other occupational areas. Since the combination resume allows you to use the best of the functional and chronological style resumes, it can easily reflect a solid career trajectory. For most social workers, this format generally works best because it allows you to market all of the best points of your social work skills, transferable skills, areas of knowledge, and achievements in a Capabilities or Professional Summary section, and then back them up with your work history in reverse chronological order.

Be sure to customize your combination style resume for each job that you apply for. You may need to reorder your capabilities or the sentences in your professional summary to fit each job. Be cautious as you do this! When you customize, you may inadvertently create employment gaps or typos. Proofread your resume carefully after each series of edits to be sure the logic and accuracy are intact.

Whatever format you choose, be sure to create a well-written chronological version of your resume to keep as a historical account of your work experience. You can then decide to include or exclude certain content and in what format to best represent or highlight how your experience relates to the jobs you are applying for.

RESUME SECTIONS AND SUGGESTED HEADINGS

The order of the sections on your resume is up to you, but it is important to think strategically based on the jobs you are applying for. Typically, for recent graduates or current students, the first three categories after your header are Capabilities or Professional Summary, Education, and Experience Highlights. Please note: the capabilities or professional summary mentioned in this section is for a combination style resume.

Other categories, what you label them, and their order depend on your experiences and their relation to the position for which you are applying. Remember, as readers review your resume, they will pay most attention to the beginning. Organize your information with this in mind. Additionally, *be intentional with all content on your resume*. We cannot emphasize this enough. It is crucial that you check the order of your headers, bullets, and each word in each section of your resume. For example, if you are applying for a leadership position, you should bring your leadership skills to the top of your resume in your summary or capabilities section. If you are seeking a position with an employer who is an alumna of your university, consider putting your education at the top of your resume. If you are seeking a position in which bilingual skills are preferred, list language skills first in your description of your work experience. All sections should be written in reverse chronological order.

Resume Header

As shown in the samples in Appendix E, your header belongs at the top of the page and serves as your letterhead for the resume and other application documents, such as your cover letter, list of references, and thank-you letters. Place your name at the top of the page and highlight it by using a slightly larger font size and/or bolding. List your name, credentials (such as degree acronyms and licensure), email address, phone number, and LinkedIn profile. The order of degrees and credentials should be degree first, then credential, with the highest credential listed last. If you have multiple degrees in social work or another field, you only need to list the highest degree or license or credential level. For example, rather than stating "Name, BSW, MSW, LCSW," you would only need to list the highest degree and credential, "MSW, LCSW." If you have multiple degrees and/or credentials in different fields, list these strategically depending on the job you are applying for. For example, if you are applying for a social work position in a hospice setting (which often hires social workers and chaplains), you would list your credentials as "Name, LMSW, M.Div." This strategic order demonstrates that you have both qualifications. Subsequent pages contain a header consisting of your last name and the page number in the top right-hand margin (e.g., "Luna, page 2").

Capabilities or Professional Summary

If you are using a combination style resume, this section will be the first thing that a prospective employer will see after your header. Because it is top and center of your resume, think of this space as ocean front property! This section will highlight a rich description of the specific qualities, skills, knowledge areas, transferable skills, and credentials that will set you apart from other candidates who are applying for the same job. You can format this section using either a Capabilities or a Professional Summary style. A capabilities section is presented in a bulleted list, whereas the professional summary is written in paragraph format. A good rule of thumb is to use Capabilities if you have an assortment of transferable skills from various experiences including non–social work jobs, volunteer positions, and professional organizations. A professional summary would be more appropriate if you have a significant amount of experience in the field in which you are applying and the skills and knowledge to back it up. Choose only one; you do not need both. To write your capabilities or professional summary, go back to the transferable skills and knowledge areas you identified in chapter 3.

If you have unique or transferable skills and knowledge areas that you would like to highlight, this is the ideal place to put them. Present this information in a bulleted format, which will make it easy for the reader to skim through. Examples of these skills might include computer proficiency, foreign languages, communication skills, team-building skills, knowledge of complex systems, leadership skills, and supervisory experience. You can also use this section to list skills and knowledge areas that are specific to social work. Here is a sample capabilities section:

- Knowledge of and strong interest in play therapy, brief therapy, and solution-focused therapy
- Excellent communication skills, including proficient knowledge of conversational Spanish and clinical documentation

- Proven leadership skills and supervisory experience in various settings
- Strong crisis management skills and comfort in a fast-paced environment
- Two years' experience conducting detailed assessments of clients for drug- and alcohol-related issues

Professional Summary

Whether you are a recent graduate or a seasoned professional, one of the best ways to make your resume strategic is to begin with a professional summary. A professional summary gives the reader a context in which to understand the content of your resume. For example, if you want to pursue a career in health disparities but your resume has a variety of experiences listed, providing a well-written professional summary will alert the reader to your most pertinent experiences and help them understand how your skills fit together to make you a strong candidate.

The bio statement that you worked on in chapter 4 will give you the information you need to craft the professional summary for your resume. The professional summary should go at the top of your resume and should be written in the first person, just like the bio statement. You might begin by stating your title, degree, or the number of years' experience you have in your field. Describe your key skills, knowledge of theories that apply to the job, practice models, and populations that you have worked with. Do your best to match these highlights to the job to which you are applying. Focus on your transferable skills, such as clinical documentation, communication, and/or supervision skills. To close, you can also briefly discuss the values, passions, and/or personal characteristics that make you unique. Here are some examples of professional summaries:

> **Generalist Example:** LBSW with experience and training in case management, children's services, and healthcare. Advanced training in case management and strong knowledge of complex systems including Medicare, Medicaid, SNAP, and local housing programs. Excellent communication skills including writing, interpersonal communication, and documentation utilizing online medical health records. Proven leadership skills in role as coordinator in volunteer and children's programs at a shelter, election to vice president of Voices for Children, and recognition as Social Work Student of the Year by the National Association of Social Workers.
>
> **Macro Social Work Example:** Highly motivated social work professional with nearly five years of experience in administrative, organizational, and leadership development. Persuasive and engaging communication style and the ability to build consensus with multiple constituents. Strong drive to assist others to grow professionally through mentorship coupled with a personal commitment to advancing the profession of social work. A proven leader who consistently forges strong collaborations based on vision and a commitment to excellence.
>
> **Clinical Social Worker Example:** LMSW with experience and training in medical social work, crisis intervention, and trauma-informed therapy. Over

two years of expertise in neonatal and pediatric intensive care case management, pediatric oncology, and programs serving parents with at-risk pregnancy. Demonstrated leadership through coordinating volunteer and children's programs at large hospital, serving as local president of the Society for Leadership in Social Work in Health Care, and building consensus among multidisciplinary teams. Effective in working with children and their families in a medical setting. Earned an Inter-Professional Health Care certificate from the University of Texas at Austin and Dell Medical School.

Experienced Social Worker Example: Versatile LMSW with over 10 years of micro, mezzo, and macro experience in social services, including behavioral health, clinical assessment, and program coordination. Strong practical and clinical foundation with commitment to trauma-informed treatment modalities. Committed to working with individuals and families to promote optimum mental and emotional health. Proven leadership qualities and the ability to engage, relate to, and manage individuals from diverse departments while promoting team values and achieving shared goals.

Career Changer Sample: LMSW with strong interest and experience in behavioral health with children and families, including over 15 years of experience in public education. Specialized in social emotional learning, family systems theory, and trauma-informed care. Excellent communication skills include teaching, presentations, documentation, and bilingual English and Spanish. Committed to working with children and families from underserved populations to rebuild trust and promote resiliency.

Education

Strategy is the key to your Education section. If you are a student, you might consider putting your education first; however, if you are not a student and have experience in the field, it would be best to list your experience first. Remember, hands-on experience is usually more important to the employer than education. Additionally, since you will list your degree acronyms or your licensure in your header, it is less important to use this valuable space at the beginning of your resume for your education. Your Education section should be clearly written, in reverse chronological order, with your most recent degree first. Always spell out the name and type of degree, followed by your major, your social work specialization (if it is part of your degree program), and any certificates or fellowships you were awarded while you were in school. It is not necessary to include colleges or universities in which you did not earn a degree, unless you have another item such as an internship or job connected to that school.

If you are a current student, include your expected date of graduation for your degree and list "Anticipated" or "Expected" before the date. If you are applying to graduate school, a research position, or a fellowship or scholarship, include your GPA, academic honors, or scholarships. If you are applying to a job outside of academia, it is unnecessary to include your GPA. In all cases, it is unnecessary to include your high school information.

Experience Highlights

Using the term "Experience Highlights" instead of "Work Experience" gives you the flexibility to include not only paid positions, but also your field placements, internships, and volunteer positions in which you gained valuable skills. The key to deciding what to include in this section is determining what is relevant to your career goals. Relevance does not necessarily mean experience in exactly the job title you are seeking, but rather skills that are pertinent to the position you are seeking.

All entries in this section should showcase a skill, a knowledge area, or an accomplishment, and must go beyond regular job duties. We cannot emphasize enough that you should be intentional when writing these statements and refer to the power words and sample skills in Appendix A. Do not include lower-level skills that should be a given for a college graduate, such as answering phones, filing, or maintaining cleanliness. Each entry will contain your job title, the name of the organization, job title, city, state, and dates of employment. To describe your experience, begin with an action verb or adjective at the beginning of every bullet point. An action verb is a dynamic verb that describes what you are doing or have done. For experience that is current or ongoing, you should use the present tense (e.g., counsel, coordinate, and facilitate), and for past positions you should use past tense (e.g., counseled, coordinated, and facilitated). In describing your work, consider including details that pack a punch into every entry—for example, size of caseload, treatment framework utilized, population description, trainings, documents created, budgets managed, results of your action (money raised, increase in clients served, etc.). Capitalization, punctuation, and date formats should be consistent for every job description. Here are a few examples of these statements:

- Facilitated grief and loss group for up to 10 students, ages 15 to 19, in a school setting
- Led community outreach and educational activities in a healthcare clinic setting utilizing a culturally inclusive lens
- Utilized trauma-informed therapy with clients experiencing family violence in a shelter setting
- Successfully wrote a $5,000 foundation grant for an after-school program, including needs assessment, budget, and rationale

For additional inspiration for action verbs and details that pack a punch, see the resumes in Appendix E.

Professional Licenses, Certifications, and Affiliations

Always include your licenses, certifications, and affiliations in your resume. There are a couple of different options for this section, and strategy is key, so let us break it down. For licenses and certifications, if you have ample space, list the name of the credential, the regulatory organization that oversees the license or certification, the state in which you earned the license or certification, the date that you received it, and the license or certification number. If you do not have enough space to include all of this information, use the acronyms of your license after your name at the top of your resume. If you have a unique certification that would make you stand out from other candidates, you could also mention this in the professional summary at the top of the resume or in the cover letter.

For professional memberships and affiliations, the organization should be spelled out with the acronym next to it, e.g., "National Association of Social Workers (NASW)." While it is not necessary to list the length of membership, do not include organizations to which you no longer belong. The only exceptions are if you held a leadership position at the membership organization or if you gained a skill while a member or volunteer. In these cases, consider listing the experience in your Leadership section, where you can list the name of the organization, dates, and leadership roles; you can also list the skills you gained in your Skills section. The following quote serves as a good example of how the Leadership section can be quite helpful in demonstrating this skill to employers:

> When hiring a director for a small nonprofit, I noticed that the leading candidate did not have any paid work experience managing budgets. However, as I read through the resume and got to the Leadership section, I saw that they had been involved in the Parent Teacher Association at their children's school for over 10 years. They served as treasurer and had worked with large budgets, reporting, and oversight. This was proof enough for me to offer them the job! (Anonymous)

We recommend that you join NASW as soon as possible, as it will be a valuable networking resource for you as a professional. If you are a student, you will be eligible for a lower membership rate at NASW and most other professional membership organizations. Some will even give you a discounted rate for a year or two after graduation.

Community Service, Service Learning, and Volunteer Experience

Have you ever been told, "It is an unpaid position, but it will look good on your resume"? Take time to consider your community service experiences and the skills that you gained from them. Because hands-on experience is so important in social work and many of us take on community service to gain skills, it is important to articulate them and demonstrate how they will be transferred to the job you are applying for. Present these activities in the Experience section using a consistent format that includes your title, name of the organization, date, and location. If your position involved leadership or significant responsibilities, it can be included in the Experience section of your resume. However, if you do include it there, make sure the reader knows that it was an internship, a volunteer position, or unpaid work so that you do not mislead the reader into thinking you were a paid employee. Here are two examples of how to list this experience:

- In the Experience Highlights section: "Volunteered at the Salvation Army as a grant writer. Researched foundations to apply for grant funding, created budget according to application guidelines, and was awarded $5,000 for free breakfast program."

- In the Community Service section: "Volunteered at Salvation Army to serve free breakfast to unsheltered families."

Professional Development

Conferences, trainings, and additional certifications can be extremely valuable for building your knowledge and expertise. These items should only be added to your resume to support and enhance your credibility. Remember, you can always showcase the full list on your LinkedIn profile. This content would include the name of the training, certification, or conference; the organization that gave the training; the location and the date.

Leadership

If you have served in leadership roles in the organizations you have been involved in, on special committees in your work, or on a board of directors, you will want to highlight this experience in your resume. This section will demonstrate your ability and willingness to take on these roles and to describe successes you have had as a leader. Be sure to use your power words to express your leaderships skills, especially if you are applying for positions requiring advocacy for a cause. For example, "Served as strong advocate and passionate spokesperson for the National Alliance of Mental Illness (NAMI), speaking to over 500 members annually."

Presentations and Publications

Presentations and Publications sections can also be included on your resume if they build a strong case for positions you are applying for. For example, if you are demonstrating your knowledge or research in a particular field, both these sections will be a powerful way to demonstrate your expertise. If you are applying for a position that requires excellent writing skills, you should highlight any published articles or reports that you have authored. If you are applying for positions that require strong public speaking skills, add any presentations or trainings that you have done. For more information on the formatting of these entries, see the Curriculum Vitae section.

Quantify Your Career Moments

Each of the headings we have reviewed describes a "moment" in your career. A strong resume will structure these moments into a strategic career trajectory. It will quantify your accomplishments in a way that speaks to your audience. This is an important tip for all social workers regardless of their level of expertise or education. With the rise of evidenced-based practice and the growing job market in nontraditional fields such as health, business, and education, we must be able to describe our impact in a way that will resonate with the right reader. For example:

- Managed caseload of up to 20 students ages 14 to 19 in a teen pregnancy program

- Conducted client satisfaction survey resulting in a 72 percent return rate
- Facilitated weekly loss and grief groups with up to 15 clients facing the death of a loved one
- Coordinated annual fundraiser for agency raising over $5,000 toward mental health awareness

Note that when you are using quantifiable statements in your resume, you should make sure the numbers are impressive and not simply outcome measures. If you have encountered a situation in which the numbers were not the highlight of the experience, focus on the skills that you utilized. For example, instead of "Case managed one high school student," you could say, "Performed case management in high school setting; identified and located resources for housing, food, and transportation."

General Formatting Guidelines for Resume and Curriculum Vitae

Regardless of whether you use a curriculum vitae (CV) or a resume, use these guidelines to ensure your document is well designed, simple to navigate, and easy to read:

- Use no less than 0.5 inch margins all around. Print out your resume, hold it at arm's length, and check that the border of white space is even on all sides.
- Use a standard font such as Times New Roman or Helvetica in no smaller than 11-point font.
- Include last name and page number in the upper right-hand corner of every page, except the first page.
- Be consistent with content, format, and punctuation with each entry.
- Use reverse chronological order and make sure that titles, locations, and dates are listed in the same order for each entry.
- Remove any information that is specific to an organization or group; for example, course numbers, group names, or acronyms that are not familiar to your audience.
- Use consistent formatting techniques such as bolding or underlining to highlight important pieces of information, including section titles. However, do not use more than two types for format styles for each header (e.g., you could use boldface and capitalization, but not boldface, caps, and underscoring).
- Do not type "Resume" at the top of the resume or "References available upon request" at the bottom. Both of these are assumed.

Resume writing is important and can be time-consuming. You must be willing to write and edit until you have a well-organized document that emphasizes your most relevant qualifications. The importance of proofreading cannot be overemphasized. One small typo or misspelled word could knock you out of the running for an interview, and often, depending on the context of the word, spell-check will not catch it. Once you have a well-written resume, everything else about your job search will get easier. Not only will you build self-confidence, you will become better at articulating your experience when the moment arrives.

CURRICULUM VITAE

A resume is a brief summary of your knowledge, skills, and experience in one or two pages. A CV is a detailed document, usually several pages long, that lists everything you have done throughout your career. The resume focuses on the highlights of your career and is succinct, targeted, and purposeful; the CV records your career history. The CV can also be an incredible career management tool (see chapter 8).

There are many professional opportunities that arise for social workers in which a CV may be in order. A CV can be used for academic job searches (including positions in research, as adjunct instructors, or as internship supervisors) or for funding or publicity purposes. The job description itself may indicate whether the prospective employer is expecting applicants to submit a resume or a CV. If you are unsure, ask your academic advisor or mentor for advice.

As with resumes, each CV is a unique document. Develop your CV purposefully by combining elements of content and format to effectively reflect your career history and trajectory. Consult Table 5.1 as you consider in what order you will list your CV's sections. We discuss each of the sections in detail next.

Education

Because a CV is primarily utilized for academia and research, the Education section should always go first. In this first section of your CV, list each degree in reverse chronological order along with the degree earned, program title, institution, city, state, and year. If you are a current student, include your expected date of graduation. If you are a doctoral student or seeking a faculty position, include your dissertation title and committee chair.

Teaching and Research Experience and Interests

The order of the remaining sections can be customized depending on the purpose of the CV. As with a resume, be strategic and tailor the headings depending on the position. For example, if you are applying to a university to teach, you may choose to list teaching interests before research. If you are applying for a job that requires you to secure funding, highlight the grants that you have acquired.

The categories Research Interests, Teaching Interests, Research Experience, and Teaching Experience speak directly to the immediate interests of the hiring committee and are most commonly used for academic positions or funding. These are four different sections on the CV and would be presented in the following order: (1) Research Interests, (2) Teaching Interests, (3) Research Experience, and (4) Teaching Experience. Hiring committees will look at these sections in terms of filling a specific need within their program and/or a good fit with the rest of the faculty.

Use a separate section for each. For research interests, list by subject area. Both teaching and research interests should align with your education, experience, presentations, and scholarly work. If you list teaching interests and/or research interests, you should then follow these sections with a bulleted list of the skills that you gained in

Table 5.1 CV Section Headers Order by Application Type

Applying for an Academic Position or Doctoral Program	Applying for Field Placement Supervisor/Instructor	Applying for a Funding Position	Applying for a Publicity Position
Education	Education	Education	Education
Research Interest	Teaching Interest	Grants	Area of Expertise or Professional Summary
Teaching Interest	Teaching Experience	Research Interest/ Experience (if applicable)	Research Interest/ Experience (if applicable)
Research Experience	Clinical/Practice Experience	Publications	Publications
Teaching Experience	Presentations	Presentations	Presentations
Publications	Publications	Clinical/Practice Experience	Clinical/Practice Experience
Presentations	Service to the Profession	Scholarships and Awards	Service to the Profession
Grants	University Service	Service to the Profession	Community Service
Scholarships and Awards	Community Service	Community Service	Honors and Awards
Clinical/Practice Experience	Professional Associations	Professional Associations	Professional Associations
University Service	Scholarships and Awards	Additional Credentials	Additional Credentials
Service to the Profession	Additional Credentials		
Community Service			
Professional Associations			
Additional Credentials			

each position. For teaching interests, list every course area in which you have taught, assisted, and developed a knowledge base or have an interest. Do not use course titles or course numbers; instead, use language that parallels the accreditation standards of the Council of Social Work Education. See Appendix E for a sample CV.

Practice or Clinical Experience

This section is very similar to the one you will write for your resume. Include the name of each organization, your title, city, state, and date for each experience, and list them in reverse chronological order. Begin each bullet point with an action verb or adjective to describe your principal tasks, skills, accomplishments, and knowledge areas. If you held multiple positions at a single agency, only list the agency name once, with position titles and dates next to it. If you were promoted, create a bullet statement that says "Promoted from case manager to clinical director within one year." You may also list social work field placements and internships in this section.

Publications and Presentations

This section can include a wide array of printed and written materials including op-eds, journal articles, technical or research reports, book reviews, book chapters, and entire books. You should list all published and unpublished manuscripts using formatting guidelines from the latest edition of the *Publication Manual of the American Psychological Association* (American Psychological Association [APA], 2020). This section can list all types of presentations, trainings, workshops seminars, panel discussions, and guest lectures.

As you get further along in your career, it may be necessary to use subheadings to strategically organize your presentations. For example, if reaching a broad geographical audience, you should use subheadings such as Local, State, National, or International. If emphasizing the style of presentations, use subheadings such as Peer Reviewed, Invited, Poster Sessions, or Trainings. If the conference is canceled, add "(conference canceled)" at the end of the listing; if the conference is moved online, use the same format as an in-person conference, including the original location. Additionally, if the conference occurs but you are not able to attend, you are still able to list it on your CV—as long as you received an acceptance by the conference review committee, it is unnecessary to state that you were not able to attend.

Funding, Grants, and Awards

List all grant projects, including title of project, name of institution, city, state, date, and amount funded. If the grant was not funded, it is still important to list the grant to emphasize that you know the application process for various types of grants; however, you should add "not funded" after the description. For each grant, list the specific skills utilized to acquire or manage the grant project; for example: "Created budget for RO1 funded grant" or "Creates timelines, meets deadlines, and manages multiple projects according to grant foundation guidelines."

Honors

In this section, include all academic honors, awards, and fellowships along with any other accolades that support your expertise and leadership. The name of the award, sponsoring institution, and date should be included in this section. If the name of the award is not self-explanatory, add a brief descriptive phrase to help the reader understand its significance.

Community, Professional, and University Service

In this section, briefly list all community and professional service (using subheadings) to include elected and appointed leadership, board positions, consulting, guest appearances on media outlets, or task force appointments. Depending on the purpose of your CV, you may reorganize these to speak to your audience. For example, if you are applying for a teaching or field instructor position, you can emphasize your connection with academia by listing university services first, such as university committees you participated in, task forces you served on, and any field liaison assignments. If using the CV for public relations, you should highlight service to the profession first to emphasize your credibility within your respective field of practice. For each entry, list the name of your role, sponsoring organization, city, state, and dates of service. See sample CV in Appendix E.

COVER LETTERS

Sending a resume without a cover letter is like giving a gift without a thoughtful greeting card. Whenever you send your resume to apply for a job, you should include a cover letter whether requested or not. If you are applying electronically and there is not a place to upload your cover letter, you can still include it as an additional page with your resume. While the resume provides an overview of your background, the cover letter allows you to highlight and explain in more detail those aspects of your background that are relevant to the organization you are contacting and/or the position you are seeking. Rather than simply reiterating what is on your resume, a cover letter is a narrative that allows you to make connections between what is indicated on your resume and the requirements of the position to which you are applying. It allows you to elaborate on certain experiences and draw attention to the particularly relevant aspects of your resume. There may be sentences or even paragraphs that will be duplicated in many of your letters (particularly if you are applying for similar positions). Yet unlike the resume, which can be tweaked and used to apply to different opportunities, a cover letter is most effective when it is tailored to the specific position and organization, from beginning to end.

How to Write a Cover Letter

Your cover letter should be written in a professional, confident, and polite tone. That said, you also want to let your personality and your enthusiasm for the employer and position shine through, so try to have a little fun with it.

The most effective way to begin your cover letter is to use the job posting as your guide. This assures that your letter is intentional and that you are connecting the key qualifications of the job to your experience. Before you begin writing, it is helpful to cut and paste the qualifications from the job posting into your letter as a reference so that you make sure to cover all the key points the employer is looking for. This helps you to prepare a letter geared specifically to the position to which you are applying and focus on the employer's interests, needs, and point of view. With this focus, describe two or three experiences, accomplishments, and/or skills that match the needs of the position as outlined in the job description. Be specific and provide examples to support your claims. By using the job posting as your prompt, you will demonstrate that you have researched the employer and are familiar with the position. Remember, never mention anything negative about your previous employers, supervisors, or colleagues. This will reflect poorly on you, even if you feel you need to rationalize something about your previous experience or why you left a job. Social work is a strengths-based profession and there is no room for negativity in any of your job application materials.

Cover Letter Structure by Paragraph

In the following paragraphs, we will review each section of the cover letter and provide advice on what to include, what not to include, and how to make a positive impression on the hiring manager. For examples of cover letters, see Appendix F.

Header and Greeting

At the top of the page, use the same header as the first page of your resume (see "Resume Header" section). If you know who the hiring manager is, address the cover letter to them, e.g., "Dear Dr. Rodriguez." Include the person's name, title, and office address. If you are unsure of the recipient's name, contact the organization to find out whom the letter goes to. If you are unable to find a contact name, do not use "To Whom it May Concern" since this may come off as cold or impersonal. Instead, use "Dear Hiring Committee," "Dear Hiring Manager," or "Dear Personnel Director."

Next, make a short list of qualifications, previous experiences, and skills you will want to include in your letter. Set this list aside—these notes will inform the content of your cover letter. Next, think about how you will organize this information to tell a story about what you have done and what you would be great at doing next.

First Paragraph

Begin by emphasizing what a good fit you are for the position. Specifically name the position you are applying for and indicate how you found the advertised position. If you were referred to the job by someone, mention them here. State how your degree, knowledge, and previous experience match the job description. If you are a recent graduate, only mention your degree; it is not necessary to tell the reader that you recently graduated, especially in the first paragraph. Mention the amount of experience from previous employment that the listing calls for, including qualifications such as certifications or licenses. The last sentence in this paragraph is critical. It is the hook that keeps the reader reading. It should indicate why you are interested in the position and what you will bring to this position. For example, "This position would allow me to continue my success in creating programs that contribute to the youth development of at-risk adolescents and use my Spanish-speaking skills."

Second Paragraph

Match your skills with the job posting. Emphasize the relevance of this experience to the job position or organization. Call attention to specific elements of your background—education, experience, leadership—that are relevant to the position. Use verbs that highlight accomplishments and results, such as "completed" and "guided."

Third Paragraph

Emphasize your transferrable skills that set you apart from others. Use your transferrable skills to highlight your unique experience from your previous jobs.

Final Paragraph

Close with a summary sentence and a positive note about the organization or enthusiasm for the job. Share what excites you about the position or organization. You can even include specific information you have found after researching the position or reading the organization's website. During your research, you will find that most organizations have either a mission statement or a description of their values publicly available.

Closing

Finish the cover letter with a closing such as "Warm Regards," "Best Regards," or "Sincerely." No need to be overly creative here. Provide space for your signature, which you can create using your cell phone, a tablet, or even an online program. (There are several free programs that let you easily create, download, and save an image of your signature.)

As with the other items in your job search marketing package, make sure that you have someone proofread your cover letter using the job posting as a guide. Reading it out loud is a great way to find errors that your eyes might miss.

Once you begin writing cover letters, each one will become easier as you build upon the framework. See Appendix F for more examples of cover letters and other career correspondence. If you are creative, engaged, and specific, you will attract the attention of hiring managers.

Table 5.2 breaks down the job description by skills needed for the job, matches these skills with the skills of a potential candidate, and gives an example of how to articulate this into sentences for a cover letter.

Now try this yourself! Read the job posting in Exercise 5.1 carefully. If you were interested in applying for this job, which information would most help you to write a compelling, relevant, and intentional cover letter?

PERSONAL OR PROFESSIONAL BUSINESS CARDS

Business cards are an excellent opportunity to promote your brand. While you might think that business cards are only necessary when you are representing your agency, they are a helpful resource anytime you are networking. Whether you are changing careers or expanding your professional network, personal business cards are a

Table 5.2 Matching Your Skills to the Job Description

Job Description	Your Skills	Sentences for Cover Letter
• Bachelor's degree in social work, psychology, or related social services field • At least two years' experience providing case management support	• Master's degree in social work • Two years' case management experience with individuals who have substance use disorders as a mental health technician before graduate school and in my field placement	I am confident that my master's degree in social work and over two years' case management experience with adults, including individuals who have substance use disorders, make me an excellent candidate for this job.
• Experience working with substance use and recovery in mental health • Understanding of residential treatment and evidence-based behavioral health treatment, including collaborative care models	• Knowledge of evidence-based practices through clinical course work • Experience using evidence-based practices in field placement • Experience on multidisciplinary teams as mental health technician in residential treatment center • Knowledge of 12-step recovery process and harm reduction programs	Before entering school, I worked as a behavioral healthcare technician in a residential treatment center for substance use where we utilized evidence-based treatment approaches in a collaborative multidisciplinary setting.
• The behavioral health clinician provides intake, support, and crisis counseling	• Over two years of experience with intake, screening, assessment, and crisis counseling in prior work experience and field placements	As a graduate social work intern, I completed an internship at The Lakes Hospital and participated in a multidisciplinary team that guided patients through a successful transition from the hospital setting to outpatient treatment centers.
• Facilitate individual and group sessions • Maintain accurate and complete documentation	• Facilitated psychoeducational and cognitive–behavioral groups • Experience with documentation according to agency guidelines and case notes.	I conducted psychoeducational and cognitive–behavioral groups at The Lakes Hospital with clients, assisted with day-to-day activities, and provided documentation utilizing electronic medical records and coding.

convenient way to share your information with new contacts. Not only do they allow you to share your contact information so that you can connect with the person in the future, they are valuable when meeting new people at a conference, job fair, or networking event.

Personal or professional business cards are an affordable way to boost your confidence when networking and serve as a keepsake of sorts that provides a sense of connection. Additionally, you do not have to be present to give them out; you

Exercise 5.1

From the Job Description to Your Cover Letter: Case Manager—Oak Hill Treatment Center

Responsibilities: This person will work closely with a collaborative care team as an embedded behavioral healthcare manager. The behavioral health clinician provides intake, support, and crisis counseling. The ideal candidate will have a working knowledge of the current behavioral healthcare landscape.

- Facilitate individual and group sessions
- Develop and implement care plans to make appropriate clinical recommendations and referrals
- Maintain accurate and complete documentation
- Provide brief interventions using evidence-based techniques

Preferred Qualifications:

- Spanish/English bilingual
- LMSW or equivalent
- Experience working with electronic medical records
- Able to collaborate with patient and care team to monitor progress and make treatment changes as necessary

Cover Letter Sample

I am extremely interested in applying for the case manager position at Oak Hill Treatment Center posted on your organization's website. I am confident that my MSW and over two years of counseling experience with individuals who have substance use disorders make me an excellent candidate for this job.

Before graduate school, I worked as a mental health technician in a residential treatment center. I conducted didactic groups with clients, assisted with day-to-day activities, and provided documentation. As a graduate social work intern, I completed an internship at South Austin Hospital and participated in a multidisciplinary team that guided patients through a successful transition from the hospital setting to outpatient treatment centers. My responsibilities included aiding in psychosocial evaluations and assessments and making referrals to local resources, psychiatric facilities, and outpatient and support groups. I gained valuable knowledge of complex systems including SNAP, Medicaid, and disability resources under the Americans with Disabilities Act.

I have applied for my licensing exam and am awaiting my test date. I am bilingual in English and Spanish and have worked with Spanish-speaking populations. Additionally, in my previous position, I was commended on my excellent communication skills including group facilitation and documentation utilizing electronic medical records.

The successful programs of the Oak Hill Treatment Center are familiar to me, and I aspire to work for a facility with a reputation as excellent as yours. I welcome the opportunity to interview with you. Thank you for your consideration.

can leave them on tables at networking events, at offices, or even include them in thank-you cards after an interview. Your business card should include the following information:

- Your name, degree acronyms, or licensure
- Employer, job title or school, student status
- Email address, cell phone number, LinkedIn profile address

Additional items on your business card might include the following:

- Personal or professional website, portfolio site link, social media profiles
- Your professional headshot from your LinkedIn profile
- Key skills, tagline, or personal mission statement
- QR code to scan through smartphone, which will take them directly to your website

Make sure your business card is consistent with your other branding materials. If you expect that there will be significant changes to your skills, power words, licensing, or other key information, print business cards in small batches so you can update them accordingly.

REFERENCES

Though checking references is usually the last step before employers make a job offer, you should identify and ask people to be a reference well ahead of the job application process. Reach out to three to five professional references in advance. They could include your field instructors, field supervisors, coworkers, work supervisors, or faculty. When considering potential references, think about not only what the person can speak to in terms of your skills, knowledge, and impact, but also whether they are reliable, articulate, and available as a reference. Do not assume that if they said "yes" a year ago that you can still use them as a reference now. When asking for a reference, do so in person if you can, or if you need to, call or send an email request. Sending your reference a copy of your resume ensures they will be looking at the same data that the hiring manager is looking at. Remember, your reference does not have your work history and accomplishments memorized as clearly as you do, so it is important to provide context. Tell them your career goals and how their input connects with the positions you are applying for. Finally, always let your reference know the results of your job search and send a thank-you note or email.

If you are applying for jobs but you do not want your current employer to know, you will still need to submit references who can attest to your work. In this case, it would be appropriate to ask a trusted colleague to write a reference for you. If you collaborate with other organizations regularly, consider asking your contact person at that organization to provide a reference. Remember, the most important information that a perspective employer is seeking is the quality of your past performance. All of your references should be able to speak to this.

The names and contact information for your references should be included on a separate document with the same header, font, and style as your resume. You will then include names, titles, and contact information for three to five references. See chapter 6 for more information about references during the interview process and see Appendix F for sample requests for references and a sample reference letter.

SOCIAL MEDIA PRESENCE

With the growing use of online platforms, your social media presence is more important than ever. It is better to control your social media presence than let it control you. By this, we mean that your social media presence should be something that reinforces your job search efforts rather than something that undermines them. When employers check social media as they are sifting through applicants, or when networking contacts Google you, you want your smartly curated professional social media presence to show up first. To ensure this happens, you must carefully prepare your social media presence *before* you begin your job search process. If you are going to share your X (formerly Twitter), Instagram, or other social media profiles, be sure there is nothing on the profiles that you would not want an employer to know. Scrub these profiles of anything unprofessional, including speaking negatively of your employer, admitting to playing hooky from work, or even worse, complaining about a hangover after a long night of partying!

The good news is you have already done much of the legwork: Using your strong professional summary, headshot, key words, power words, and your resume, you can establish a strong social media presence with relative ease.

LinkedIn is the most powerful professional networking site available today. The site helps social workers make connections to people, organizations, careers, and community partners. It strengthens and extends existing networks of trusted contacts and provides a means to engage with professionals from multiple disciplines. This makes LinkedIn a career management tool that you can use throughout the span of your career. As social workers, we connect clients, organizations, interdisciplinary professionals, and systems. In that connector role we navigate complex systems for our clients, and we are constantly seeking solutions to human problems that may require significant learning curves. LinkedIn can serve as an efficient shortcut to making those connections. Additionally, it is an outlet for demonstrating your experience, increasing your credibility, promoting your cause, and building connections with experts in the field.

Whether you are new to the field or a seasoned professional, the following sections will help you to translate your resume to a strong LinkedIn profile, build meaningful connections, and utilize the platform to advance your career.

Your Profile

LinkedIn is one of the most powerful networking tools you can use in your career, but before you begin to explore the benefits, it is important to update your profile just as you would your resume. Your LinkedIn profile, which is accessible to millions of users, can enhance your visibility and manage your reputation. LinkedIn also allows you to document your career, follow trendsetters in your field, and find and share interesting posts.

To get started on LinkedIn, follow these four steps:

1. Create a LinkedIn profile and claim your personal URL (which includes your name; e.g., https://www.linkedin.com/in/yourname). This direct link makes it easier for employers to find you.
2. Use the information provided in chapter 4 to create a good professional headshot and use it as your LinkedIn profile photo.
3. Choose a background cover photo that is professional and gives readers a glimpse of what you are looking for. Think of LinkedIn as a virtual networking event and your cover photo is where you show up. For example, if you are seeking a geographical move, use the skyline of the location you want to move to. LinkedIn also provides many samples to choose from if you cannot find one.
4. Complete the various sections of your profile, as detailed next.

Your Headline

Your 220-character LinkedIn "headline" appears immediately below your name on the top of your profile. Be strategic about your headline to ensure you can be found by current and future connections. Many people make the mistake of using their job title for this section. This can make you appear as if you are not open to new opportunities and it is redundant with your job title listed just below it. Think of your headline as the words or phrases that you want to be found by. For example, rather than having a headline that reads: Social Worker, Any Social Service Agency Inc., use strategic key words that speak to your audience; for example: LMSW | Older Adults | Loss and Grief | Chicago, Illinois. Remember to use these same keywords throughout your profile.

About Section

The About section under your professional headline provides an opportunity to showcase your experience and expand on the professional summary that you created earlier in this chapter. While the professional summary on a resume is typically a brief paragraph, the About section of LinkedIn allows for more freedom in terms of length, content, and formatting. If you write it intentionally, you can use key words and search terms that will catch the algorithms of recruiters, contacts, and potential collaborators. Write your summary in a narrative format, with good transitions that explain your career journey. This can be organized in different ways. If you have a logical career trajectory, you may want to start with your most recent position and describe how you got there. If you have had some gaps or major shifts, do not be afraid to put these into context. Everyone learns something from change and transition, and by writing this section as a journey, you will have the opportunity to explain how the career events of your life make you uniquely qualified for opportunities to come your way. Depending on the purpose of your summary, you might make this section longer or shorter. For example, if your audience comprises recruiters for a job, then you may want to make it longer so that you can insert more key words. If the purpose is for professional networking to enhance your career or gain clients, you may think about making a briefer, more compelling summary.

Consider these tips when you write your About section:

- Use a catchy first line—you want your first sentence to be interesting and compelling so that viewers want to read more about you.
- Go back to your power words, key terms, and other phrases from your toolbox and make sure these words are used in your summary and throughout your profile.
- Be authentic, and do not be afraid to let your personality shine through.
- Do not be shy. Lead with your most significant accomplishments. This can be as simple as the number of years of experience you have, honors and awards you have received, or accomplishments that can be quantified.
- Make it easy on the eye. Regardless of how long the summary is, make it easy to read by using spaces between paragraphs or bullet points.

Finish with a call to action. For example, if you are seeking a new position, you might finish your summary with, "If you are looking for a macro social worker with skills in policy and program development and a strong background in executive leadership, please send me a DM."

Skills and Endorsements

The next step in completing your LinkedIn profile is to identify the skills that will match up with the job opportunities you want. *Skills* are key words or phrases that describe your areas of expertise, such as "clinical social work," "case management," "mental health counseling," and "community outreach." LinkedIn makes this easy, since you can add them when you add the descriptions of your job duties. As with the other sections of LinkedIn, the app will populate these skills for you if you do not do it yourself. You can add up to 50 skills, but your top 10 are the most important. Make sure that you use skills and terms that are applicable to your career goals. If the skill is not listed by LinkedIn, make up your own. For example, there may be a clinical framework that you are knowledgeable about that may not be listed, but you can easily add this. LinkedIn gives you the option of pinning your top three skills so that when your connections view your profile, they will pop up. You should make completing this a priority, after the other sections that have already been mentioned. The sooner you get these skills listed and pinned, the more they will come up for your connections to see and the more endorsements you will get in these key areas. You can also rearrange your existing skills or remove skills that are no longer relevant.

Endorsements are a way for your connections to vouch for your skills and expertise. They can be given by anyone you are connected to on LinkedIn, and they appear as a list of skills on your profile with the number of endorsements next to each one. Endorsements help to validate your skills and demonstrate to others that you have the knowledge and experience necessary to succeed in your field.

Once you have added your skills, you can begin to receive endorsements from your connections. You can also request endorsements from specific connections by clicking the "Ask to be endorsed" button next to a particular skill on your profile. Keep in mind that endorsements are more meaningful when they come from connections who have worked with you directly and can attest to your abilities.

LinkedIn's Skills and Endorsements features are valuable tools to help you showcase your expertise and build your professional network. By highlighting your specific areas of expertise and gathering endorsements from your connections, you can demonstrate your qualifications and stand out to potential employers or clients.

Connecting

Now that you have updated your profile, added your skills, and written a strong About section, it is time to start making connections! You can connect with current and former colleagues and managers, folks you have met at conferences and networking events, vendors you have partnered with, and friends whose careers you are curious about. LinkedIn will make suggestions based on connections you already have. Do not be afraid to use LinkedIn to branch out. Use the "mutual connections" function on LinkedIn to connect with people whose careers you admire. Be sure to send a personalized message with your connection request. See Appendix F for a sample connection request.

WRITING SAMPLES

Writing samples may be part of the application materials requested from you during the interviewing process. This is another great opportunity to showcase your skills! Usually, the type of writing sample requested is reflective of the job you are seeking; for example, a policy paper for a macro job or a sample case study for a direct practice job. Follow the directions (if provided) in terms of the number of pages, whether the writing sample should be an excerpt or a complete paper, and whether the interviewer wants to see markups from an instructor or a clean copy. If there are no detailed instructions, pick a sample that is approximately three to five pages to demonstrate your best, most relevant writing. The bottom line is that they are looking to see if you have the writing skills necessary to be successful in the job. Sometimes employers incorporate writing activities during the interview process to gauge writing ability specific to the role:

> Instead of a writing sample, I usually ask final candidates to complete an exercise relevant to the position—a brief proposal, presentation, etc. I am looking for a logical presentation of their expertise and thinking and a reflection of their professional tone and style. I do not want something overly polished, but instead want to make sure what I have been hearing in the interview process is reflected in the product presented. (Sarah Cluggish, chief program officer at Project Bread)

CONCLUSION

By preparing this job search marketing package before you begin applying for jobs, you will feel more confident and informed about the types of jobs you are looking for and what you bring to the table. The advice given in this chapter is designed to get your foot in the door for an interview. While you might use templates or AI to create these materials, you will need to be able to articulate your skills in person for your entire career when you are interviewing for new jobs or promotions, giving presentations, or advocating for resources.

Finally, we recommend that you reevaluate your professional brand and other materials annually to ensure you are prepared for your next opportunity. A job search is a huge undertaking, but it is also a learning experience and an opportunity to assess your career and present yourself in the best possible professional light.

CHAPTER TAKEAWAYS

- Apply your professional brand to all aspects of your job search marketing package including your resume or CV, cover letter, LinkedIn profile, and more.
- Intentionality is key. Identify your audience, use power words and industry language, and start early.
- Reevaluate your brand annually, edit your materials accordingly, and be consistent across all platforms.

CHAPTER 6

Implementing Your Job Search Plan

What You Will Learn
- ❒ How to use key words to identify job opportunities
- ❒ How to create a networking plan to support your job search
- ❒ How to successfully apply for jobs and interview

Action Plan
- ❒ Create a job search support system
- ❒ Make a list of key words that will enable you to find job opportunities
- ❒ Create a list of people you would like to add to your network
- ❒ Prepare for job interviews

Now that you have conducted self and career assessments, established a career direction, laid the foundation of your professional brand, and updated your marketing materials, you are ready for action. You have probably heard the expression, "Looking for a job *is* a job!" This is indeed true. A proper job search takes time, commitment, consistency, and determination. When done this way, your search will yield better results. Moreover, you are better prepared to take advantage of opportunities that come your way unexpectedly.

This chapter will take you through the major steps of a job search. We will show you how to use key words to find the jobs you want and how to apply for those jobs. We will discuss the advantages of networking to better inform your job search, make connections, and build relationships throughout your career. The chapter will end with tips and techniques for interviewing.

In addition to being time-consuming, job searches can also be stressful. It is important to identify a group of people that can support you through the process. This group can consist of your career advisor, field supervisor, or classmates if you are still in school, or friends, family, and colleagues if you are already in the professional world. Your support team can help you review your application documents, brainstorm career strategies, and practice for interviews. The members of this group may be job searching themselves—you can be their support system as well. Join together to celebrate the high and lows of a job search!

FINDING OPPORTUNITIES

Let us start our discussion by looking at the case study of Marisia and how she executes a comprehensive action plan to find a new career role.

CASE STUDY

Marisia

Marisia graduated with her MSW five years ago and wants to explore a career pivot. Since her final field placement, Marisia has been working in medical social work. Recently, she has been feeling the need to do something different, but she did not know what. To help determine her next steps, she spoke with her university's career advisor who helped her identify which aspects of her current job she wanted to continue doing in her next role and what she wanted to let go. Based on Marisia's responses, her career advisor recommended a four-part action plan:

1. Reflect on her work experience and conduct a self-assessment of her current skills, knowledge, and values.
2. Using the information gleaned from the self-assessment (skills and knowledge she wants to use, the office culture she finds most rewarding, priorities around salary, work schedule, etc.), create a profile of the important elements she will be looking for in her next position.
3. Network with others to explore career options. Marisia needed to ask others about the details of their jobs—role, pace, salary, stress, variety of tasks—and determine why those roles appealed to her. Through these conversations, Marisia could identify gaps in her experience that she could fill to make her more qualified to pivot to something new. She could also get advice from these professionals on the best way to find jobs in their area of expertise and ask them for referrals to others to talk with.
4. Update her marketing materials (LinkedIn, resume, etc.) to reflect the new roles she was seeking.

It took a few months to network, but after completing these four steps, Marisia was able to identify that she wanted to continue with some clinical, client-facing work, but that she wanted to work outside the hospital setting. She had done some program management and social innovation work in the past and was interested in having part of her role incorporate these skills. She was looking for something a little slower paced. Through networking with alumni, Marisia discovered an opportunity at a college research center working on depression prevention. She applied for the position and got it! In this new position, Marisia is applying her assessment and supervision skills, using her knowledge and experience with depression, and interacting with clients. The position also allows her to develop her programmatic and research interests and provides a new setting to do her work outside of a hospital. Marisia is excited about this new opportunity.

Get Organized

You are going to be collecting a lot of data during your job search, and the best way to stay organized is to begin organized. We suggest you set up a folder on your computer labeled Job Search and the year. Add application materials (e.g., resumes, cover letters, interviewing preparation) and each job description or posting you have applied to. This folder will become your toolbox, allowing you to access documents quickly to create your materials for each job application. For example, if you keep all of your cover letters in one place, you can easily copy and paste sentences from one cover letter to another and tailor the material for the job you are applying to.

Job Search Key Words

Key words are terms used for job searches that include your areas of interest (e.g., a social issue, cause you are tied to, or population), skills, setting, roles, or job titles. As we explored in chapter 3, your self-assessment will help you discover the role you want to play as a social worker (e.g., therapist, case manager, community organizer) and the social issue you want to address (e.g., health disparities, food insecurity, anxiety). Your self-assessment helped you identify your specific knowledge, skills, and credentials and those needed to perform the job. Your exploration efforts revealed job titles that correspond to your work interest and skills; for example, community outreach coordinator or domestic violence advocate.

You will use the results of your self-assessment to begin searching for agencies that do work in your area of interest and with your skill set. Through this thoughtful and intentional assessment process, you will create a starting point for your research that will save you time, energy, and stress as you target organizations that align with your career goals and increase your likelihood of job satisfaction.

A simple internet search can result in a list of organizations tagged with your key words in their mission, program work, or agency name. For example, if you type your key word (e.g., education, community development) along with a specific geographic location into a search engine, you will get a long list of organizations/employers doing this type of work, including their names, locations, and websites. This information may inform you about the organization and its work, provide the names of employees to contact for informational interviews, or lead you to job postings on the agency website.

Searching the web by job title or skills or knowledge areas can produce the same result—a list of organizations to target. Job titles (e.g., clinician, grant manager, volunteer coordinator) are useful key words on job search websites, agency-specific job portals, job boards, and social media platforms such as LinkedIn. Skills and knowledge areas can also be part of job titles (e.g., bereavement coordinator, crisis intervention coordinator, or researcher) and are important to utilize in your search. A modifier can help refine your search using setting, population, intervention, or social justice issue. For example, *school* social work, *in-home* therapist, *outpatient* clinician, and *health* policy.

If you are interested in a macro-focused job, using the right key words is critical to locating the organizations and job opportunities that you are seeking. Paradoxically, we do not recommend using "macro" or "social work" as key words. Many jobs labeled with the title "social work" are clinical or in direct services. Similarly, jobs that are macro focused are generally not titled "macro social worker." Instead, apply the previous instructions for using key words that describe the role you want to play, the skills you want to use, and the population or issue you want to focus on. Start with the most widely chosen paths of macro social work, such as advocacy, community organizing, program development, research and evaluation, policy, and leadership.

CASE STUDY

Owen

After volunteering for several nonprofit organizations, Owen decided to go to graduate school to obtain an MSW. In the short term after graduation, Owen wanted to make an impact by advocating for the community. In the long term, he thought about becoming an executive director of a nonprofit organization. Owen focused on community organization and management in the MSW program and enjoyed his field placement working to address the gaps in public education for low-income communities. Upon graduation, Owen wanted to move to California to work at a children and family services organization, but he was unsure how to begin his search.

After some self-assessment and research, Owen learned that youth development work was a key area of interest and that his target geographic area would be the San Francisco Bay Area. Owen typed "youth development in the Bay Area" into a search engine, and it returned the names of over 20 potential organizations. Owen researched each organization's website to learn about its mission, work, and programs. He used his university's career services office to identify alumni he could connect with to learn more about this work and set up virtual informational interviews with several recent graduates. Through these discussions, he learned about the many settings in which he could work with youth and families around academic success, including community-based organizations and city-supported partnerships with the local schools. Owen identified job titles that corresponded with the work he was interested in doing, like "youth development specialist" and "youth advocate." Using these job titles as key words in a job search board, Owen found a position as a youth connector for a nonprofit organization that allowed him to create relationships with both families and adolescents. The person in this position would create and execute youth programs, build relationships with school-based staff to identify and connect youth to programs, support families, conduct outreach, evaluate programs, and develop marketing plans. Owen was excited to find an opportunity that was the stepping stone he needed to launch his social work career.

Use Exercise 6.1 to organize your own key words to use in finding job opportunities.

Exercise 6.1

Sample Key Words

1. Using a chart like the one in Table 6.1, organize your key words (from your self-assessment in chapter 3) by the following filters: Skills, Area of Interest, Population, Job Title/Role, Setting, and Location.
2. Using a search engine, play around with a combination of the words to elicit organizations or job postings that fit your interests.
3. Dive deeper by visiting each organization's website to uncover more detailed information about the organization such as its mission, core values, programs, staff listing, and career or job posting portal.
4. Add these to the spreadsheet of organizations in your job search folder.
5. Target these organizations for potential job opportunities, informational interviews, and volunteer and/or internship options.

Table 6.1 Sample Key Words Chart

Skills	Area of Interest	Population	Job Title/Role	Setting	Location
Individual therapy	Gender-based violence	Refugees	Resettlement coordinator	Domestic violence shelter	United States, West Coast
Advocacy	Trauma	Women	Family advocate	Mental health clinic	International
Prevention	Mental health	Families	Case manager	Nongovernmental organization	English/French-speaking countries
French speaking	Trafficking	Francophone	Bilingual therapist	Faith-based nonprofit	Boston
Crisis intervention	Healthcare	Displaced persons	Social worker	Hospital	Los Angeles

(continued)

> Sample Job Posting Results:
>
> - Psychosocial caseworker—Francophone
> - Family support social worker—bilingual English and French or Haitian Creole
> - Resettlement case manager—refugee services
> - Anti-trafficking caseworker
> - Social worker/advocate for violence prevention and recovery

Job Search Tips by Area of Practice

The following are specific job search pointers for the main areas of social work practice, described in chapter 1.

Clinical Social Work Positions

- Use the key word "social work(er)" to elicit clinically focused job opportunities.
- The type of clinical role you want to play may be refined by a population you want to work with (e.g., adolescents, older adults with dementia, victims of violence), the acuity of their challenge (e.g., major mental illness, early intervention, depression), or the setting where you want to work (e.g., partial hospital, community health center, outpatient clinic).
- Your clinical role is also defined by your level of licensures, so make sure to pay attention to the license requirements indicated in job postings to ensure you are qualified.

Macro Social Work Positions

- When searching for macro positions, you will not find jobs with the title "social work/social worker" as these will yield positions that are clinical or direct service jobs. Use key words that describe the skills you want to use (e.g., evaluation, advocacy, fundraising) and/or the issues you feel passionate about (e.g., domestic violence, health, education).
- Search for organizations, agencies, and think tanks that have a mission of interest to you such as child welfare, domestic violence, women's health, or immigration.
- Check out state nonprofit associations, which often list their membership and post jobs on their websites.
- Network within trade or professional organizations such as the American Evaluators Association and the Network for Social Work Management.
- Online journals such as *The Chronicle of Philanthropy* and *The Chronicle of Higher Education* are helpful resources.

- Do not rule out organizations that do clinical or direct service work. They may have opportunities for administrative and leadership roles.

International Social Work Positions

- Be an assertive and actively engaged job searcher. International work is generally a challenging field in which to get a job, especially a first job.
- International experience is required for most global positions, so find opportunities to gain experience through internships, fellowships, or volunteer positions.
- International work is a field in which you are expected to pay your dues, and first jobs are typically difficult assignments in unstable and nonsecure areas of the world. You will need to demonstrate a willingness to do the work where it needs to get done. Agencies like the Peace Corps and Catholic Relief Services place you where they need you—you do not choose where you work.
- Because international work is dependent on dynamic global situations (e.g., geopolitical factors, natural disasters, humanitarian crises) you need to be comfortable with ambiguity around your job description and demonstrate flexibility, resourcefulness, and adaptability.
- U.S.-based jobs at international nongovernmental organizations typically go to those who have worked in the international field for a while. These are not positions someone right out of school can usually land.

Nontraditional Social Work Positions

- Be able to answer the question "Why should I hire a social worker?" If you are applying for a job that does not ask for a social work degree, you should be able to articulate what a social work degree provides that is relevant to the job requirements that another degree does not—you want to set yourself apart from an MBA or MPA. While each person may answer this in a slightly different way depending on career focus, motivation, and personality, some common social work themes to highlight include
    - a social justice focus
    - a strengths-based approach
    - a systems approach
- Job seekers should research as much as possible about the industry in which they are applying, including the history, industry language, funding streams, key responsibilities, stakeholders, constituents, customers, and other disciplines that work in this industry.
- Social workers must learn to articulate transferable skills into industry language and try not to use social work jargon.
- Networking is imperative to gain insight into these fields, increase visibility, and learn of industry trends. Research should go beyond entry-level positions to predict a typical career path or promotion trajectory within the industry.

- It may also be important to take additional classes or earn credentials that are needed for these jobs, such as mediation certifications, business/budgeting courses, and research methods.

Finding Job Listings

With key words in hand, you are ready to search for job listings. Take a multipronged approach when searching for job opportunities, keeping the following in mind.

Job Boards

Large, general job websites such as Indeed.com require you to filter the jobs posted with key words to return jobs relevant to your job search. There are also specific job boards that contain certain types of jobs, such as usajobs.gov for federal positions or NASW's job board for social work–related positions. Job boards such as usajobs.gov or Indeed.com allow you to refine the types of jobs you are looking for and post your resume so employers can find you. If you would like to identify more online job sites, consider asking your informational interviewees, "What job boards does your organization use?"

Job Fairs

Job fairs are another avenue for job searching, professional networking, and information gathering. Usually, the organizers of the fair will post a list of employers on the fair website for those who have registered. This will allow you time to preview and learn about the employers expected to be in attendance and the type of jobs they are recruiting for. Once you have researched the list of prospective employers, prioritize the organizations you want to visit at the job fair. On the day of the fair, dress professionally and explore as much of the event as possible so you have time to engage with all of the organizations that interest you. Have copies of your resume, including any variations of your resume that feature different skills, so that you can share your experiences with prospective employers and move quickly on available jobs that interest you. Be prepared to speak concisely about your interest in the organization and ask questions about its expectations, opportunities, and hiring process. Collect the recruiter's contact information for follow-up. If the event is virtual, keep in mind that there may be a time limit to your interaction with a prospective employer and that you may have to schedule a more detailed follow-up conversation with the recruiter.

Volunteering, Temporary Work, and Internships

Finding your dream job may take some time. While you search, consider a volunteer position, temporary work, or an internship that will allow you to gain skills, make connections, demonstrate what you have to offer, and evaluate the office culture that may lead to further employment. Use all of these methods to get your proverbial foot in the door!

Lesser-Known Organizations

Many job seekers know about the larger, well-marketed organizations, but they miss out on opportunities at lesser-known but valuable organizations doing great work. Job openings at these smaller agencies may only be listed on the agency website and not advertised widely online.

Networking

Networking is the exchange of information, advice, and connections among people. It requires strategy, motivation, and, for some, courage. Job seekers often think, "I do not need information, I need a job!" It may feel that way, but networking can lead to a job by

- informing you of unadvertised job openings.
- connecting you with people who are in a hiring position.
- introducing you to a mentor or colleagues who can help support and guide your career.
- revealing hiring insights that allow you to better present yourself through your cover letter, resume, and interviewing.
- helping you feel more confident that your career field is good match.

Networking is critical to a successful job search. Informational interviews may reveal where jobs are posted for a specific agency, what hiring managers are seeking, the office culture, and typical starting salaries. Through conversations with people in your targeted career field, you may find out about opportunities that might not be advertised publicly, such as project or consulting opportunities or filling in for an employee on medical leave. You may learn about opportunities coming in the future from a grant or other funding. This inside information is especially critical for social workers seeking employment in areas that serve an immediate social need and have received local, state, or federal attention; for example, housing needs when the economy declines.

Last, social work is a people-oriented field in which work is often done collaboratively. Agencies want to hire people who are a good match with the requirements of the job, complement the skills of the other employees, and are aligned with the values of the agency. Making a connection with someone allows you to introduce yourself professionally *before* applying for a position. Remember, people want you to succeed, and social workers inherently want to help people. If you make a good impression or have a good connection, that person could tell you about job opportunities at their agency, pass your resume along to the hiring manager, or connect you with other professionals at other agencies in the field.

Overcoming Networking Obstacles

For some people, networking seems inauthentic, as if you are talking to someone because you want something from them or because you are trying to impress them.

Some introverts shy away from networking because it conjures up thoughts of a big room of strangers in which you do not know whom to approach, or if you do, you don't know how. Networking does not need to be any of these things. While you can certainly strike up a conversation spontaneously with a stranger and find commonalities that lead to a useful connection, more often networking is done intentionally and with someone you have some initial familiarity or commonality with; for example, an alumna of your college or a referral from a colleague. For those who are more introverted, networking can feel more comfortable if it takes place in a one-on-one conversation, not a big room of unknown people. With the right preparation of open-ended questions, these conversations can be enjoyable, energizing, and reassuring.

Why would someone take the time to meet with you? What do *they* get out of it? Maybe someone is willing to meet with you because they enjoy talking about themselves or your shared career interests. They might be a seasoned professional who remembers when they were starting out as a social worker or figuring out their next career move and are willing to give back and share their expertise. Often these connections can be fruitful to both parties.

Help, Inform, Relate

If you are new to networking or you struggle to make a connection in these settings, here is a helpful approach to strike up a conversation with someone you would like to network with:

> **Help:** "I noticed you are looking for a place to sit. There is room at our table if you would like to join us!"
> **Inform:** "Looks like it is raining outside. Hopefully it will pass by the time our training is over and we head out for dinner."
> **Relate:** "I see on your name badge that you are from Ohio . . . me too! What part of the state did you grow up in?"

In the following case study, Makeyela uses networking to better inform her job search for school social work opportunities.

CASE STUDY

Makeyela

Makeyela was a final year MSW student interested in pursuing a career as a school social worker. Her field placements taught her that she preferred working at a middle or high school in an urban setting. She was aware of the challenges of landing a school social work position as a recent graduate, and knew that her preferred geographic area compounded the challenge. Makeyela was advised by her school's career counselor to pursue the following networking strategy:

Cast a Wide Net: Makeyela should talk with school social workers at public (urban and suburban), charter, and therapeutic schools, as well as those who work as school social workers at an agency that contracts with the public schools. This will allow for the gathering of information and advice about the roles, opportunities, salaries, and advancement at these different settings for a recent MSW. Makeyela can also grow her network by asking contacts for suggestions of other people to talk with.

Get the Inside Scoop: School systems can be large and bureaucratic, and are often unionized. It can be helpful to understand how these factors might impact the job application process. Networking can provide important information on the best way to get your application through human resources and to the hiring person, how the salary system works, and how this might affect salary negotiations.

Learn about Unadvertised Opportunities: In a school system, there are often temporary opportunities because of maternity and medical leaves, or other hiring opportunities that might allow a recent grad to get their foot in the door. These opportunities are often spread by word of mouth rather than officially advertised. Networking may reveal these opportunities.

Explore Other Options: If Makeyela's dream scenario does not play out, what is a good Plan B? What other jobs should Makeyela consider for a year or two that will put her in a better position to land her dream school social work job in the future? Networking can inform this decision. Talking with those in the field will provide great recommendations from current school social workers.

Create a List of People to Network with, Including

- Her current field supervisor and coworkers
- Her faculty advisor (who is also a school social worker)
- Last year's field supervisor at the Department of Children and Families
- Alumni, classmates, and the professor of her school social work course, as well as the chair of her school department's children, youth, and family concentration

After following this advice, Makeyela made several important discoveries:

- A job board dedicated to school social work jobs
- A biannual school social work conference sponsored by her NASW state chapter and active special interest group (or SIG)
- An annual local school job fair and on-campus recruiting at her graduate and undergraduate colleges
- A clearer understanding of the state school social work license process

---

Use Exercise 6.2 to create your own networking plan of action to identify people to talk with, create a timeline, and execute a successful outreach.

Exercise 6.2

Creating Your Network Plan

1. Generate a list of contacts:
   - Start with classmates, professor, relatives, and coworkers.
   - Add former supervisors and coworkers.
   - Use your college's career or alumni office to identify alumni to speak with. Often this connection alone will start the ball rolling.
   - Look to NASW state chapters, which often have special interest groups that allow you to connect with social workers with shared career interests.
   - Use LinkedIn and internet searches to find groups, associations, and conferences for people who share similar career interests. It is important to "get in the same place" virtually or physically as others who share your job interest.
2. Create a networking spreadsheet to stay organized (see Table 6.2).

Table 6.2 Networking Spreadsheet

Name	Agency	Job Title	Phone	Email	Address	Connection	Contacted	Notes
Simone Calas	Boston Medical Center	Dir. of Social Work	617-555-1234	s.calas@bmc.org	One Boston Medical Center Place, Boston 02118	BC alumna	emailed 11/3/21	met at networking event 11/2020
Richard Webber	OCD, McLean Hospital	Social Worker	781-345-8899	rwebber@mclean.org	Belmont campus	referred by S. Calas		

3. Create a plan of action and timeline to reach out and schedule a time to talk to each contact (see chapter 3 for further instruction on informational interviews). Plan at least two networking conversations per month, preferably several months before applying for jobs.
4. Use your elevator pitch created in chapter 5 as a basis for your outreach email.
5. Plan to share an updated copy of your resume (see chapter 5) with the contact for feedback.

Timing

Networking can take time to bear fruit. Creating a network of others who are willing to make time to meet, keep an eye out for opportunities, or forward your resume to someone at their agency takes time, so plan to start the networking process several months before applying for jobs to get the most out of your efforts. Networking contacts are more likely to help if you have established a connection before applying for a job. If you apply and then try to connect with someone for help, they may be less likely to respond positively because they do not know you. They may also not want to interfere with their organization's job search process. Having a good plan will save time, increase potential opportunities, and allow you to make a great impression on others.

Remember that these professional relationships are precious. Those with whom you are networking are extending their own professional reputation by helping you, so make sure you follow up with a thank-you immediately, and let them know how your job search works out. Here's some advice from a leader in the nonprofit world to make the most of an interaction:

> If the networking is one-sided and you're on the side benefiting—be flexible with your schedule and easy to reach. Someone else is doing you the favor and that person is likely very busy. Networking over LinkedIn is awesome and very accessible. Networking with alums always goes well—people are generous with their time to help the success of another alum. When I want to network, I'm very personalized with my message if I know the person. Generic has no place with someone you are already familiar with—that's for strangers. Even acquaintances get personalized messaging. I also try to celebrate something about people when they reach out to me or I reach out to them—it's important in this field to build each other up and be each other's cheerleaders. My compliments are always genuine, but I try to be very present and conscious about making them happen. Networking that feels like a sales pitch is a total turnoff to me, and I won't respond. The world is much smaller than you think, be kind or it can come back to bite you. (Susan Keays, president and CEO, Italian Home for Children, Inc., Boston, MA)

APPLYING FOR JOBS

Now that you have spent time job searching, you should be uncovering job opportunities that align with your career aspirations. Before you submit your application or documents, let us discuss some recommendations for optimal success.

Document the Job Requirements

Pay attention to the job requirements. Better yet, take notes in your job search spreadsheet (see Table 6.3) about what requirements are needed and note the deadline, if indicated. If no date is indicated, set a goal date by which to apply so that it does not fall off your radar. Do not wait too long to apply; some job postings will state that the organization will take applications until the position is filled. If you wait too long, you may miss out.

Follow Instructions

Follow the instructions indicated by the organization or as indicated in the job posting. And yes, this is a test! Instructions might include referring to a job code in your cover letter or including a specified subject line in your email. Employers want to hire competent people who can follow simple directions. In the field of social work,

Table 6.3 Job Search Documentation

Job Title	Agency Name	Location	Application Deadline	Application Requirement	Date Submitted	Response	Follow-Up
Social worker	Community Care	Topeka	8/21	Resume, cover letter	8/16	Interviewed 9/1. No 2nd interview	Interview thank-you
Clinician	Topeka Medical Center	Topeka	9/25	Resume, cover letter	9/23	Application acknowledgment 9/23	
Intake specialist	ABC Community Services	Kansas City	Posted 9/20	Application, resume, cover letter	9/23		

following directions is often pivotal to the work done—for example, grant applications, court documents, and case notes to qualify clients for services. You may have to submit your application to an online portal, and you want to be sure it goes to the correct person and with all of the requested information.

Contact Your Network

If you have networked with someone within an organization that is hiring, contact them to find out more about their organization's application process. This is informative not only about their specific organization, but other, similar organizations, which may use the same processes and techniques. Your contacts can offer advice about how to get noticed and avoid the red flags that get applicants rejected or weeded out of the process. Taken a step further, your network contacts can become advocates and recommend you for jobs by informing their colleagues about your application or serving as a referral in your cover letter (e.g., "I am applying at the recommendation of [insert contact name here]."

Work with Recruiters

In some instances, particularly later in your career, you may receive an unsolicited inquiry from a recruiter. Often this outreach occurs if you have profiles on networking platforms such as LinkedIn. There are software features that allow recruiters to use key words, such as location, degree, skills, licenses, and credentials, to search for potential viable candidates—like you! If you are contacted by a recruiter, you should always respond quickly. If the title of the job or the organization interests you, respond to the recruiter in a favorable manner and ask for a meeting to discuss the position in more detail. Utilize this meeting to find out more about the position and organization and if this opportunity is a good fit. If the recruiter thinks you are a fit, they will invite you to apply—often asking you to submit a cover letter and resume to send to a hiring manager for review and a possible interview. If you are not interested, still respond quickly. Thank the recruiter for the outreach. Let the recruiter know that you are not looking for a job at this moment, but would like to stay in touch and connect later if your plans change. If the recruiter has contacted you about a job that is not a good fit, let them know what you are looking for. Now you have an ally in your job search!

INTERVIEWING

Though every job and organization is unique, employers generally have three criteria in mind when they interview candidates:

- Does the applicant have the skills and experience to do the job?
- Is the applicant motivated and hardworking?
- Is the applicant a good fit with the agency work environment and other employees?

Knowing that these are the fundamental questions that employers are trying to answer will help you anticipate the questions they will ask and prepare your responses.

Anticipate Questions and Prepare Answers

In preparing for an interview, think about your skills and strengths and how you are going to communicate them to the employer. Begin by brainstorming all that you have to offer based on your self-assessment in chapter 3. Then, using the job description as a guide, identify the responsibilities and qualifications necessary to be successful in this position. Select which of your skills, experiences, and personal characteristics you will highlight to demonstrate your qualifications. Go beyond what is indicated on your resume by demonstrating what motivates you, your accomplishments, and how you solve problems. Tell stories about your past experiences to demonstrate your claimed abilities. For example, if you are going to highlight your oral communication skills, think of a time you demonstrated success in this area, such as presenting at a meeting or co-facilitating a training. When you prepare this way, you will have concise, well-thought-out answers already constructed for whatever question is asked of you. This strategy will help you to feel more in control of the interview, as opposed to trying to think about all the answers to all the questions that could be coming.

It is also important to anticipate areas of questioning based on the job posting. For example, if an ability to work in a fast-paced environment is included in the description, the interviewer may ask questions about time management, thinking on your feet, or staying organized under pressure. If working successfully with a diverse client population is mentioned, prepare to demonstrate your understanding of antiracism and its role in your ability to make perceptive assessments and effective treatment plans.

The truth is, sometimes employers are not skilled in interviewing, and you want to make sure you get across what makes you a good candidate, even if they forget to ask. For some interviewers, you may be the first person they have interviewed, or you may be the first social worker they have interviewed. Even if you are meeting with a skilled interviewer, they may feel anxious, just like you! Be personable, conversational, and engaging, just as you would like for them to be with you. Interviewing can be tedious and exhausting for the interviewer; keep this in mind as you enter the interview.

By preparing your interview stories ahead of time, you will be able to finish with a strong last impression by responding to the following question:

> My very favorite question is the last one I usually ask, and it goes like this: "Often we prepare for an interview by anticipating questions and drafting our responses. We want to humble brag to make sure our skills get across. Then, the interviewer may not ask certain questions and we are disappointed that some of our best responses never had a chance. So, is there anything about you that we haven't asked that you'd like us to know?" (Susan Keays, president and CEO, Italian Home for Children, Inc., Boston, MA)

Research the Organization

It is important to research the organization before the interview. You should be familiar with the organization's mission and general structure. Use the internet and speak with social work students, alumni, or faculty who are knowledgeable about the agency or field of practice. Doing your homework and integrating this information and language into your interview are important ways to demonstrate your interest in the position. It is also important to research the person (or people) who will interview you. You may find information about them on the agency website or on the interviewer's LinkedIn profile. This research allows you to know how long the interviewer has been at this agency, their background, and if you share any similar experiences. You might have attended the same school or appreciate the same TED Talk speaker. This information could be helpful in creating small talk or better understanding your future colleagues.

Dress for Success

The way you are dressed creates a first impression on your interviewer. You want to convey confidence, professionalism, and that you understand the expectations of the agency you are interviewing with and have prepared for the interview process. You want the interviewer to focus on what you are saying and not how you are dressed. The best way to do this is to dress professionally. And remember, it is always better to be overdressed than underdressed.

Oftentimes when we consider a job interview, we either spend too much time worrying about what to wear, or we wait until the last minute to decide, adding to our anxiety. Researching and preparing your interview attire should be a part of your overall interview preparation. You can save time by setting aside a few clothing options that you will use for your interviews. Here are a few tips:

> **Dress Professionally Yet Comfortably:** This cannot be overemphasized. If you are wearing something that does not fit right or needs constant adjusting, you will not be able to concentrate fully on the interview. Choose something else.
> **Do Your Research:** Ask your networking contacts what attire is appropriate for the settings/agencies where you are interviewing. Be observant when interacting with others in the field. Working in a hospital setting or with

older adults might require more traditional attire than working with children or in a home.

Get Details: Ask about the format of the interview ahead of time, so that if, for example, they plan on giving you a tour of the facility, you will know to wear comfortable shoes, or, if you are meeting with the board, you might add a jacket.

Interview Rehearsal

The best way to prepare for an interview is with a dress rehearsal. Put on the clothes you picked for the interview. Grab your resume, cover letter, and prep sheet, and practice the interview. Some career offices offer mock interviews for students and alumni or have software you can use to simulate an interview. If you are interviewing remotely by Zoom or another virtual meeting platform, practice with someone else to make sure the background, sound, and lighting are optimal. Have your mock interviewer give you feedback on your nonverbal cues (e.g., nervous habits, posture, facial expressions, volume of voice) as well as the content of your responses. Practicing does not mean your answers will sound over-rehearsed or unnatural but rather well thought-out and articulate.

Second Interviews

Often, there will be multiple rounds of interviews in the hiring process. If you have been invited back for a second interview, congratulations! This indicates that you impressed them in the first interview. In these interviews, you can expect new faces, more specific questions, and perhaps a tour of the organization. Sometimes the first interview is conducted by someone in human resources and serves as a screening interview to make sure you meet the minimum qualifications of the position. Second interviews might be with the supervisor, unit leader, and even coworkers, together or in small groups. You may be asked to do a presentation or complete an assignment to assess your knowledge and your communication skills. If presenting, always practice with someone who will give you honest feedback and coaching on your presentation skills.

Sample Interview Questions

Regardless of the position you are interviewing for or your occupational field, there are usually some basic questions asked during an interview that you should have prepared responses for. Table 6.4 provides some examples of basic interview questions and ways to think about your responses.

Tough Questions: Addressing Limitations or Weaknesses

Interviews will always include tough questions—some predictable, others not. You want to be prepared for any challenging question, whether it be about gaps in

Table 6.4 Basic Interview Questions

Question	Preparing Your Reply
Tell me about yourself.	This response will be a combination of your elevator pitch (see chapter 5) and why you are interested in the position.
Why do you want to work here? or Why are you interested in this job?	Demonstrate your research of the agency and familiarity with the job description while sharing your related values, skills, and experience.
Why should we hire you?	Talk about how you can contribute your skills, experience, attitude, and passion.
What are your recent accomplishments?	Offer details about one or two accomplishments and why they are important to you. They do not need to be award winning or large scale; rather, they should demonstrate your values, skills, and/or impact.
Why are you leaving your current position?	Keep responses positive. Do not bash your current manager, team, or organization. Instead, talk about professional development, career interests, and opportunities.
What kind of work environment do you thrive in?	Talk about your values and your relationship with your colleagues and supervisor.
If you were a dessert, what kind of dessert would you be?	If you get a quirky question like this, just roll with it. There is no right or wrong answer!

employment, missing credentials, or concerns about your age. The following pointers will help you prepare.

- Have an answer prepared ahead of time so you do not fumble through the response
- Keep the response positive and never lie
- Provide examples of how you have addressed the situation

Table 6.5 provides examples of tough questions and ways to think about your responses.

The "Weakness" Question

In almost every interview, you will be asked to describe your weaknesses, limitations, or areas of growth. As you consider this question ahead of the interview, prepare a statement of your limitations confidently and turn them into a learning opportunity or even a reason why this new opportunity excites you. For example, if the job requires creating and facilitating a group on grief and loss, and you have not had the opportunity to facilitate a group by yourself before, you might answer, "While I am very knowledgeable about grief and loss and I have co-facilitated groups in my previous position, I have not had the opportunity to create and facilitate a group

Table 6.5 Sample Tough Questions

Topic	Question	Preparing Your Reply
Age	Given that you are a recent graduate, how comfortable are you with providing services to adult clients?	Share that in your first field placement you worked with older adults. You learned to establish rapport by not coming in as the "expert" telling clients what to do but rather acknowledging their life experience as an asset to our work together. Describe how you found ways to demonstrate your clinical knowledge in conversation to assure them you knew what you were doing.
Missing credential, minimal experience	Please tell me about your experience with our XYZ medical records system.	Be honest that you are not familiar with the XYZ system, but convey confidence that you can overcome this deficiency. Provide an example of a time you were not familiar with something and got yourself up to speed through research and working with others. Indicate a willingness and interest in learning.
Absence or gap in employment	Your resume indicates a few years since you last worked. How have you stayed prepared for this position?	Highlight volunteer, continuing education, and other activities that have allowed you to stay in tune with the field and gain new skills, knowledge, and experience.

by myself. This is why I am so excited about the possibility of working for this organization, as I would love to gain this experience." This question, if answered in the correct way, can be an asset to your interview as you demonstrate self-reflection and a desire for self-improvement. Remember: weaknesses are only things that you have not learned yet.

When asked about weaknesses, avoid using clichés that are self-compliments in disguise, such as "I am a perfectionist." Instead, point to an area that you improved upon recently, such as stepping up your social media presence, brushing up on the *Code of Ethics*, or asking a supervisor to give you pointers on dealing with conflict. If possible, do not answer with habits or personal characteristics that can only be addressed by you—for example, punctuality, attitude, or ability to work with others. This may make the interviewer wary that you will not be able to change all by yourself.

Clinical-Specific Interview Questions

Clinical questions will likely revolve around your client relationships, your interest in specific populations, your knowledge of those populations, interventions you have used, how you like to be supervised, and your self-care. Table 6.6 provides examples of clinical-specific questions and how to prepare your responses.

Presenting a Case Study

In clinical job interviews, you might be asked to present a case study. A case study is a brief presentation demonstrating your knowledge, skills, and abilities as they relate to providing clinical services or therapy for a client. Your presentation should be no more than about five minutes. Your case should be a real-life example that you are familiar with, both its history and progression. Follow these tips to help you prepare:

- Give your example a title: "Treatment Addressing Client with X Diagnosis/Presenting Problem"
- Describe how the client was referred to you, the agency, or the hospital
- Provide some basic demographic information about the client (age, race/ethnicity, sex/gender, marital status, etc.), but do not provide any identifying information
- Discuss intake, initial meetings, and engagement
- Discuss decisions on treatment, including any evidence-based treatment, techniques used, and why

Table 6.6 Clinical-Specific Interview Questions

Topic	Question	Preparing Your Reply
Relationship with clients	How do you build rapport with your clients?	Describe your experience with and style of building rapport and trust, challenging clients, setting boundaries, and discussing confidentiality and the Health Insurance Portability and Accountability Act (or HIPAA)
Population/issue focus	Why are you interested in focusing on this population or issue?	Talk about your experience, rewards, and motivations with this work
Knowledge of clinical interventions	What clinical modalities do you feel most skilled at? How do they apply to your population?	Demonstrate understanding of and comfort level with specific modalities and when and with whom they are most effective
Clinical supervision	What style of supervision have you found most rewarding?	Be able to articulate preferred supervision style, including communication, feedback, availability
Self-care	What do you for self-care?	Have a self-care plan in place and articulate it confidently
Diversity	How have you demonstrated a commitment to diversity, equity, and inclusion?	Give specific examples of efforts and outcomes and how you have learned from past mistakes

- Discuss progression and outcomes, if any
- Describe other problems or challenges, systems issues, and how you addressed them

Macro-Specific Interview Questions

Macro-specific interview questions are likely to focus on skills such as teamwork, leadership, and advocacy. Table 6.7 provides examples of macro-specific interview questions and ways to think about your responses.

Behavior Interview Questions

Many aspects of our day-to-day jobs in social work will be situational; for example, how you address a client who shows up under the influence, or how you prioritize competing demands. In the past, interviewers would address these subjects using hypothetical questions, which in turn resulted in hypothetical answers. To gain insight into a candidate's actual level of experience and potential to handle difficult situations, employers will likely use behavioral interviewing as a strategy. The philosophy behind this type of interview is that past behavior is a predictor of future behavior. Behavioral interviewers ask you to present a situation relevant to their question, describe what action you took, and share the result. This scenario allows you to give

Table 6.7 Macro-Specific Interview Questions

Topic	Question	Preparing Your Reply
Value of social work degree versus other master's degrees	Why should I hire a social worker?	Talk about strengths-based and systems approaches and how they align with your social justice values. Convey an understanding of how macro interventions play out on the micro level.
Leadership	Describe your leadership skills.	Discuss style and values around motivation, delegation, decision making, team building, critical thinking skills, and communication.
Evaluation	What is your approach to evaluation and how would you implement that in this position?	Articulate your technical skills, your familiarity with the *Code of Ethics*, the type of research you have conducted (e.g., participatory, community focused, quantitative, qualitative), and your experience with the internal review process.
Collaboration	Tell me about a teamwork experience, what you learned, and how you might do things differently.	Reflect on past experiences, such as consensus building and delegating; describe group work done in classes.

examples of past experiences to illustrate how you demonstrated a skill or handled a particular situation. To prepare yourself before the interview, think about the skills required for this job (start by reviewing the job posting) and write out examples from past employment during which you best demonstrated these skills. Table 6.8 provides examples of behavioral interview questions and ways to prepare your responses.

STAR Method

The STAR method provides an easy-to-remember acronym that provides a framework for answering behavioral interview questions:

> **Situation:** Describe the situation that you were in or the task that you needed to accomplish. This situation can be from a previous job, a volunteer experience, or any relevant event.
> **Task:** What was *your* responsibility? What role did you play?
> **Action:** Describe the action you took, keeping the focus on you. Even if you are discussing a group project or effort, describe what you did—not the efforts of the team. Use the pronoun "I" not "we" to emphasize this; for example, "I wrote . . ."
> **Results:** What happened? How did the event end? What did you accomplish? What did you learn?

Table 6.8 Sample Behavioral Questions

Topic	Question	Preparing Your Reply
Adaptability	Tell me about a time when things did not go according to plan. How did you handle the situation?	Focus on the solution, not the problem. Demonstrate your adaptability, ability to learn from mistakes, and how you make use of supervision.
Time management	Give an example of a goal you reached. How did you achieve it?	Think about times you set goals (or goals were set for you) and discuss how you met them, such as using your organizational skills, managing your time differently, and seeking out a mentor.
Teamwork	Relate a time you dealt with conflict among team members.	Focus on the solution, not the problem. Share skills in conflict resolution, interpersonal skills, and leadership.
Initiative	Describe a time when you saw a problem and took the initiative to correct it.	Describe the steps you took in a specific situation and then generalize, indicating initiative, problem-solving skills, and innovation.
Ethics	Ethical dilemmas can arise in social work. How have you handled such a dilemma?	Have a good example on hand, and in your response incorporate the *Code of Ethics*, the policies of the agency you were working for, professional standards, and your own integrity and use of supervision.

CASE STUDY

Garrett

Garrett was a recent MSW graduate seeking a job as a school social worker. They had obtained their BSW and gone straight into graduate school the following semester. In preparation for a job interview as a school social worker, Garrett prepared by studying the organization's "six core values." Based on these values, they came up with three stories from their volunteer work, internship, and academic experience to use if asked behavioral interviewing questions. In the interview, Garrett was asked to describe a time when they disagreed with a supervisor and how they handled it. Garrett answered using the STAR method:

> **Situation:** "While I have not had a situation like that with a direct supervisor, there was a time in graduate school when I disagreed with a grade I was given by my professor."
> **Task:** "It was a group project, and while my portion of the project was done well, according to the professor's comments, one of my group members plagiarized a couple of paragraphs and the whole group was docked 10 points."
> **Action:** "I sent my professor an email and scheduled an appointment to discuss my concerns with her."
> **Results:** "She informed me that according to the syllabus, students are expected to work collaboratively as a team and share accountability for the final product. While I was not able to get my grade changed, I appreciated the opportunity to gain clarity about the importance of understanding the syllabus for future courses, the expectations of a graduate-level group project beyond just the grade, and the importance of collaboration and professional accountability."

The story that Garrett chose to use in their interview contained many of the possible elements of a behavioral interview question. While the situation presented was about conflict with a superior (disagreeing with a grade given by a professor), there were also elements of ethics (plagiarism) and policy (the syllabus for the class). These elements could have been used interchangeably while describing the situation, but not without good planning ahead of time to think through and practice the examples that Garrett chose to use. Additionally, it is important to point out that Garret's answer displayed honesty, strength, and an openness to learning. Do not ever underestimate the power of authenticity and humility!

Questions to Ask Your Interviewer

An interview is a two-way conversation. As important as answering the questions put to you is having your questions answered. At the end of the interview process, you should feel that you have the information you need to determine whether this is the right job for you. This involves first analyzing yourself. What is important to you in your job? This depends on individual preferences. For some, flexible time might be more important than not sharing an office space with someone. For others, gaining particular skills might be more important than a particular salary. Think about what you are looking for first, so that you can make sure this job and organization is a good fit for you. Come to the interview prepared with questions that revolve around these major themes:

> **Position:** What will I be doing and what are my responsibilities?
> **Organization:** What is the organizational/departmental environment?
> **Supervision:** What is my supervisor's management style?
> **Team or Colleagues:** What is the team culture?

General Interview Tips

What to Take with You

Bring extra copies of your resume if your interview is in person, including a copy for you to refer to. If the interview is virtual, be sure to have a copy of your resume on hand. Whether interviewing remotely or in person, mute your phone. Better yet, put it in another room so it does not distract you. Have pen and paper to takes notes or document important information. Use the interview prep sheet in Table 6.9 to capture the key information you have prepared for the specific interview. Review it before an in-person interview; have it in front of you to look at during a remote interview.

Take Time to Think

Do not feel you have to start talking the minute the interviewer stops. If you need time to think about the best response to the employer's question, give yourself a minute—it is better than rambling on until you find your point! Be prepared with what you will say when you pause. For example, you might say, "Let me take a moment to think about that," or you might repeat the question back to the interviewer to clarify and then ask for a moment to think about it.

Be Yourself

When interviewing, you want to put your best image forward, but you also want to let your personality show through. It is important for both you and the employers to decide whether you are a good fit with the office environment and coworkers.

Discuss Salary at the Right Time

The issue of salary may or may not be brought up during an initial interview. It is best for you not to bring up the subject in a first interview, but you should be prepared to discuss your salary expectations if asked. Present a range that reflects your

Table 6.9 Interview Prep Sheet

Date of interview	
Job title	
Agency name and location	
Names and contact info for interviewers	
Key info about agency/department	
Key info about position	
Why am I excited/well suited for this role	
Three points I want to make	
Three stories to use for behavioral interviews	
Area(s) of growth specific to this position	
Questions to ask	
Next steps and timeline	

understanding of typical salaries for this position or career field. Salary conversations often occur when you become one of a few final candidates or before a final offer. Further salary negotiation tactics can be found in chapter 7.

Interview Follow-Up

What you do after the interview is just as important as what you do during the interview. The following are our recommendations for documentation, thank-you notes, and post-interview networking.

Document the Interview

Jot down notes after the interview so that you capture both your first impressions and important facts about the job and organization. If you do not write down this information right away, things will start to blend together, especially if you are interviewing at more than one place. Is there information you are still lacking? Did you communicate all the important points about yourself? These are things you will want to cover in the next round of interviews.

Thank-You Communication

Be sure to send a thank-you letter to your interviewers within 48 hours of your interview. Hiring managers agree that this is an important component in their hiring decision making. It makes a good impression, allows you to reaffirm your interest in the position, and demonstrates respect for the time they took to interview you. Use this opportunity to remind them of your skills and to articulate something that stood out about the interview or the organization. Make sure you use the correct spelling of names and titles. You can ask the interviewers or receptionist for this information, ask for business cards, or look at the interviewers' LinkedIn profiles. For most employers, sending a thank-you by email is acceptable. Follow a formal business letter style. Subject heading can be "Thank you for the interview" or "Follow-up to interview." Refer to Appendix F for samples.

Connect through LinkedIn

Now that you have finished your thank-you letter, it is time to connect with the interviewer and other participants through LinkedIn. This will indicate your continued interest in the position and agency and keep the lines of communication open. It will also allow you to learn more about the organization through the employee's lens; for example, how they describe their work. Take the time to send a personalized invitation! When you send the invitation, let them know you enjoyed the interview and that you would like to connect. This does not take the place of a thank-you letter, but it is a nice touch. For more information on connecting on LinkedIn, see chapter 4.

Update References

If you are in the final stages of interviewing and the employer has asked for a list of references, now is the time to reach out to each of your references with an update. Confirm with each reference that they are currently available to be contacted. Share the job posting and your resume with them so that they are prepared to talk about you within this context. Make sure to let them know when you accept a position.

Next Steps

Always close the interview by asking what the next steps are and what the interviewer's timeline is. Write this down on your interview tracking sheet, as it will be very important for following up. If they do not contact you either way, send the interviewer an email within three weeks, asking about the status of your application. An email is much better than a phone call, as you do not want to catch the interviewer off guard. Unfortunately, there will be interviewers who neglect to contact candidates who were not chosen. While this is considered poor form, it does happen if hiring managers are overwhelmed with applicants, but you may want to consider it a red flag in terms of future employment with the organization.

Keep Applying

Once your interview is finished, especially if you did well, it can be easy to let your guard down and take a break from the job search while you await an offer. Do not let this happen to you! Celebrate your success, then gear up for the next application or interview. Remember that your job search does not end until the first day of your new job. Imagine how wonderful it would be to have multiple job offers at one time and negotiate for the one you really want! The best way to have multiple offers is to go on multiple interviews. Keep moving forward, and your hard work will pay off in the end!

CONCLUSION

A job search can feel like a roller coaster ride of ups and downs. You may think an interview went really well, but then not hear back. You may rush to submit application materials, only to wait weeks or longer for acknowledgment or contact. Our advice: Embrace the fact that you can only control what you can—let go of the rest. Keep yourself motivated by rewarding yourself for achieving small goals. Involve others in the process by having a job search partner or group with whom to share ideas and keep each other going. Learn from each other's experiences, good or bad. Things will work out! Make a plan; enjoy the journey.

CHAPTER TAKEAWAYS

- Networking is a valuable use of your time that can help you connect with unadvertised opportunities, build relationships with those in the field, and gather information that allows your application materials to be effective.
- The interaction can happen spontaneously or through careful planning—plan to do both.
- Following up is critical to maintaining the professional relationship, even if you are hired elsewhere.
- You got this! Whether you are extroverted, introverted, or a little of both, find a way to network that is comfortable for you and then stretch yourself a bit. Do not necessarily start with a big room of unknown faces.
- In preparing for your interview, *use the job description as a guide* to what skills and experiences you should highlight.
- Use the prep sheet, dress for success, and practice.

- An interview should be a two-way conversation that involves you answering questions for the employer's evaluation and you asking the employer prepared questions to see if this is the right position for you.
- Follow up with a thank-you note, document the interview, and continue applying for jobs until you secure an offer and decide to accept it.

CHAPTER 7

Evaluating and Negotiating Job Offers

What You Will Learn

- ❐ How to evaluate and manage job offers
- ❐ How to assess organizational culture
- ❐ How to negotiate a financial package
- ❐ How to successfully onboard with an organization

Action Plan

- ❐ Create a personal budget to help you with salary negotiation
- ❐ Learn the lingo regarding salary and benefits
- ❐ Practice your script for negotiating

Congratulations! You have been offered a job. Your first inclination may be to accept right away because you do not want all your hard work to go to waste. In addition, this may be your first "real" job offer after college, your first job offer after changing careers, or your first job offer in a position that will advance your career.

We strongly suggest that you take a moment and not accept immediately. You want to evaluate a job offer holistically by determining if the job matches your personal values, your career goals identified through your self-assessment (chapter 3), and your financial requirements.

If you are feeling rusty or unsure about how to do this, do not dismay! This chapter contains valuable tools to help you examine job offers, negotiate a fair salary, assess organizational culture, accept a job on the best terms possible, and successfully onboard with an organization.

EVALUATING WORK CULTURE

Evaluating workplace culture is important because a great predictor of how successful you will be in your new job is how well your values and goals align with the organization's culture. Lauren Davis, director of diversity, equity and community at the University of Michigan School of Environment and Sustainability, stated, "When your values and goals align with a workspace, you do not have to spend so much time stressing over whether or not you 'fit' in, you can spend more of your time doing your work and being productive" (personal communication, June 21, 2023). And it is better to find out whether an organization is a good fit for you during the job search or interview process than after you have invested time and energy into working for that organization. Assessing workplace culture goes beyond reviewing the organization's website and job description. Here are five ways you can assess workplace culture.

1. Determine what is important to you in terms of workplace culture. What type of workplace environment do you thrive in? Where do you want your career to progress and does this organization provide the type of support you are seeking? Do you see any red flags to indicate that this organization is not suitable?
2. Seek out employee feedback. Websites such as Glassdoor post feedback and ratings from employees about culture, communication, and issues within the organization. You can also gain insight through informational interviews with employees or within your social and professional networks.
3. Interview the organization. During the interview, it is vital that you have questions to ask the employer. Suggested questions that may give you clues about the workplace:

   - What do you like best about working here?
   - What are the biggest challenges in working here?
   - What advice would you give a new employee to your organization?
   - Why is this position vacant?
   - How often are the same positions open at this organization?
   - What characteristics make employees successful at your organization?

4. Explore employee orientation/onboarding. Ask your interviewer what orientation is like. Do orientation and onboarding seem engaging to you?
5. Keep communication open. How easy was it to ask and receive information during the interview? Did the employer respond positively and in a timely manner to your questions?

See Appendix G for an extensive list of questions for assessing workplace culture, as well as an exploration of an organization's diversity, equity, and inclusion practices.

EVALUATING COMPENSATION

First, let us discuss the elephant in the room—money! Everyone hates to talk about money, but money is one of the most important reasons we find new jobs. The National Association of Colleges and Employers (NACE; 2023), which provides current information about employment trends, states that one of the top reasons candidates choose to work for an organization is the salary and benefits it offers its employees. Everyone wants to be compensated fairly for their work and feel valued as an employee. This begins with feeling valued as an applicant.

The "B" Word: Budget

What do you think of when you think of the word budget? For many people, a personal budget may have a negative connotation or bring up feelings of fear or deprivation. As a recent college graduate, or a social worker who has been struggling with their job search, you may have been living month to month just trying to make ends meet. Whether our situation is stable or changing, many of us avoid thinking about a budget at all. Rather than avoid these feelings, we encourage you to get comfortable with finances and budgeting. If you do, you will be able to solve your budgeting problems and make more informed decisions about finances. To that end, we encourage you to create a budget of monthly expenses with a paper or electronic spreadsheet. Begin by documenting your current monthly expenses. Remember, information is power—just knowing what your expenses are and how much money you will need will bring you a sense of relief.

Creating a Budget

Using the template in Appendix H, make a spreadsheet of categories/items you pay for each month. Next to that category/item, list how much money in dollars that category/item costs you each month. Review past bills, credit card statements, and bank statements for estimates. Once you have a complete list, add up all the dollar amounts, and you will have an estimated budget for a month. If you multiply your monthly budget by 12, you will have an estimate of your yearly expenses. If you are planning to relocate for your new job, websites such as salary.com can assist you with estimating the cost of living for a geographic area.

Once you have an idea of the total amount of expenses you have for a month and for a year, review those numbers and ask yourself these questions to become more comfortable with your personal budget:

- How do you feel about the monthly number?
- Did you discover anything new about yourself and your spending habits?
- Does the total amount shock you? Why or why not?
- How did reviewing expenses in written form affect you?

Creating a budget helps you to be more effective at evaluating offers and determining whether the job offer will cover your living expenses, allow you to build your savings and retirement, and provide you with stability and self-worth.

Research the Market and Consider Intangibles

Many job postings will not disclose the salary range for open positions. Before you can negotiate your salary, it is beneficial to learn what salary employers are generally paying for the position you are seeking. With this information, you will be able to judge the fairness of an offer and gauge how much you can negotiate and have your counteroffer backed with evidence. It is optimal to conduct this research well before applying for jobs or going into an interview. In the next section, we will discuss avenues and resources to help you research salaries; refer to Exercise 7.1 for an activity to help you identify salaries for positions you are seeking.

It is also important to note that many factors determine the pay scale of positions: geographic location, agency setting, union versus nonunion, public versus private, and agency/organization size and age. Differences in pay for similar positions vary by geographic location to match the cost of living in those areas. If you are searching for positions in expensive cost of living areas (e.g., New York and San Francisco), the pay scale will be higher than in lower cost of living areas, (e.g., Detroit). Settings such as hospitals, schools, community mental health agencies, and grassroots organizations may pay slightly different wages because these settings rely on different funding streams to support their operation. Some organizations (such as public schools) have a unionized history that has impacted their pay scale, whereas a charter school may not have to adhere to the same restrictions. Agency size and years of operation may affect staff pay due to reputation and longevity, variety of funding streams, and complexity and variety of services offered. You want to be aware of differences across settings so you can make appropriate comparisons.

There are several sources to use in researching salary information:

- The Bureau of Labor Statistics is a federal agency of the United States whose mission is to track economic, employment, and labor information. There you can find information about employment trends and careers, as well as occupational development. In addition, this agency tracks data on unemployment rates, hiring rates, and salaries for different occupations by state and region of the United States.
- Often when you are participating in informational interviews (see chapter 3), you are meeting with hiring managers at organizations where you wish to work or you are meeting with people who are working in a position you wish to obtain. Use this time to ask about salary ranges for your job interests; benefits packages; and professional development opportunities such as training, conferences, licensure, and exam support.
- Many states have a nonprofit association that acts as a membership collective serving nonprofits in that state. Often these organizations provide online job boards and collect salary information for nonprofit jobs from their members.
- Governmental agencies (federal, state, local) and other public institutions such as schools, universities, and hospitals often publish their salary information on their website.
- Public colleges and universities often have salaries listed with the job titles/positions of everyone hired, from the president to the groundskeeper.

- Job-related and employer review sites such as LinkedIn, Indeed, ZipRecruiter, and Glassdoor have salary information.
- College and university career services offices and alumni associations keep data on salaries of graduates.

Exercise 7.1

Research Salary Range

In Table 7.1, write down at least two positions that interest you. These prospective positions can be positions you have seen in recent job postings, positions you are seeking upon graduation, or dream positions. First, ask yourself whether you are looking for a specific practice setting (e.g., medical, school, nonprofit, or government). Indicate this next to the position. Then list the size (number of employees) of the agency/organization and what geographic location you are interested in. Then, try to find out the salary ranges for these positions using some of the resources we have listed. What did you find out? Did you find a salary range? Most of the time you will find a range but there will be a clear low starting point and a clear maximum amount.

Table 7.1 Salary Ranges

	Type of Setting	Size of Organization	Geographic Location	Salary Ranges
Position A				
Position B				

Salary Negotiation Lingo

To communicate effectively, it is vital that you understand the terminology often used in job applications, negotiations, and job offer reviews. Key terms include:

Salary Requirement: Sometimes employers ask you during the application or interview process to state your salary requirement. Never state one specific amount because you may reduce your ability to negotiate. Offer the employer a range of about $5,000 that is based upon your research; for example, $40,000 to $45,000, negotiable.

Salary History: Usually, an employer wants you to provide your hourly rate or yearly salary for each job listed on your resume. Know your rights! In some states, such as California, Delaware, Massachusetts, and Oregon, there are laws preventing employers from asking about salary history. Websites such as salary.com keep track of state bans related to salary questions.

Annual Salary/Base Salary: Base salary is a fixed amount of money paid to an employee by an employer in return for work performed. Base salary does not include benefits, bonuses, or any other potential compensation from an employer.

Net Salary (Take-Home Pay): This is the amount an employee receives after all deductions are made (taxes, benefits, etc.).

Benefits Package: This can vary by employer but may include vacation time, sick time, holiday time off, paid time off, retirement contribution matching, professional development or training, medical/dental/vision plans, and flexible spending or health savings accounts.

How to Negotiate/When to Negotiate

Job seekers are often nervous about negotiating an offer. There are many opinions about negotiations, and it can be difficult to decipher what is valuable. We have two important pieces of advice gained from discussions with employers and human resource professionals:

1. **Always Negotiate.** Know that negotiation is a natural part of the employer/employee job acceptance process. When an employer extends an offer to you, they are expecting you to review it, often hoping you will accept it, but understanding that a negotiation may occur. You can negotiate salary and, in some instances, benefits. We will discuss how to negotiate salary and/or benefits later in the chapter.
2. **Never Negotiate Before an Employer Extends an Offer.** This timing is extremely important because you want to make sure the employer has decided that they want to hire you. This is when you are in your best negotiating position.

Reviewing Offers and Contracts

Once you have created a budget and researched the job's salary range, you will be in a better position to review an offer. In addition, based upon your research, you will know if the offer you have received reflects industry standards. When an offer is first extended (often by a phone call and followed up with an email), you do not need to immediately accept or decline. It is appropriate to ask for time to evaluate the offer. Employers will give you time—usually from a few days to a week—to review the offer. Two sample job offer letters are provided here.

Sample Offer for Clinical Position in Private Practice

Dear Chantail Johnson:

As discussed by phone, we are happy to officially extend this offer to you. The offer being extended is for a contractual position as a therapist providing clinical services to children and adolescents. Your appointment will be a full-time caseload (at least 25 clients per week), which amounts to $62,400 per year. Our rate for services is $120 per billable hour. Your salary will consist of a 60/40 split with 60 percent of the billable hours going to the practice to cover administrative costs, which include office space, management of client referrals, appointments, billing, and clinical supervision. Your share is 40 percent. No benefits are provided. However, we offer options for group health, dental, disability, life, and liability insurances. You must also cover your own malpractice insurance. We also provide monthly in-house group consultation and professional development.

If you have any questions, please feel free to contact me.

We look forward to you joining our team.

Sincerely,

Mindful Counseling, INC

Sample Offer for Macro Position in Nonprofit Organization

Dear Jose Ortega:

As discussed by phone, we are happy to officially extend this offer to you. The offer being extended is for a full-time regular appointment as a program coordinator, with a full-time equivalent salary of $45,000 ($21.63/hour). You will be paid ~$1,730 gross on the biweekly pay schedule. Please see the attached benefit handbook which explains the health, retirement, and other benefits offered by our organization.

Your appointment will be a full-time (40 hrs/week) regular position and you will report to Brenda Smith. Your regular duties will include the monitoring of program, fiscal management, and community engagement. Your work hours will usually be 8:00 A.M. to 5:00 P.M., Monday through Friday with a one-hour lunch; however, you may change this schedule in consultation with your supervisor.

Please confirm your acceptance of this position in writing by September 19.

If you have any questions, please contact me.

We look forward to you joining our team.

Sincerely,

Human Resources Representative

As you read everything over, compare the offer letter to your research and write down everything that you want to negotiate (within reason). Note why you want to negotiate or the reason behind your decision or counteroffer. What do you want to negotiate? What is important to you? In Appendix I you will find an offer evaluation grid to help you review employment offers. As you evaluate your offer consider the following:

- How do you feel about this offer? What does your gut say?
- How does this position compare to what you articulated through your self-assessment in terms of values and career goals?
- Considering your market research, how does this offer compare?
- What are the pros and cons of the benefits package?
- Is anything missing that is of importance to you?

Reviewing Benefits

Benefits packages vary by organization. A benefits package may include:

Medical/Vision/Dental Insurance: These are types of health insurance that often require co-payments depending upon your coverage level and number of dependents. You may be offered choices of health plan, including ones with higher and lower deductibles. Review the insurance benefits carefully to determine which plan is right for you, whether your current providers are covered, and whether you will be using out-of-network (and therefore, more expensive) providers. Understanding your current healthcare expenses is essential to understanding how a new plan will impact your budget.

Flexible Spending Account or Health Savings Account: These are untaxed accounts to which you contribute funds to cover co-pays or other out-of-pocket medical, dental, and vision costs. Employers may make contributions to these accounts, or, in the case of health savings accounts, allow you to invest those funds.

Retirement: These plans could include a traditional pension (specific amount paid to a retiree for a certain number of years of service) or a defined contribution plan such as a 403(b) or 401(k) in which both the employer and employee pay into the plan.

Vacation Days: Bankable days off earned each pay period.

Holiday Time: Specific days the organization is closed each calendar year.

Sick/Personal Days: Set number of days an employer can use for sickness, family care, etc.

Paid Time Off: A growing trend is for companies to offer paid time off (PTO) generally, and not break it down into vacation, sick, or personal days. Think about whether PTO works for you and be sure the organization has a culture that encourages using PTO.

Life Insurance: Some organizations offer policies for purchase or offer a policy payment based upon your salary for a beneficiary.

Liability/Malpractice Insurance: Most organizations cover this as part of their own administrative costs. However, social workers employed as part of a private practice often must purchase their own liability/malpractice insurance.

Tuition Reimbursement: Specific amount of money paid toward student loans or specific amount of money paid toward additional classes or degrees.

Professional Development/Expense Account: Specific amount of money an employee can use for training, conferences, certifications, professional memberships, license fees, and licensure supervision costs.

Additional Equipment: Organizations may pay for computers and software for remote work, work cell phones, or the use of a car for site visits.

Mileage Reimbursement: For social workers who use their own vehicle for company business, some employers offer mileage reimbursement.

Relocation Costs: Moving can be costly and some organizations will provide funding to help offset some of the related expenses.

Hiring Bonus: This is a one-time payment to a new hire. We caution against giving too much weight to a hiring bonus. It is a nice touch. While attractive at the outset, it does not increase your wages year over year.

Some benefits are nonnegotiable because they are based on seniority or union contracts. However, many benefits are negotiable, such as vacation days, hiring bonuses, and relocation costs. As part of your review of an offer, it is vital that you understand what is offered in addition to your salary so that you will have a realistic picture of your net salary or an additional cost you may have to incur that is not covered by your employer.

Other Negotiables

In addition to salary and benefits, there may be other aspects to consider when negotiating or finalizing a job offer, including

Start Date: Do you need time to finish school, relocate, or give extra notice and extract yourself from your current position?

Vacation: Do you have a vacation already scheduled? Be sure to inform your potential employer before you accept the offer.

Licensure and Credentials: Will the employer pay for licensure and professional development, including continuing education requirements to maintain your license? Is there a set salary bump if you attain your independent and/or clinical license?

Always take time to review the offer letter—both the salary and the benefits. When a deadline is given for reviewing the offer, be sure to note the date on your calendar. Call the employer back before or on that date to discuss your counteroffer. Do not fail to follow up when promised!

Your Counteroffer

When you contact a prospective employer with a counteroffer, it may be difficult to put into words what you wish to say and have confidence behind your request. When thinking about why an employer should increase their salary offer, you should keep in mind the following:

- You have the knowledge, skills, and personality strengths that made you the final candidate. They are offering you the job and want you to join their team—you are in a great negotiating position!
- You demonstrated the ability to make or save employers money. Have you been awarded grants for programs? Raised money? Met targets that are directly related to revenue gains? Have you streamlined a process, saving the employer time? All these outcomes point to money gained or saved, which would be very valuable to a prospective employer, who wants you to achieve the same outcomes for their organization.
- You met the goals, outcomes, and objectives of your current employer. You are productive and will bring the same energy to the new organization.

Here are some suggested counteroffer responses. Note that each response shows enthusiasm and appreciation for considering your request.

> **Example 1:** I am very excited about the program coordinator position. Regarding the base salary, I think my experience and education warrant a salary closer to $47,250. The additional $2,250 is only 5 percent above what you are offering me and I believe that I would bring value to your organization, such as my demonstrated ability to save organizations money by process improvement and earn additional money by obtaining outside funding.
>
> **Example #2:** Thank you so much for the offer. This position is a great fit for me. I am excited to work assisting children and families to address mental health concerns and thrive, which I learned is a major focus of your clinic. Given my extensive knowledge, experience, and skills in art therapy and dialectical behavior therapy, I would be a great contributor to the clinic. In addition, I have just passed my clinical exam and am close to obtaining my clinical license. I was looking for a fee split of 55/45 as a starting salary and hope that you will consider it.
>
> **Example #3:** I am hoping there is room to negotiate my start date and reimbursement for professional development opportunities. First, I have a vacation planned and would like my start date to be on June 15 after I return. Second, I am hoping that some of the professional development money utilized for this position go toward costs associated with licensure. My licensure fees are $430, including the cost of the application fee and exam fee.

Some employers will need time to consider your counteroffer. Do not be surprised if they ask for time to consider whether they can fulfill your request. Once an offer is finalized, make sure to get any agreements in writing (email is acceptable).

COMMON JOB SEARCH DILEMMAS

While your job search and offer negotiation may seem complex, they are likely variations on a common theme, such as balancing more than one offer or managing a counteroffer from your existing employer. In the following sections we describe some common scenarios.

More Than One Job Offer

Occasionally, you may find yourself in a situation in which you have more than one job offer. This is a great situation to be in, but it can be stressful. When you are considering more than one offer, it is important to ask each employer for time to review their offer so that you can adequately review and evaluate each one specifically and make comparisons. If there are differences between the offers, you may be able to leverage one against the other. For example, you may receive an offer from organization A for $50,000 plus benefits and an offer from organization B for $47,000 plus benefits. Upon your review, you decide that you are more drawn to organization B than organization A. In negotiation, you can contact organization B to let them know that you have an offer from organization A, and ask if they can match it.

Second-Choice Offers

In some instances, you may receive an offer for your second-choice job before hearing about your first-choice job. This is not an easy position to face. If you have interviewed for your first choice and are waiting on a response, ask your second-choice employer for more time to decide. In some instances, you may be able to contact your first-choice employer for an update, giving you more insight into how to proceed. Sometimes, you may have to decide whether you want to risk waiting on your preferred employer or proceed with a firm offer from another organization.

Backing Out of an Offer

Formally accepting an offer for a job is something you should only do in good faith and when you fully intend to honor that commitment. Backing out of an offer can have serious career consequences. The world of social work is smaller than you might think, and you do not want to burn any bridges on your journey. However, life is unpredictable, and in some instances, such as a partner getting transferred or an illness in the family, you may have to back out. As soon as you have made this decision, you should contact your employer right away to apologize and decline the offer. If possible, provide the employer with an explanation of why you are backing out of the position. Do whatever you can to smooth the situation over and back out on good terms.

Asking for a Raise

In many instances, asking for a raise is like researching salary information for a new job. In fact, sometimes job seekers use a job offer to negotiate a higher salary with their current employer. When asking for a raise, you should consider the following:

- What is your strategy? Build your case for why you deserve a raise, such as positive performance reviews, awards received, new credentials and licenses obtained, additional responsibilities absorbed, and success with important projects.
- What is your timeline? Will you ask during your annual review? During a major restructuring of your department? After you have logged a big success? Keep in mind timing as it pertains to the financial strength of your workplace and the economy.
- Are you being compensated fairly? In this case, you are asking for equity in compensation with someone in the same or a similar position.
- Are you asking for a raise because you have another offer? One strategy is to go on the job market or answer a call from a recruiter, interview, and get an offer from a potential employer and use that as leverage to ask for a raise. Your current employer may not want to lose you!

Sometimes, organizations are constrained and cannot increase your salary while you have the same job title. However, if you have taken on more responsibilities or your position has evolved since your hire, you may be able to successfully negotiate a change in your title, thus giving you the opportunity to make a higher salary.

Onboarding

Congratulations! You have accepted an offer and now you have a start date. You want this new relationship to be successful and meaningful and to start off on the right foot. You also do not want to miss out on any opportunities as an employee. We suggest the following:

- Create a file on your computer specific to this job. Keep a copy of your job description, annual reviews, accomplishments, awards, and other work milestones for future reference. It is too easy to forget our accomplishments when we are busy with our day-to-day work. If you are tracking this information, when you need to update your resume or CV, create a bio statement, or ask for that raise, you already have gathered historical information.
- Obtain a copy (written or online) of the employer's organizational chart. Become familiar with the areas/departments of your workplace and the people who work in those areas.
- Note the key leaders in the organization. How are they leading? What is important to them? It is great to know this strategically as you maneuver within the organization. In some instances, you may find a mentor.

- Learn how information is communicated. Does the organization rely heavily on email? Social media? Manuals? Do not get left behind.
- When comfortable, volunteer on a committee or take the lead on a small project to become more engaged, get to know your coworkers, and build your reputation.
- Meet your coworkers. Are there opportunities to have lunch outside your desk? Attend office events? Network during staff meetings?

CONCLUSION

We recognize that negotiating job offers can be overwhelming, especially when you are starting a new job. You may not be able to do all this right away, but we hope that at some point—earlier and not later—you spend some time acting upon these suggestions.

We hope that you have gained some invaluable information on how to evaluate job offers, negotiate a higher salary, and make a positive impact as an employee when you start a new job. So, we ask—when can you start?

CHAPTER TAKEAWAYS

- When offered a job, take time to consider whether it is a good career move, a good organizational fit, and a satisfactory salary and benefits before accepting.
- Creating a personal budget and researching salary puts you in a good place to evaluate a compensation package.
- If you want to accept an offer, negotiate!
- Always act professionally whether accepting, declining, or negotiating.

CHAPTER

8

Mapping Your Legacy as a Social Work Agent of Change

What You Will Learn

- ❐ How to use the Professional Development Cycle of Social Workers to prepare for your mid- to late career
- ❐ How to embrace your inner leader
- ❐ How to reassess your professional brand
- ❐ How to advance your career through LinkedIn, annual performance evaluations, communication skills, CEUs, and leadership skills
- ❐ Ideas for establishing and preserving your legacy

Action Plan

- ❐ Reassess and update your professional brand
- ❐ Leverage your annual performance evaluation
- ❐ Hone your communication skills on multiple platforms, including social media, writing, and presentations
- ❐ Update your LinkedIn profile to reflect mid- to late-career developments
- ❐ Create an action plan to move your career forward

Now that you have established your career as a social worker, you can truly appreciate your role as a change agent, but your journey is not over. The profession of social work is committed to lifelong learning and professional development. To be an agent of change, social workers need to keep up with our evolving societal problems, political climate, social justice issues, and the advancement of technology. To this end, many successful social workers maximize their contributions to the field by pursuing continuing education, seeking professional advancement opportunities, networking, and sharing their expertise with others. This chapter will cover the key components of social work career development that will help you to navigate stages 4, 5, and 6 of the PDCSW (see Figure 8.1) and will offer several tips to increase your visibility and grow your professional brand beyond your workplace.

AGENT OF CHANGE CAREER TIP #1: MAXIMIZE YOUR ROLE AS A LEADER

Whether the next step in your career advancement is as an executive director, an influencer, an instructor, or a subject matter expert, you will require leadership skills. Even if you do not consider yourself a leader of people, at this point in your career you are a leader of thoughts, ideas, opinions, and professional accomplishments. Acknowledging your expertise and leadership in the field gives you a framework to apply to your professional brand and will increase your credibility and image among your circle of influence.

What Is Your Leadership Style?

In today's competitive environment, social work leaders are expected to go beyond the status quo, do more with less, and think outside the box. Unless your organization regularly invests in professional leadership development, there is very little time to maintain and evolve your professional brand as a leader. One of the first steps to maximizing your role as a leader is to know what your leadership style is. Your leadership style has evolved over time, and you may have changed your leadership behaviors depending on your work circumstances. However, in this stage of your career, you should have a clear idea of how you would articulate this to others, along with specific stories that demonstrate your mastery of these skills. The following section will provide you with resources and strategies to clearly define your leadership style.

Leadership Assessment Tools

The leadership assessment tools described next are designed to help social workers gauge their leadership capabilities and potential. These tools help individuals understand their strengths, identify areas for improvement, and articulate their leadership style to others.

CliftonStrengths Assessment

CliftonStrengths is an assessment tool that focuses on identifying an individual's top strengths out of a list of 34 key attributes (Rath, 2007). This tool's strengths-based approach is a great fit for social workers because it focuses on strategies to leverage your strengths and overcome your weaknesses. The tool utilizes four domains

Stage 4
Conveyed Knowledge:
Entry Level to Mid-Level Social Work

Stage 5
Imparted Knowledge:
Demonstrated Expertise

Stage 6
Explored/Examined Knowledge:
Subject Matter Expert

Stage 4
- Add value to your organization and colleagues.
- Supervise interns.
- Provide clinical supervision.
- Participate and lead committees.
- Build expertise in client population, policy, or systems.
- Build upon management and leadership skills.

Stage 5
- Submit proposals for conferences.
- Serve as an adjunct professor.
- Serve in elected positions within membership organization.
- Demonstrate advanced communications skills, including writing and speaking.
- Consider DSW or PhD for advanced education.

Stage 6
- Serve as an author or keynote presenter.
- Research and name policies or interventions.
- Create a course, contribute knowledge to the profession.
- Reflect on your legacy and preservation of expertise.

Figure 8.1: Professional Development Cycle of Social Workers, Stages 4–6

to frame these attributes into actions: relationship building, influencing, executing, and strategic thinking.

Emotional Intelligence Assessment Tools

Emotional intelligence is a critical aspect of effective leadership. It is the ability to recognize, understand, manage, and effectively express emotions. Higher emotional intelligence fosters healthier relationships, enhances stress management, and improves overall effectiveness in personal and professional circles. Emotional intelligence assessment tools not only help individuals understand their emotional intelligence, but also help them to develop it. Like the CliftonStrengths assessment, emotional intelligence tools strongly align with social work values. Social workers naturally recognize that emotional intelligence can be cultivated and refined through self-awareness, practice, and a commitment to growth. Emphasizing emotional intelligence in leadership can have a transformative impact on individuals and the teams they lead, improving self-awareness, self-regulation, motivation, empathy, and social skills.

DiSC Assessment

The DiSC assessment (Marston, 1928) assesses behavioral styles and preferences and categorizes individuals into four primary personality types: dominance, influence, steadiness, and conscientiousness. By identifying one's dominant style, individuals can gain a better understanding of how they interact with others and lead teams by adapting their communication and behaviors to work more effectively with others.

360-Degree Feedback

360-degree assessment involves gathering feedback about your leadership skills from various sources, including supervisors, subordinates, peers, and other stakeholders. Since 360-degree feedback solicits critique from many different sources, it can provide a well-rounded review of individual performance.

As you consider an assessment tool, also consider having a qualified career coach to help you interpret and apply the knowledge you have gained. A coach can also help you to apply the knowledge and create a plan to further develop your skills.

Become a Thought Leader

A thought leader in social work is recognized as an authority and influence on a certain topic or area of practice. This may be due to their innovative ideas, expertise, and/or contributions to advancing their respective area of practice. Thought leaders in social work often contribute to the development of innovative ideas, approaches, and trends that shape the direction of the profession.

At this stage in your career, you already possess many of the characteristics of a thought leader. As with most stages of the PDCSW, we usually land in this position without even realizing it! Table 8.2 shows the qualities, attributes, and actions of a

Table 8.1 Qualities, Attributes, and Actions of a Thought Leader

Qualities of a Thought Leader	Attributes	Actions
Influence	Provide insights that have a significant impact on the profession, shaping policy, practice, and education in social work	• Create and name a model of a theory, policy, or process • Serve as an expert witness • Grow your audience on all platforms
Visibility	Remain visible and active in professional settings, including conferences, workshops, universities, and online platforms	• Present at conferences • Stay active within academia • Share your knowledge on online platforms, LinkedIn Groups, Clubhouse, etc.
Expertise	Demonstrate deep understanding of your field, based on experience, research, and education	• Gain maximum educational requirements • Engage in research • Gain additional certifications
Collaboration	Create partnerships with like-minded individuals to address challenges, solve problems, and expand professional networks	• Participate in work groups beyond your workplace • Engage in dialogue with people outside of your organization to gain exposure to diverse ideas, knowledge, and skills
Engagement	Share knowledge and expertise with others through presentations, writing, social media, guest lectures, etc.	• Create blogs for LinkedIn to demonstrate knowledge • Share and comment on posts and posts from others providing guidance in online discourse • Participate in podcasts, present at conferences, and offer guest lectures at local educational institutions
Lifelong Learning	Participate in continuing education, seek additional certifications, and appreciate new ideas and perspectives	• Stay abreast of current trends, commit an allotted amount of time to participate in continuing education units • Negotiate certifications as part of your performance evaluation
Advocacy	Align your work and expertise with causes you care about	• Serve as a spokesperson for your organization or the population you serve
Innovation	Introduce new concepts, theories, and approaches that question the usual way of doing things and push the limits of how people normally think in the field	• "Name it and claim it" in terms of the concepts, models, or approaches that you are introducing

thought leader. Take a moment to consider each one and in what areas you would consider yourself a thought leader. Additionally, take time to assess what you could improve.

Becoming a thought leader takes time, dedication, and a consistent effort to contribute meaningfully to the field of social work. Thought leadership is not just about having knowledge, but also about sharing that knowledge in ways that positively impact the profession and the communities it serves.

Lead with Authenticity

As you have learned throughout this book, the challenge becomes how to "package" your competencies in a strategic manner that allows you to become intentional about your own professional growth and development. If you are given leadership opportunities in your career, you will undoubtedly begin to think about your legacy as a social worker. Leaving a legacy is one of the most powerful things you can do in your career and life, because it enables you to have influence in the future, well after you are gone.

AGENT OF CHANGE CAREER TIP #2: REASSESS YOUR BRAND WITH INTENTION

As you enter your mid-career, you may be wondering if your professional brand has changed. The answer is yes! While authenticity will always be the foundation of your brand, your professional brand is not static. Your professional brand will evolve with you as you gain more years of experience and grow to reflect advancements and changes in your career. We recommend revisiting your professional brand every year and with every job change to ensure you are updating your brand to reflect your latest experiences and prepare you for whatever is coming next.

The defining moments and career roles that we discussed in chapter 4 will help you to shape your personal brand. But what if you are a mid-level professional or considering a significant leadership position? What other significant achievements would you like to incorporate in your brand? As you enter the mid- to later stages of your career, let us take an inventory. At this point in your career, you have acquired years of experience, achieved major accomplishments, and earned awards or special recognitions. You have imparted information to others through presentations and trainings. Perhaps you have earned additional certifications or degrees or served as a leader in professional organizations that are pertinent to your field. Throughout your career, you have gained recommendations and/or testimonials regarding your leadership, work, or other professional contributions.

This next case study will demonstrate the importance of taking inventory of your career to determine what you need to advance your career and pursue your goals.

CASE STUDY

Shondra

Shondra has been working for seven years with older adults in a variety of settings. After she received her BSW, she was an activities coordinator in a nursing home. She worked for three years and then decided to go back to school to get her MSW and obtain more clinical skills and knowledge to apply to her work with older adults. After receiving her MSW, she began working in a nonprofit that serves older adults with case management, counseling, and other wraparound services. Now, with 15 years in the field, she aspires to apply her experience and knowledge to the field through presentations, writing opportunities, and teaching. She is also considering pursuing a DSW to gain additional expertise and credibility. She realized that to begin this journey, she will need to reassess and update her professional brand. Shondra used the PDCSW Assessment Tool (see Appendix B) to gauge where she is in her career. See Table 8.2 for the results of her assessment.

As you can see from this example, Shondra has had a very productive career and lots to add to her resume! Based on the PDCSW Stages 4–6, Shondra is entering stage 5 of career development. The next logical step would be stage 6. In Table 8.2, Shondra has identified the actions she needs to take to fully reach this stage of career advancement.

While there are many experiences and opportunities that will advance your career, the PDCSW serves as a framework for assessment. See Appendix B for a blank form of this exercise. Evaluate your most recent work experiences by reviewing the competencies listed in the first column of the chart. "None" indicates that you have no experience in this area. "Some" indicates that you have some experience, but you have not quite mastered it. "Mastered" indicates that you are proficient in this competency and you are ready to go on to the next goal. Documenting the dates will help you to keep track of your goals and gauge where you were in your career when you reached these milestones.

AGENT OF CHANGE CAREER TIP #3: MAKE THE MOST OF YOUR ANNUAL PERFORMANCE REVIEW

Whether you have been in your job for several years or are beginning your first position after graduation, chances are you will have a performance evaluation every year. An annual performance evaluation provides the best context to have a discussion with your supervisor about your career. This is an opportunity to talk to your supervisor about your career aspirations, your challenges, and, most importantly, your accomplishments throughout the year. The results of this process can propel you to a promotion or raise, or provide leverage for applying for other jobs. You should view annual evaluations as a regular part of career management, not only to record your accomplishments, but to keep track of your growth areas and what you need to succeed in your current role and ultimately your career. This is a great opportunity for both you and your supervisor to reaffirm performance metrics and supervisor expectations.

As you begin to prepare for your evaluation, ask yourself:

- Have your career goals changed?
- Have you outgrown your job?
- How does your organization define "peak performance"?
- Are you being challenged to your fullest potential?

Table 8.2 Shondra's Professional Development Cycle of Social Workers Assessment

Stage 4: Entry-Level to Mid-Level Social Work	None (Date)	Some (Date)	Mastered (Date)	Notes on Skills	Next Goal	Next Steps
Add value to your organization and colleagues			X (12/2023)	Over seven years of experience in social services, including nonprofits and public service Coworkers have commented on my enthusiasm, collaborative nature, and sense of humor when tackling big projects		
Supervise interns			X (2014–present)	Created BSW and MSW internship program Received Field Instructor of the Year award		
Provide clinical supervision			X (2020)	LCSW-S		
Participate and lead committees		X (2021–2023)		Served on employee engagement committee to create diversity and inclusion program for staff in large nonprofit	Seek additional committee assignment, start a committee, or ask to lead a work project	
Build expertise in client population, policy, program, clinical framework, or systems			X (2020–present)	Five years of expertise in behavioral and cognitive assessments, grief and adjustment counseling, and narrative therapy Created health and wellness program for older adults Developed and implemented short-term counseling program for older adults		
Build on management and leadership skills	X				Seek leadership training opportunities	Apply for upper-level position in current job

Stage 5: Demonstrated Expertise	None (Date)	Some (Date)	Mastered (Date)	Notes on Skills	Next Goal	Next Steps
Submit proposals for conferences	X				Submit proposal for NASW conference	Choose area of expertise to present about at conference
Serve as an adjunct professor	X				Create CV for adjunct professor positions Apply for adjunct professor position at local university and online	Continue to grow communication skills, teaching abilities, and network with local universities through internship programs and university/community opportunities
Serve in elected positions within membership organization	X				Seek leadership position within NASW and/or university alumni association	Apply for nomination of leadership position in state NASW chapter
Advanced communications skills, including published writing and public speaking		X		Created and facilitated training for interns regarding services, agency protocol, and loss and grief	Submit proposal for internship instructor's workshop regarding internship training program	Write article for university newsletter regarding internship program and designing protocol for interns
Consider DSW or PhD for advanced education	X				DSW education and/or leadership training	Explore advanced education including DSW programs

Table 8.2 Shondra's Professional Development Cycle of Social Workers Assessment (*continued*)

Stage 6: Subject Matter Expert	None (Date)	Some (Date)	Mastered Date	Notes on Goals	Next Goal	Next Steps
Serve as an author or keynote presenter	X				Determine expertise and conferences in which presentation would be pertinent for a keynote speech	
Research and "name" policies or interventions	X				Create a "name" for model internship training program	Research techniques utilized or theories utilized in training model; may use an acronym, e.g., Student Intern Training Program (SITP)
Create a course, contribute knowledge to the profession	X				Create a training manual applicable for any organization to establish protocols for interns	Submit presentation to CSWE regarding protocol
Serve in state or national leadership role or run for public office	N/A				Serve on National Internship Development Committee for CSWE	Set informational interviews and send emails to current and former members of this committee to understand nomination process
Reflect on your legacy and preservation of expertise	X				Continue to articulate contributions to the field in online discussion, in bio statement, on LinkedIn, on CV, etc.	Self-nominate (or ask for nomination) for NASW Pioneer, Lifetime achievement or other awards that pay tribute to your career

These questions will help you to write your self-evaluation with intention and to understand what you need from your employer to move forward in your job. Make sure you are prepared and include notes regarding career advancement; for example, a training that you would like to attend, a certification you would like to obtain, an opportunity you have identified to work with a specific population, or a specific project that would add crucial skills to your career toolbox.

When you meet with your supervisor, you will have the opportunity to set goals for the following year. While negotiating these goals, tell your supervisor why they are important to the success of your organization and to you professionally. For example, if you are seeking to present your work on a project at a professional conference, explain the importance of developing your communication skills and giving visibility to the program or agency you are working for.

If you are hoping to gain leverage for a raise, a certificate, or other opportunities, know what you are going to ask for before you go into your evaluation. Even if you are not sure how your evaluation will turn out, you will be prepared. Ask yourself these questions:

- What do you want to ask for?
- Why do you deserve it?
- How will it benefit both you and the organization?

Some performance review areas to consider are presented in the following lists:

Financial

- Salary increase
- Annual bonus
- Travel funds
- Allowance for automobile, cell phone, internet
- Funds to pay for licensure fees or licensure examination

Professional Development

- Clinical supervision
- Conference registration
- Certifications, e.g., school social work certification, case management certification, or nonprofit management certification
- Professional memberships, e.g., NASW, School Social Work Association of America
- Premium LinkedIn account

Leadership

- Leadership training
- Change in title or position in organization
- Opportunities inside your organization and outside (committees, coalitions, or other opportunities to collaborate and grow your network)

- Leadership assessment, e.g., DiSC, CliftonStrengths, 360-degree leadership evaluation
- Executive coaching

Working Conditions

- Flextime for special projects
- Permission to work remotely
- Additional staff to support your role
- Upgraded office equipment (computer, laptop, ergonomic chair, standing desk)
- Modified work schedule

As described in chapter 4, use power words and numbers to create curiosity about your performance and leave the supervisor with a desire to learn more about what you are doing and how you are doing it. Remember to express your performance as part of a strategic career trajectory. For example, "I created a budget for my department to prepare for leadership positions in the future." The more prepared you are for your evaluation, the more confident you will become in articulating your successes and experience. Engage in the conversation, be transparent, and discuss your strengths with confidence and humility.

If you receive critical feedback or you are caught by surprise, do not take it personally. The better you understand your supervisor's feedback, the better able you will be to interpret what they are looking for and how you can improve. Do not be afraid to ask questions, seek clarification, and ask for examples of what success in various areas would look like. It is also important to set up a feedback loop for the upcoming year so that you can improve on these issues and address them head-on in your next evaluation.

These strategies ensure that you will have a successful evaluation, a good sense of how you are performing in your role, and an opportunity to advocate for yourself. In turn, your evaluation will make you a stronger advocate for your clients and your organization!

AGENT OF CHANGE CAREER TIP #4:
SEEK OUT LIFELONG LEARNING WITH CONTINUING EDUCATION

While continuing education is required to maintain social work licensure for most clinical practicing social workers, it also has a deeper meaning for us as social workers, especially if we want to continuing growing in our career. Many of us entered into this career because we are lifelong learners and want to continue to apply the most effective, evidence-based approaches to those we are working with. We enjoy learning about people, organizations, systems, and policies. The key to continuing education is to be intentional about what we learn, how we learn it, and what we do with that knowledge once we have it.

For macro social workers, continuing education can take many forms outside of the traditional CEUs needed for licensure, such as advanced research, crisis communication, leadership, or organizational technology. Since there are many fewer macro-level social workers, those seeking CEUs that align with licensing may have a more challenging time finding them. In this case, one strategy is to focus on the special populations, systems, or areas of practice that you serve as opposed to clinical interventions.

In seeking continuing education, many social workers will take what they can get when they are scrambling to meet their licensing requirements. We recommend a more intentional approach through research and discussion with your networking contacts, well ahead of any licensing deadlines. The following are a few tips to be intentional in your continuing education:

- On LinkedIn, join relevant groups, study professional profiles that intrigue you, and read your news feed daily. If you find a role model who has a professional career path you would like to emulate, view their profile to see what conferences they have attended, what they are trained in, and how they have used this knowledge.
- Research professional associations that align with your skills and interests. They often offer conferences, trainings, and opportunities to connect with professionals who share your career interests. View their offerings and reach out to colleagues or connections on LinkedIn to learn if these trainings would be a good fit for you and your needs.
- Determine what activities will take you to the next level. This could be clinical supervision, a certificate program, or additional techniques that will give you expertise and credibility to move forward.

Next, it is important to know how you like to learn. Do you enjoy going to conferences and meeting new people? Would you prefer to attend a workshop with coworkers, with colleagues in a professional association, or at your alma mater? Do you learn best in online trainings in the comfort of your own home? Regardless of your learning style, you will absorb the information better if you are in your element.

Finally, as you consider various learning opportunities, figure out how you will finance them. Will your organization pay for it? Could you submit a conference proposal that might get your employer to pay for the conference, and use the rest of the conference to learn and network?

Regardless of what you decide for your professional development, make sure that it is intentional. Do not wait till the last minute to choose an opportunity that could propel your career. These are not only learning opportunities, they are also networking opportunities. Make the most of them!

AGENT OF CHANGE CAREER TIP #5: INCREASE YOUR VISIBILITY THROUGH SOCIAL MEDIA

Now that you have had time in the field, let us put that new professional brand to use on social media. If it has been a while since you have checked your online profiles, take a moment to upload a fresh headshot and use the information in chapter 4 to create an engaging bio statement. The following social media tips will keep your profile fresh and help you advance your career.

Connect and Engage with Groups and Professional Associations

LinkedIn, Facebook, and MyNASW are just a few online sites with informal communities tailored to like-minded individuals, specific areas of practice, and professional organizations. There are many different groups to join of all different sizes, and any LinkedIn member can create one. Joining a group helps you to keep up with trends in the field, ask and answer questions, meet new connections, and find resources for your clients. One of the best ways to begin looking for groups is to research the groups that your connections are members of—chances are some of those groups will match your interests. You can also search groups based on your specialty area of practice, geographical area, or topics of interest to you, such as special populations, interventions, policy interests, or advocacy efforts. By participating in groups, you can identify resources and professionals that can help your clients, your organization, and your own career advancement. For example, if you seeking expertise from a social worker who has experience on East Coast expertise in trauma-informed therapy, you might post this question to the group. For example, "Seeking recommendation for CEUs regarding trauma-informed therapy on the East Coast." Upon getting recommendations, you can easily look up the workshops. You can also take the additional step of looking up the people who recommended the workshops and the workshop instructors on LinkedIn to find more opportunities for learning and connection in trauma-informed care on the East Coast. That extra research and outreach will ensure that you make the most out of the recommendations that you get.

Post Blogs

Online platforms also allow you to gain professional visibility and demonstrate your expertise to a wider audience. If you are knowledgeable in a topic that is presented, do not hesitate to contribute to the conversation by making comments or sharing articles and posts to your feed or groups. Additionally, you can share the knowledge you have gained from your group to your own news feed, again reinforcing your knowledge and interest in the subject at hand. A word of caution: When sharing your knowledge in groups always demonstrate professionalism and humility. It is extremely important to come across as genuine and helpful rather than as an annoying advertisement for yourself.

Broaden Your Connections Geographically and across Industries

If you are seeking to advance or change your career, reach out on your social media platforms to seek helpful advice about your desired career move. Use the tips and strategies in chapter 6 regarding informational interviews. Along these same lines, be a resource for others.

Regardless of where you are in your career, social media can serve as a powerful tool to make professional connections, find jobs, demonstrate your knowledge areas, and locate resources for your clients.

AGENT OF CHANGE CAREER TIP #6: MAXIMIZE YOUR COMMUNICATION SKILLS

At every level of your social work career, you will need good communication skills. As you become a seasoned professional, presentation skills are a must. We encourage you to seek opportunities to present, whether in-person or online, at conferences, networking events, or your own organization. Now that you are in the mid-to-late stage of your career, you have gained a level of expertise and years of experience that will be recognized before you engage the audience. The best way to prepare for this stage of your career is to hone your presentation skills and know how to prepare for presentations. Some people may think they can speak off the cuff, but this is a rare skill, and you do not want to risk your reputation for lack of preparedness.

If you are new to presenting, ask your supervisor if you can do a presentation at a staff meeting or an organizational training. Additionally, if you are in touch with your local university, many professors are looking for guest lecturers for classes on specific topics. This is a great way for professors to bring practice into the classroom and for presenters to get practice.

You might also consider submitting a proposal for a conference. Membership organizations will put out a call for proposals and have various tracks in which you could choose to tailor your presentation. They will also give you guidelines for submitting the presentation, which usually includes a title, a 50-word abstract, learning objectives, and the names and bio statements of the presenters.

Remember these simple tips when preparing for presentations:

Start Off Strong: Remember, this is the first impression that your audience will get of you.

- Storytelling is a great way to engage your audience and begin a compelling presentation. Tell a brief story related to your topic and why it is meaningful to you. Choose relatable stories from your own experience or the lived experiences of others, stories that will impact the audience and draw their attention to your presentation.
- Ask the audience a question. Make sure to pause to give your audience time to digest the question and answer it.
- Start with a bold statement, such as, "More than 70 percent of social work job seekers fail to negotiate their first job offers."
- Get their attention! Contradict their expectations of the presentation. An example of this might be, "Now as social workers, we are not really in it for the money, right?"
- As with all things social work, authenticity is key, and the story must relate clearly to the point you are trying to make.

Set the Order of Your Learning Objectives and Be Sure to Meet Them: Your learning objectives could be to teach a practice skill, present a theory, or describe research findings. After you have identified the objectives, create an outline, which will help you to assess the order of your learning objectives so that the information makes sense. Setting and meeting learning objectives is particularly important if the presentation is accredited for CEUs.

Consider Incorporating Visual Aids and Activities: Most adult learners have an attention span of 10 to 15 minutes. Visual aids such as infographics, photographs, or short video clips can make the information interesting and add variety to your presentation. If appropriate, activities can be a great way to break up the content of the material, allow participants to network with each other, and encourage audience participation. These activities could be small-group exercises to practice a skill or a team-building activity that produces useful information to share with the entire group. If doing a virtual presentation, you might consider incorporating polls or a whiteboard for audience members to participate in. Always explain the activity thoroughly to the participants and be clear about the amount of time allowed for the activity.

Create Opportunities for Participants to Learn More: It is also wise to provide handouts, a website, or even a QR code through which your audience can follow up on the information you are presenting to them. Knowing that the information is available in handouts or online allows them to listen to you rather than worrying about taking excessive notes.

Find a Way to Leave Your Audience Inspired: Many presenters will end with participant questions; however, this often leaves the audience flat. Always follow the final question with concluding key points, a quote, a call to action, or a vision for the future. A strong finish will make a lasting impression on your audience.

These are just a few ideas to get started, but remember, the more you engage in public speaking, the less nervous you will feel and the more confidence you will gain. And do not forget to add these to your resume immediately so you do not forget the details!

AGENT OF CHANGE CAREER TIP #7: WRITE TO DOCUMENT YOUR LEGACY

Throughout every stage of the PDCSW, writing is a key skill. Writing skills are crucial to the success of our careers, regardless of our area of practice. Social workers in the clinical field will need to write clear clinical documentation, case notes, statistics for grant applications, and training materials. Macro social workers write policy briefs, research reports, talking points, community outreach materials, and evaluations. These examples of writing are usually the minimum expectations for social work jobs, but as you begin to prepare for your legacy, you may feel even more compelled to engage in writing projects that will preserve your thoughts, ideas, policies, and interventions.

There are many ways to preserve these ideas. If you are just getting started, write a blog for your organization's website or your own social media profile. There are many websites that will provide you with ideas on how to write a blog, but, generally speaking, blogs are a great way to express your knowledge of a certain field of practice, tips for solving a problem, or how to work with a specific clientele.

Writing for online and hard copy newsletters or publications is also another way to practice your writing skills. These are generally brief articles that pertain to the membership organizations, industry news, or even organizations in which you are involved in your personal life, such as your church, university, or civic group. Many industry publications are looking for subject matter experts to write on various topics. Take note of their submission requirements, especially minimum and maximum page requirements. This will help you to evaluate the extent of depth you want to go into about your topic.

If you are involved in research, a much deeper commitment to learning the writing process is required, and mentorship from faculty, researchers, or collaborators can be most helpful. All journals will have author guidelines that address grammar, style, and formatting. While academic/research writing is much different than other types of writing, one of the best ways to prepare for this type of writing is by reading journal articles regularly and becoming familiar with APA style. Additionally, many journals are looking for reviewers of articles, which is another way to learn best practices for writing this type of content.

AGENT OF CHANGE CAREER TIP #8: CONTRIBUTE TO THE PROFESSION

Now that you have reached this point in your career and you have honed your communications skills and professional visibility, it is time to give back to the profession. While there are many ways to give back throughout your career, the following ideas are ways to increase your visibility and build your reputation based on your expertise and credibility.

> **Serve as an Adjunct Professor:** Adjunct professors are crucial in social work education. Not only do they fill an important gap when university budgets are tight, but adjuncts bring real-life experience to the classroom. As an adjunct professor, you will have the opportunity to teach students based not on your education (usually an MSW or graduate degree), but also on your expertise. This is also a great way to connect with your local school of social work, enhance your professional network, and serve as a role model for the future members of our profession.
>
> **Serve on Boards or Take Other Elected Positions:** Often, board members are strategically selected to serve. You might be selected for your expertise in a certain area such as finance, connection to the community or service

industry, or because you are a leader in your field. Serving on a board can yield many professional benefits. You will enjoy the satisfaction of contributing to a cause that matters, enhance your leadership skills, and build your resume. While some boards are more of an advisory model, others are working boards and may require much more time and responsibility. Make sure you understand the time commitment and expectations before you join.

Become an Expert Witness: Social workers who provide oral testimony as evidence in trials are expert witnesses. These social workers utilize their knowledge and expertise in the courtroom to interpret information gathered in complex cases. These cases can include family law, mental health, criminal law, and death row cases.

Facilitate Continuing Ed Course or Deliver Training: At this stage in your career, your knowledge is highly valuable to others in the profession. As a trainer you have the opportunity to not only share your knowledge but to teach skills as well. Social work is built upon lifelong learning and continuing education, so as a leader it is critical that you share your knowledge with others in some form or fashion.

While these are just a few examples, contributing to the profession ultimately helps all social workers. While some of these opportunities are paid and some are unpaid, they are all valuable resume builders and will enhance your reputation as a social worker and expert.

AGENT OF CHANGE CAREER TIP #9: PURSUE AN ADVANCED EDUCATION

In terms of social work education, the master's degree is the terminal degree in our profession. However, if you are seeking to become an expert in the field, an advanced degree will give you the opportunity to expand your knowledge and gain the credibility you need to move forward.

You may be considering a PhD or a DSW. A PhD focuses on theoretical, scholarly research and academia. A DSW focuses on practice, supervision, applied research, and leadership.

A DSW is generally a shorter time commitment and it prepares students for advanced training in specific areas. DSW programs are offered primarily online, which makes them a good option for working professionals. This degree is tailored for micro, mezzo, and macro social workers to expand their expertise in a specific field of practice, population, or intervention.

For those who seek to teach or conduct research, the PhD in social work prepares students to be scholars who function as "stewards of the discipline" (Group for Advancement of Doctoral Education in Social Work, 2023). The primary purpose of the PhD in social work is to prepare students for tenure track faculty positions, research, and administrative careers in academia. PhD programs are offered both in-person and remotely and generally take three to four years to complete.

AGENT OF CHANGE CAREER TIP #10: PRESERVE YOUR LEGACY

By this point in your career, you are recognized as the expert in your field of practice. You may have written about your expertise in journals or other industry publications or been invited to present at membership conferences as a keynote speaker. If you are a scholar, you may have engaged in published research and/or named a policy or intervention. You may also have served as an expert witness for multiple cases or a consultant for organizations in your field. In other cases, you may have held multiple leadership roles. In any case, your experience, communication skills, expert knowledge, and influence have been recognized and have made a positive influence in the field. You have a solid professional brand and are widely known in professional circles.

Consider how you will preserve your legacy. This might be writing a book in your area of professional expertise. You may also create a class or a certification to impart the knowledge you have shared with others. Other professionals may recognize you by inducting you into the NASW Social Work Pioneers or another notable recognition specifically in your area of expertise or with the populations that you have served. Consider this quote from a social work thought leader:

> Looking back on the past 26-plus years, it is clear that the most rewarding jobs have been the ones that valued my skills and interests. Throughout my career, I've focused on two areas: suicide and technology. After nearly a decade of working with suicidal youth and their families, I went back for a PhD so I could learn how to develop interventions to better serve families of suicidal youth. During my doctoral program, I combined my passion for connecting with people and my fascination with technology to start the Social Work Podcast. Through the podcast I have been able to meet and learn from experts, and share information and connect with listeners all around the world. I've been invited into communities of like-minded tech enthusiasts, and have been privileged enough to be part of many of the revolutions of technology in social work. Whether it is through my work in suicide prevention or technology (or sometimes the intersection of the two), I have found endless satisfaction in bringing people together, whether that's a family torn apart by crisis, the global community of social workers on social media and my podcast, or simply gathering with colleagues at conferences. (Jonathan B. Singer, PhD, LCSW, Social Work Pioneer, National Association of Social Workers, professor, Loyola University Chicago School of Social Work, founder and host of *The Social Work Podcast*)

When you are considering your legacy, it is important to remember that we all started in the same place: the beginning. While creating a legacy is a lifetime of hard work, learning, and growing, most of us began with a desire to help people and make a difference. While it may feel like we are only making a difference one person at a time, each experience contributes to the foundation of our legacy. Every social worker can be an agent of change, and with the right tools, perseverance, and tenacity, we can all leave a legacy of excellence.

AGENT OF CHANGE CAREER TIP #11: LIFT WHILE YOU CLIMB

As a leader in social work, you have many options to support the work of your colleagues. Social work teaches us to help others, and if we are to build a legacy that shapes the future of the profession, we must remain committed to influencing our colleagues along the way. Follow these tips to raise the profiles of your colleagues.

> **Highlight the Contributions of Everyone on Your Interdisciplinary Team:** When you are working on a team with professionals from other disciplines, they may not be fully aware of the role social workers play. Regardless of whether you are the leader or a team member, demonstrate graciousness by introducing colleagues to each other and informing other team members of how your colleague contributes to the team. For example: "This is John, he is our intake specialist and he's an outstanding first point of contact for our clients."
>
> **Write a Note or Send a Card:** In today's world of endless social media and 24/7 email access, the art of the handwritten note is fading fast. Recognize your colleague by sending them a note or simply leaving a card on their desk. Writing by hand is a conscious action that shows authenticity and intentionality and demonstrates appreciation for another's work. Writing also takes *time*, which often feels scarce in our profession. Your colleagues are certain to feel appreciative of this gesture.
>
> **Nominate Your Colleague for an Award:** There are many different awards for social workers, especially during March, which is the NASW-designated Social Work Month. While this takes a little effort from the nominator, it can make a world of difference to the recipient. Being nominated for awards makes us feel valued and respected, not to mention that it is a great resume builder. In addition to NASW, there are many other professional organizations that recognize social workers from various areas of practice. You might also consider nominating your peers for an award from their university, such as Alumni of the Year. When someone receives an award, they are more likely to nominate someone the next year. It keeps the momentum going!
>
> **Invite Your Colleague to Present:** Everyone appreciates being recognized for their expertise, and there is no better way to recognize someone's knowledge, skills, and abilities than to ask them to impart their knowledge to others. This could be done in the form of a staff training, a webinar, or simply attending a staff meeting and making a short presentation. Additionally, this will give your colleague the opportunity to network, learn from others, and build their resume.
>
> **Provide Mentorship:** "Lifting while we climb" was the motto of the National Association of Colored Women at the end of the 19th century (Tarr-Whelan, 2009). Stepping into the next phase of our careers, we must embrace our duty to mentor emerging social workers and pave the way for future leaders. Just as we have benefited from the guidance of mentors, we now stand ready to impart wisdom and support to those who will carry

our profession forward. In this spirit of continuity and growth, we affirm our commitment to fostering a legacy of empowerment and advocacy in the field of social work.

CONCLUSION

The journey of a social worker extends far beyond initial establishing one's career. Rather, the journey evolves into a lifelong commitment to learning, leading, and contributing to the profession. Navigating stages 4, 5, and 6 of the PDCSW is essential, and this chapter has provided a comprehensive guide for mid- to late-career social workers. By embracing your inner leadership qualities, reassessing your professional brand, and leveraging tools such as LinkedIn and annual performance evaluations, you can intentionally advance your career. Excellent communication skills across various platforms, from social media to presentations, will further your professional growth. The emphasis on continuing education, seeking advancement opportunities, and building a professional legacy underscores the ongoing commitment to your career. It is a reminder that, regardless of your career stage, proactive steps taken now can significantly impact future success, meaning it is never too early to think about your legacy.

CHAPTER TAKEAWAYS

- You will need leadership skills as you progress through your career. You should constantly nurture these skills through assessments, developing a niche or expertise, and applying the PDCSW. Authenticity is key.
- Reassess your personal brand every year to make sure you are perceived professionally the way you intended. Enhance your communication skills to convey your message across all platforms.
- Plan your career with the end in mind, much like a treatment plan. Consider your legacy and lift up other social workers along the way.

APPENDIX A

Comprehensive List of Social Work Skills

Following is an inventory of skills that will help you articulate your experience when writing your resume, updating your LinkedIn profile, and preparing for interviews.

The skills are organized by functions most widely used in social work including direct practice; community development and organizing; consulting; corporate social work; management; policy; research; supervision; teaching; and diversity, equity, and inclusion. Also listed are general social work skills common to several functions and some general performance skills. Skills specific to presentations, writing, and information management are listed separately.

No list is exclusive. Use this list to generate ideas about your own acquired skills. When stating a skill that cuts across functions, try to give it more meaning by attaching it to a specific knowledge area (for example, "conduct needs assessments for low-income housing, transportation, and employment for three communities"). When using to prepare for an interview, think of at least one example that demonstrates that skill. Edit the items to fit your language and experience or the language of your field of practice.

SOCIAL SKILLS BY FUNCTION

Generalist Social Work

- Advise clients, patients, and families on accessing services
- Advocate for groups, consumers, clients, and patients
- Assessment skills
- Build consensus

- Client-centered approach
- Collaborate with local, regional, and national organizations
- Communicate with grace and patience
- Community outreach
- Conduct needs assessment
- Contribute as part of a multidisciplinary team
- Demonstrate realistic expectations of self and others
- Demonstrate a sense of professional mission
- Design, plan, and lead programs
- Determine barriers to access of services
- Develop and implement service plans
- Facilitate groups: clients, consumers, families, staff, task forces, collaborations
- Follow agency and professional protocols
- Identify and resolve ethical issues
- Identify strengths
- Incorporate knowledge of theory with research and practice experience
- Interpret laws and policies
- Knowledge of human behavior and theory
- Maintain confidentiality in oral and written communications
- Manage crises
- Navigate complex systems
- Provide case management
- Recruit and manage volunteers
- Think clearly about complex problems
- Understanding of group dynamics
- Use comprehensive systems thinking
- Verbal, oral, and written communication skills
- View work through a social justice lens

Clinical Social Work

- Analyze social support networks
- Apply different treatment approaches: brief therapy, family therapy, play therapy, solution-focused therapy, etc.
- Apply *Diagnostic and Statistical Manual of Mental Disorders* (DSM) criteria
- Assessment and diagnosis
- Assist clients in processing information and issues
- Assist individual clients and families with developing coping skills
- Base interventions on evidence-based practice or best practices
- Build effective client relationships
- Collaborate with a treatment team
- Complete intakes or detailed assessments of clients including psychosocial assessments and social histories
- Conduct effective termination and referral
- Conduct individual and group therapy

- Construct genograms and family maps
- Contract with clients or consumers
- Create and manage client files according to rules of employer and NASW *Code of Ethics*
- Crisis intervention
- Deal with client resistance
- Demonstrate cultural humility
- Design treatment to achieve short-term outcomes in a cost-conscious context
- Determine client eligibility
- Determine insurance eligibility and manage billing
- Develop and implement intervention, treatment, care, and discharge plans
- Discharge planning
- Documentation
- Educate clients, consumers, and patients about health risks, retirement planning, substance use issues, medical compliance, and other pertinent information
- Educate and empower family members, care providers, and staff
- Explain Health Insurance Portability and Accountability Act (HIPAA) regulations, client confidentiality, and mandatory reporting
- Facilitate family team meetings and partner with community
- Follow up on treatment
- Grief and loss theory
- Group facilitation
- Identify, evaluate, and compile list of references to community resources
- Identify and intervene with clients who are at risk
- Identify outcomes measures
- Intervene with clients or patients in crisis
- Interview clients, consumers, patients, and families
- Knowledge of cognitive conditions, mental health issues, and the DSM
- Lead a treatment team
- Manage permanency planning, family group conferencing, or victim–offender dialogues
- Measure caregiver strain or stress
- Monitor changing functional levels
- Organize and facilitate a support group or educational group
- Provide case consultation
- Provide case management
- Provide culturally appropriate services
- Recruit, select, train, and prepare foster or adoptive parents, guardians, respite care providers
- Set and collect fees, including sliding scale
- Shape the context with diagnostic expertise
- Supervisory experience and training
- Treatment planning
- Understand an individual in their environment

Macro Social Work: Community Organizing

- Acquire financing for a community project
- Build consensus with community coalitions and grassroots groups
- Collaborate with groups
- Collaborate with key stakeholders, e.g., chambers of commerce, small business owners, neighborhood associations, religious institutions, and recreation programs
- Communicate with diverse neighborhood residents
- Compile a community resource list
- Construct a community map
- Coordinate and train volunteers
- Counsel homeowners and small business owners about the loan acquisition process
- Design a campaign strategy for social change
- Develop community, neighborhood, and social networks
- Develop policies and plans that integrate social and economic development efforts
- Develop a strategic plan
- Educate community members on intent of outside groups
- Educate corporate staff and other groups on how their messages are received in the community
- Engage community members in leadership training
- Engage in fundraising
- Establish a plan of incremental goals that can sustain a long-term collaborative effort
- Evaluate target community's assets: individual, organizational, and geographical
- Evaluate target community's strengths, interests, and needs
- Examine formal and informal service delivery systems
- Facilitate community-building efforts
- Foster a commitment among organizations and individuals to improve the community
- Function as a liaison with the business community and local institutions
- Gain acceptance in the community
- Identify barriers to starting businesses and making improvements in the community
- Identify and connect residents with resources in the community
- Identify local leaders for collaboration and training
- Identify media events, public hearings, elections, and strategic initiatives
- Identify and work with investors and other potential sources of capital and credit
- Interpersonal development (e.g., communication and engagement)
- Manage finances
- Manage varying interests of coalition and collaboration members
- Navigate and work effectively within local political systems

- Optimize search engines
- Plan and execute events
- Problem solve and make decisions
- Provide consultation for community development banks, microloan funds, community development loan funds, or community development credit unions
- Provide technical assistance and support to community organizations, coalitions, collaborations, or neighborhood associations
- Train and manage talent
- Write grants

Macro Social Work: Policy, Evaluation, and Research

- Access and use governmental publications and data sets
- Advocate for policies and regulations
- Analyze community strengths, assets, resources, and needs
- Analyze data using quantitative and qualitative techniques
- Analyze impacts of federal and/or state policy on local level
- Analyze and interpret statutes, regulations, policies, and programs
- Analyze an issue
- Analyze policy in political and financial terms
- Appreciate the complexity of the larger system
- Approach policy with a win-win mindset rather than all or nothing
- Articulate connections across disciplines
- Articulate opposite viewpoints
- Articulate political feasibility and funding realities
- Assess and document intervention outcomes
- Build consensus and coalitions
- Collaborate with coinvestigators, research center colleagues, and research assistants
- Collate a wide variety of sources and source types
- Collect, clean, code, input, analyze, and manage data
- Conceptualize areas of knowledge
- Conduct structured and unstructured interviews
- Conduct surveys
- Consider systems approach to community or societal problems
- Convey a compelling picture of what policy might accomplish
- Coordinate research and evaluation projects
- Create infographics to present data
- Critique and assess data, articles, and reports
- Curate best sources for a given project
- Define agendas
- Define problems and issues
- Design and conduct needs assessments, feasibility studies, program evaluations, and clinical practices
- Design, improve, and critique questionnaires

- Design research studies
- Develop data profiles
- Develop legislative strategy
- Develop and maintain relationships with key stakeholders
- Develop measures
- Develop relationships
- Develop research proposals
- Formulate policy recommendations
- Frame questions
- Generate hypotheses
- Get beyond passion and process to make difficult decisions and complete tasks
- Handle frequent and extensive critiquing, editing, and rewriting of your work
- Identify common ground to advance the agenda
- Interpret quantitative and qualitative empirical results
- Lobby for or against legislation
- Locate, explain, and apply relevant statistical data
- Locate, review, and summarize literature
- Prepare action alerts and legislative fact sheets
- Prepare and deliver testimony to legislative committees
- Prepare proposals for technical amendments to a law
- Present options and defend positions orally
- Present research clearly to different audiences (academic, industry, public)
- Run general statistical packages, such as SAS, SPSS, and specific packages for structural equation modeling, network analysis, cluster analysis, and qualitative analysis
- Secure and analyze consumer feedback
- See connections across the big picture rather than focusing on a single issue
- See long-term implications
- Think agilely about public policy
- Think from a generalist perspective
- Tolerate frustrating political situations
- Understand current public policy issues
- Understand the language of other players and opponents
- Understand pitfalls of extrapolating data from local to national level
- Use data accurately
- Use descriptive, inferential, and multivariate statistics
- Work with institutional review boards to satisfy criteria for protection of human subjects
- Write grants
- Write in a quick, concise, clear style

International Social Work

- Assess and respond to safety concerns including those related to abuse, neglect, exploitation, and other interpersonal violence

- Be resourceful
- Build capacity of field teams to deliver successful programs
- Build community partnerships
- Collaborate with local agencies, nongovernmental organizations, and community members
- Communicate in languages other than English
- Conduct evaluations
- Conduct trainings
- Demonstrate ability to be adaptable
- Demonstrate dedication to the human rights of refugees, immigrants, asylum seekers, and displaced people
- Manage programs
- Practice cultural awareness and humility
- Provide technical oversight
- Provide trauma-informed intake evaluations and holistic treatment plans
- Translate data into actionable insights to inform program evaluation, strategic planning, and funding
- Understand frameworks for measuring and monitoring systemic change in complex systems

Nontraditional Social Work: Corporate Social Work

- Advocate for disabilities and accommodations
- Apply knowledge of organizational policy development and review
- Communicate, counsel, problem solve, set goals
- Conduct community outreach
- Conduct employee engagement and satisfaction surveys
- Conduct mental health assessments and referrals
- Consult on workplace bullying and harassment prevention
- Create programs for employee wellness programs
- Demonstrate ability to address conflict resolution and mediation
- Evaluate programs
- Facilitate training on employee empowerment and self-advocacy
- Incorporate social responsibility
- Integrate wellness
- Offer crisis intervention and trauma response
- Promote work–life balance and programming
- Provide coaching on career development and work–life balance
- Provide employee counseling and emotional support
- Provide family and caregiving support
- Provide mediation/dispute resolution
- Provide referrals on substance abuse and addiction support
- Provide workforce planning and restructuring support
- Skilled in social responsibility and community engagement initiatives
- Teach employee financial literacy and assistance
- Train and educate on diversity and inclusion policies

Nontraditional Social Work: Diversity, Equity, and Inclusion

- Advocate for social justice
- Commit to ongoing self-reflection, learning, and growth to better understand the complexities of diversity, equity, and inclusion
- Conduct outreach to internal and external groups
- Continuously improve diversity, equity, and inclusion practice
- Demonstrate ability to identify personal bias while ensuring fairness and impartiality
- Develop and execute events, programs, and trainings
- Embed diversity, equity, and inclusion goals in agency strategic plans
- Engage with the community and build relationships
- Identify specific goals and continually assess and modify educational offerings toward aims
- Manage up and across
- Practice anti-oppressive social work
- Practice cultural competence
- Practice trauma-informed social work
- Provide allyship and solidarity
- Utilize intercultural communication to facilitate open and inclusive dialogue and active listening,
- Utilize intersectional analysis to recognize and address various forms of oppression

TRANSFERABLE SKILLS

All social workers have transferable skills. These are skills that are valuable in many different work contexts and roles. They can be acquired through jobs, lived experience, volunteering, or participation in a professional organization. The examples that follow will help you start to articulate what you have learned outside of social work–specific skills and how this might apply to your next career move.

Communication: Writing

- Collaborate with others to streamline multiple writerly voices
- Create training or education materials
- Edit materials for different purposes: brevity, tone, and clarity
- Edit written material quickly
- Prepare briefings on issues, meetings, or legislation for an executive or leader
- Prepare case plans with interdisciplinary teams
- Prepare talking points on an issue for leaders or groups
- Provide constructive criticism
- Script an executive or leader to conduct a meeting or event (written and verbal step-by-step preparation)

- Summarize a large volume of information
- Update old written materials for present and future use
- Write affidavits, documentation, case notes, executive summaries, reports, mission statements, sound bites, treatment plans, minutes, legislation, regulations, press releases, brochures, newsletters, letters, journal articles, op-ed pieces, business plans, project reports, memos, direct mail pieces, marketing plans, option papers, and proposals
- Write appropriate material for social media, video, audio, and multimedia projects
- Write in different styles for different genres: grants, academic papers, promotional, journalistic (features and news), technical, legal, regulatory
- Write in styles appropriate to a leader, the purpose of a project, the culture of the organization, or the situation
- Write quickly, concisely, and clearly
- Write technical material and reports using statistics and financial data

Communication: Presenting

- Conduct informative, educational presentations: public forums, workshops, and seminars
- Conduct in-service trainings
- Debate issues effectively, alone or with co-presenters
- Defend an opinion or argument
- Deliver extemporaneous speeches or presentations
- Engage audiences with interactive activities (small group discussions, polls)
- Facilitate town meetings, focus groups, neighborhood meetings
- Interview effectively: listen, reframe, reflect, and attend
- Lobby in person, by telephone, and by mail
- Make case presentations
- Persuade different audiences on the same topic
- Persuade diverse groups: neighborhood associations, small and large businesses, local and state governments, school systems, healthcare providers, funders, and social services agencies
- Present in front of a camera: recorded or live coverage
- Present testimony to legislative bodies
- Provide court testimony
- Provide relevant and intentional context for key points
- Respond to impromptu questions: points of data, controversial issues
- Serve as liaison between agencies, organizations, and communities
- Serve as point person handling questions about issues and projects
- Serve as spokesperson with media and other audiences
- Speak a language other than English or sign language
- Speak to large and small audiences
- Use effective interpersonal communication: active listening, open-ended questions

- Use governing body procedures accurately
- Use memorable examples to illustrate abstract ideas
- Use multimedia technology for presentations: computers, smartphones, audio, and visual
- Use negotiation techniques

Technology and Social Media

- Address issues of confidentiality and information management
- Be knowledgeable of computer software programs and smartphone apps
- Conduct outreach using social media, Listservs, etc.
- Conduct virtual meetings, online therapy, or virtual interviews
- Consult with users to develop information systems
- Gather data for reports, identify trends, and apply for funding
- Manage databases
- Manage a Listserv social media group
- Produce online (live and recorded) presentations
- Serve as a webmaster: design and maintain pages, create interactive sites
- Store data in the cloud or in other agency-provided online storage
- Train staff and managers to input and retrieve data
- Use AI when appropriate
- Use computer platforms for case management, treatment, and reimbursement
- Use computer software to record, access, analyze, and report information
- Use electronic recordkeeping
- Use statistical software

Teaching and Training

- Analyze learning difficulties and recommend action
- Command knowledge of the subject area
- Compare course content for overlap and continuity
- Create learning assignments and group learning activities
- Define parameters of a course
- Design assignments that develop critical thinking, practical skills, and creative skills
- Design distance learning (online) courses
- Develop abstracts, learning objectives, and proposals for presentations
- Develop course-evaluation surveys
- Evaluate teaching techniques and seek outside consultation on teaching style
- Facilitate discussions and debates
- Facilitate self-directed, independent learning
- Foster safe, respectful, and productive classroom climates
- Generate skill-building resources (e.g., learning guides, worksheets)
- Identify appropriate theoretical and practice readings
- Incorporate diversity, equity, and inclusion material into courses

- Manage disagreement and conflict among participants
- Provide constructive criticism
- Select course readings, books, and visiting speakers
- Think conceptually about educational curriculum design
- Utilize various types of media including recordings, message boards, and polls
- Write exams or evaluations that measure levels of learning and knowledge and skill mastery

ADVANCED SOCIAL WORK SKILLS

This next section of skills is for any social workers in leadership positions or who are later in their career.

Consulting

- Analyze client resources, strengths, problems, and needs
- Conduct assessments
- Conduct SWOT analysis
- Create reports
- Create timelines and action plans
- Deliver products and reports by deadline
- Determine fees
- Develop a network
- Draft and negotiate contracts
- Educate client staff on issues, terminology, and meaning
- Establish rapport with clients
- Facilitate discussions with clients on problem clarification and solution options
- Identify and investigate potential clients
- Identify and package specific services to offer
- Identify potential and future consulting needs of clients
- Manage budgets
- Negotiate contracts and deals
- Prepare and present business and marketing plans
- Research, develop, and recommend solutions
- Strategically plan
- Train or collaborate with client staff to implement new solutions
- Troubleshoot and implement solutions

Management

- Access and work with the media
- Analyze an annual report
- Analyze unit costs

- Assess risk, liability, and legal issues
- Collaborate with board members in strategic planning and directing the organization
- Communicate with outside groups: funders, governments, consumer groups, media
- Conduct feasibility studies
- Contribute to the development of an organization's culture
- Coordinate multicommittee events and projects
- Create and facilitate interorganizational entities: partnerships, networks, and collaborations
- Create a vision for the organization
- Design and evaluate services that meet varying funders' requirements
- Design services, programs, and projects that produce measurable outcomes
- Develop a high profile in the community
- Develop and monitor budgets
- Develop a network of contacts
- Develop and oversee a marketing plan including social media outreach
- Develop policies and procedures
- Develop quality assurance measures
- Develop, select, train, and direct a board
- Evaluate programs, projects, services, and agency structures
- Formulate and direct a fundraising strategy: special events, capital campaigns, annual funds, volunteer programs, and grant writing
- Formulate and follow a project work plan
- Formulate and implement public relations strategies
- Interpret federal, state, and local policies and regulations
- Manage a complex composition of funding sources and reporting requirements
- Manage large volumes of information, including organization statistics and outside data
- Manage multiple departments and programs
- Manage organizational change
- Move a pilot project to a mainline service
- Negotiate and secure contracts
- Organize committees, groups, and special events
- Prepare cost-benefit analyses, budgets
- Provide data and testimony for law and policymakers
- Reconcile conflicting values among multidisciplinary teams, agency and funders, agency and regulators
- Recruit, supervise, evaluate, promote, and terminate employees
- Recruit, train, organize, and motivate volunteers
- Represent the organization in public arenas
- Secure financing
- Set agendas, organize, and run meetings
- Stay current on policy and service delivery trends

Supervision

- Collect organization and service statistics
- Consult with and inform management about progress; crisis situations; personnel issues; staff, client, community assets and needs
- Critique oral assignments: case, project presentations, public speeches, in-service training
- Differentiate tasks and supervision for professional, paraprofessional, student, and volunteer staff
- Draft and make recommendations on content for job descriptions
- Edit written assignments: documentation, reports, treatment plans, proposals, grants, assessments, articles
- Educate staff on professional development opportunities
- Evaluate staff work: interventions, treatment plans, documentation, projects, programs
- Fine-tune services, procedures, and staff performance to meet outcome objectives
- Handle staff development: identify training preferences and needs and provide training
- Interpret organization objectives, policies, procedures, and outside trends and issues affecting the agency
- Make decisions: crisis situations, ethical dilemmas, reduced or expanded resources, changing demands
- Manage conflicting needs of management, staff, and clients, consumers, and communities
- Match staff abilities with work assignments
- Motivate and direct staff performance
- Organize, delegate, and schedule work
- Orient new employees
- Review resumes and interview job candidates and make recommendations on hiring
- Serve as liaison between staff and management
- Set performance expectations
- Suggest changes in services, policies, and procedures

APPENDIX

B

Assess Your Career Stage with the PDCSW Assessment Tool

The Professional Development Cycle of Social Workers (PDCSW) is a model of career development based on six stages of career advancement in the profession of social work and is described in detail in chapter 2. Use the assessment tool provided in Table B.1 to gauge where you are in the professional development cycle of social work. In the last column, document any significant information relevant to these milestones, such as your next goals, notes for improvement, or anything else that you feel is important about completing this milestone and moving on to the next. Evaluate your most recent career experiences by reviewing the competencies listed in the first column of the table. "None" indicates that you have no experience in this area. "Some" indicates that you have some experience, but you have not quite mastered it. Perhaps you are just learning this competency or have limited experience, however, you are being *intentional* about gaining exposure to these skills. "Mastered" indicates that you have mastered this competency and you are ready to go on to the next goal. Logging the dates will help you to keep track of your goals and help you to gauge where you were in your career when you reached these milestones. Use the blank rows at the end to list your own goals, competencies, or milestones. For an example of a completed PDCSW assessment tool, refer back to Table 8.2.

Table B.1 PDCSW Assessment Tool

Stage 1 Generalized Knowledge: Find Your Calling	None (Date)	Some (Date)	Mastered (Date)	Notes on Skills	Next Goal	Next Steps
Drawn toward a meaningful career						
Desire to advocate for a cause based on learned or lived experiences						
Explore various issues and populations						
Gain practical exposure through volunteering or internships						

Stage 2 Theoretical Knowledge: Pursue Your Education in Social Work	None (Date)	Some (Date)	Mastered (Date)	Notes on Skills	Next Goal	Next Steps
Learn theoretical foundations and practical skills						
Learn the NASW *Code of Ethics* and other professional standards						
Deepen knowledge and understanding of cultural humility						
Enter first practicum experience						

(continued)

Table B.1 PDCSW Assessment Tool (continued)

Stage 3 Specialized Knowledge: Paraprofessional Social Work	None (Date)	Some (Date)	Mastered (Date)	Notes on Skills	Next Goal	Next Steps
Join a corps of professionals						
Enter first professional job or second practicum experience						
Demonstrate leadership skills						
Continually seek learning opportunities						

Stage 4 Conveyed Knowledge: Entry Level to Mid-Level Social Work	None (Date)	Some (Date)	Mastered (Date)	Notes on Skills	Next Goal	Next Steps
At least 2–5 years of experience						
Participate on and lead committees						
Build expertise in client population, policy, or systems						
Deliver a strong professional brand						
Add value to your organization and colleagues						
Supervise interns or provide clinical supervision						
Build on management and leadership skills						
Demonstrate a self-care plan						

(*continued*)

Table B.1 PDCSW Assessment Tool (*continued*)

Stage 5 Imparted Knowledge: Demonstrated Expertise	None (Date)	Some (Date)	Mastered (Date)	Notes on Skills	Next Goal	Next Steps
Facilitate formal trainings						
Submit proposals for conferences						
Serve in elected positions within a membership organization						
Serve as an adjunct professor						
Demonstrate advanced communications skills, including published writing and public speaking						
Serve as an expert witness						
Cultivate the talents of others						
Consider a DSW, PhD, or other advanced education						

Stage 6 Explored/Examined Knowledge: Subject Matter Expert	None (Date)	Some (Date)	Mastered (Date)	Notes on Skills	Next Goal	Next Steps
Recognized as an expert						
Serve as an author or key-note presenter						
Research and name policies or interventions						
Create a course, contribute knowledge to the profession						
Serve in state or national leadership role						
Reflect on your legacy and preservation of expertise						

APPENDIX C

Sample Informational Interview Questions

No matter what stage of your career you are in, informational interviews can inform, guide, and inspire you in your next steps (learn more in chapter 3). An informational interview with a person who inspires you gives you insight into what they do, their responsibilities, their career history, how they obtained their position, and how they navigated obstacles along the way. Gathering this information can help you to make more informed career decisions.

Your responsibility is to arrive at the interview prepared with open-ended questions for the person you are meeting. Staying within the agreed-on time limit shows respect for your interviewee. The following questions can be used directly or customized to fit your interviewee.

Field of Work

- What does a typical work week entail?
- What are your favorite and least favorite parts of the day?
- What are the biggest challenges that you encounter?
- What do you find most rewarding about your work?
- What other jobs did you have before this one?
- What work do you plan to do in the future?
- If you could change two things about your job, what would they be?
- What do you wish someone had told you about work when you were in school?
- How much flexibility do you have regarding being in the office, dress code, work hours, and vacation schedule?
- Does this type of job require evening or weekend work?

Preparing for the Field

- How well suited is my background for this type of work?
- What skills or talents are essential for effectiveness in this job?
- What can I do to best prepare myself for a job like yours?
- What university experiences are most relevant?
- What credentials, educational degrees, or licenses are required for entry into this career?

Job Search Advice

- What is the typical beginning salary range and longer-term earning potential in this field?
- How do people find out about openings in this field?
- Is there a great deal of turnover in this field?
- If you were hiring right now, what would be the most critical factors in determining your selection?
- Are there peak hiring seasons?
- What is the best way to conduct a job search in this field?
- How does one find out about job openings at your agency?

APPENDIX
D

Career-Defining Moments, Patterns, and Professional Themes

To begin the process of defining your professional brand, use this exercise to identify (1) consistent patterns of performance you have applied in all your professional interactions; (2) personal characteristics you incorporate into your professional and personal lives; (3) feedback you have received from others about your work, including recognition from your colleagues, clients, supervisors, mentors, and anyone else who has impacted your career; and (4) what makes you stand out among your peers.

To begin this process, review your career-defining moments, the career roles listed on your resume, and the career development exercises you have done thus far. See Table 4.1 in chapter 4 for an example of this exercise.

Table D.1 Career-Defining Moments, Patterns, and Sample Professional Themes Inventory

Career-Defining Moments	Patterns	Personal Characteristics	What Others Said	What Made You Stand Out

Common professional themes:

APPENDIX E

Sample Resumes and Curriculum Vitae

A resume is a critical piece of your job search application materials. In chapter 4 we provide detailed resume and curriculum vitae (CV) writing guidance. The samples included here can be helpful references as you write or rewrite your own.

Sample #	Resume Format	Resume Type
1	Combination	MSW Clinical (Recent Graduate)
2	Combination	MSW Macro
3	Combination	MSW Nontraditional Macro
4	Combination	BSW
5	Combination	MSW Macro/Clinical (Experienced)
6	Chronological	MSW Micro
7	Chronological	MSW Clinical
8	Chronological	MSW Macro
9	Chronological	MSW Micro (Recent Graduate)
10	Functional	BSW
11	Functional	MSW Macro
12	Functional	MSW Clinical (Experienced)
13	Chronological Modern	MSW Macro
14	Curriculum Vitae	

ASHANA SUBRAMANIAN, MSW
9 Poplar Terrace, Cambridge, MA 02140 • 617-777-7777 • asubra44@gmail.com

SUMMARY OF QUALIFICATIONS
- Fluency in English, Hindi, Urdu, and Bengali; basic understanding of Spanish
- Neuroscience and Social Work Certificate
- Interest in connection between trauma, substance use, and neuroscience
- Ability to understand and address complex treatment needs of dually diagnosed patients
- Comfortable with both crisis and longer-term work
- Experience with clients and coworkers from diverse backgrounds, including immigrant and multilingual populations

EDUCATION
Master of Social Work, Clinical, Mental Health, Certificate in Neuroscience and Social Work, Expected May 2025
Boston College, Chestnut Hill, MA
- Relevant electives: Substance Use Disorders, Cognitive-Behavioral Therapy, Advanced Trauma Theory, and Treatment Modalities

Bachelor of Arts, Psychology, Minor in Women's Studies, *magna cum laude,* June 2021
University of Massachusetts Boston, Boston, MA

EXPERIENCE
Social Work Intern, Outpatient Addictions Services, Cambridge Hospital, Cambridge, MA   Sept. 2024–Present
- Conduct comprehensive intake evaluations for new clients and determine appropriate level of care
- Provide individual therapy using motivational interviewing and strengths-based model
- Provide case management for patients in Intensive Outpatient Program
- Facilitate weekly psycho-educational and recovery-centered groups
- Collaborate with multidisciplinary team of treatment providers (social workers, psychiatrists, doctors, and nurses)
- Maintain client documentation records in EPIC and complete insurance pre-authorization paperwork
- Create and update treatment plans for clients

Social Work Intern, Casa de la Comunidad, Boston, MA   Sept. 2023–May 2024
- Provided survivor-centered, empowerment-focused individual counseling and advocacy to shelter and community clients using strengths-based/supportive model
- Facilitated weekly domestic violence psycho-educational/empowerment groups
- Provided crisis intervention and ongoing support to shelter clients
- Developed and renewed safety plans with clients
- Provided referrals to clients for services internally and in the community

Student Mentor, Above the Influence (ATI), Boston, MA   Sept. 2021–June 2023
- Collaborated with Substance Abuse Youth Coalition to implement ATI campaign
- Trained in ATI facilitation, advocacy, public speaking, health issues, and relationship between substance use and high-risk populations
- Facilitated focus groups with urban youth to understand issues and implement programming
- Built strong, authentic relationships of compassion and mentorship with youth

Shelter Intern, Asian Task Force Against Domestic Violence (ATASK), Boston, MA   Sept.–Dec. 2020
- Managed client cases in collaboration with staff; regularly checked in with clients, offering support pertaining to mental/physical health, parenting, and legal concerns
- Assisted clients with housing search, job search, goal setting, and enhancing life skills
- Covered crisis hotline and provided office support

Research Assistant, Dr. Leslie Wainright, Worcester, MA   Jan.–May 2021
- Assisted in researching best practices for application of Mindfulness Based Stress Reduction for clinical depression

Figure E.1   MSW Clinical (Recent Graduate)

Scott Brandon, MSW

123 Sunny Road, Ypsilanti, MI 48197 • 734-123-4567 • Brandon@email.com

SKILLS SUMMARY

PROGRAM EVAUATION AND RESEARCH

- Created protocol for and organized key informant interviews and focus groups
- Analyzed qualitative and quantitative data for several projects
- Produced data visualization/dashboards for organizations
- Conducted literature reviews and market analysis to better inform research and report writing

PROJECT MANAGEMENT AND PROJECT COORDINATION

- Spearheaded several projects and met administrative deadlines and goals
- Facilitated strategic planning exercises with key stakeholder engagement
- Served as part of an interdisciplinary team to plan events, works

GROUP FACILITATION AND TRAINING

- Utilized best practices for facilitating intergroup dialogue—cultural, inclusive, and social justice frameworks
- Co-facilitated groups for substance abuse treatment and recovery programs
- Organized training sessions for agency participants and staff

TECHNOLOGY

MS Word, Excel, Access, and PowerPoint, SPSS, NVivo, Qualtrics. Knowledge and use of social media platforms: LinkedIn, Facebook, Instagram, TikTok, YouTube

EDUCATION

Master of Social Work, University of Michigan School of Social Work, Ann Arbor, MI, April 2020
Bachelor of Arts in Psychology and Sociology, University of Michigan, Ann Arbor, MI, April 2017

EVALUATION AND RESEARCH EXPERIENCE

Program Evaluator April 2020–Present
Curtis Center Program Evaluation Group, University of Michigan School of Social Work, Ann Arbor, MI

Collaboratively worked on several formative, implementation, and outcome evaluation projects and community needs assessments in different capacities by performing literature reviews and market analysis; evaluation planning; key informant interviews and focus groups; data collection and analysis; report writing and dissemination. Most notable evaluation projects worked on:
- Retooling Michigan's Child Support Enforcement Evaluation, *evaluator*
- Detroit Substance Abuse Prevention, Treatment, and Recovery Needs & Assets Assessment, *project coordinator*
- Washtenaw County Sheriff's Office, Street Outreach Program, *lead evaluator*

Research Assistant and MSW Intern September 2019–April 2020
Intergroup-Social Change Agents, University of Michigan School of Social Work, Ann Arbor, MI

Conducted research activities on social and educational policies concerning educational disparities and cultural competence for an intergroup dialogue program in four local high schools; quantitative and qualitative data collection and analysis and program evaluation; co-facilitation of the after-school intergroup dialogue program in two local high schools; and planning and implementation of fundraising activities for those schools.

Research Assistant January 2019–September 2019
Family Education and Support Training Program, Eastern Michigan University School of Social Work, Ypsilanti, MI

Assisted in experimental pretest and posttest design, quantitative data analysis of over 11 years of data collected through the Family Education and Support Training program, a psycho-educational program for family members of those with mental challenges offered by the National Alliance on Mental Illness of Washtenaw County.

(continued)

Figure E.2 Combination MSW Macro

OTHER SOCIAL WORK–RELATED EXPERIENCES

Resident Aid September 2017– September 2019
Dawn Farm, Washtenaw County, MI

Began as an intern and then hired as permanent staff. Monitored and cared for clients undergoing detoxification from alcohol and other drugs and inpatient treatment and recovery services; intake prescreening, admissions, treatment planning, bio-psychosocial assessments; facilitation of substance abuse–oriented and AA-centered groups and attention to the practical needs of clients. Created and implemented a new data collection and entry system for the monitoring of client encounters with treatment staff; provided clients with recovery support and recovery-oriented systems of care specialized case management services.

Community Organizer/Volunteer February 2015–April 2016
Washtenaw County Infant Mortality Coalition, Ypsilanti, MI

Organized and facilitated seminars focused on Washtenaw County's high African American infant mortality rates and disparities among under-represented racial and ethnic minority groups. Presented prenatal and postnatal pregnancy, mother, and infant support; and provided safety method materials to mothers and concerned community members to prevent and mitigate infant death.

Body Safety Training Coordinator/Volunteer May 2014–September 2014
Washtenaw Area Council for Children, Ypsilanti, MI

Created a database of Washtenaw County's preschool- and kindergarten-age daycare and educational facilities and facility educators, directors, and principals; performed administrative and scheduling tasks; presented information and materials to children, educators, daycare workers, and parents on body safety and sexual abuse prevention through the Body Safety Training Program.

CERTIFICATIONS AND TRAININGS (2017–2020)

- Programs for the Education and Evaluation of Responsible Research and Scholarship (PEERRS), UM
- Responsible Conduct of Research and Scholarship (RCRS), UM
- Geographic Information Systems (GIS Mapping) for Social Workers, UM
- Executive Leadership Skills in Human Service Organizations, UM
- Understanding Diversity and Social Justice through Dialog, UM
- American Evaluation Association & Centers for Disease Control and Prevention Summer Evaluation Institute

PROFESSIONAL ORGANIZATIONS

National Association of Social Workers • Michigan Association for Evaluators • American Evaluation Association

---

Figure E.2 Combination MSW Macro (*continued*)

Yvonne Salas

555-123-4567 YSalas@sampleemail.com

PROFESSIONAL SUMMARY

MSW graduate student focusing on direct services with marginalized communities with an interest in life skills development with teens and effective therapeutic practice with families and women. Over 20 years of combined experience serving the community with a keen focus on advocacy, empowerment, education, and mentorship. Strengths include sound project management, building positive relationships, creating pathways from people to resources, effective communication skills, strategic planning, embracing diversity, and efficient case management.

EDUCATION

University of Southern California, Los Angeles, CA (online cohort)
Master of Social Work (Expected May 2025)
University of Michigan, Ann Arbor, MI
Bachelor of Arts, English and Psychology (May 1999)

PROFESSIONAL DEVELOPMENT AND TRAINING

- Self-Care Conference – September 2022 (Detroit Wayne Connect)
- Abuse and Neglect Training – March 2022 (Detroit Wayne Connect)
- Medicare Fraud and Abuse Training – February 2022 (Detroit Wayne Connect)
- Youth Suicide QPR Prevention – January 2022 (Detroit Wayne Connect)
- Certificate: Diversity Equity & Inclusion in the Workplace (Online – University of South Florida Muma College of Business) – May 2021 (Detroit Wayne Connect)
- Crucial Conversations – June 2018 (Henry Ford Health System)

SKILLS AND COMPETENCIES

CASE MANAGEMENT

- Assessed HIPAA violation complaints to determine information breach status and proper course of action
- Managed an average of 20 ongoing privacy cases per month
- Maintained appropriate documentation for privacy-related cases, including a detailed log of allegations, investigation activities, patient notifications, related verbal and electronic communication, and breach risk assessments, and relayed pertinent information to affected parties
- Participated in a bi-weekly work group to review complex specialized privacy cases with system legal advisors to determine proper courses of action for investigation and reporting

MANAGEMENT

- Managed systemwide project to review and update notice of privacy practices for redistribution to patient population
- Managed systemwide communication plan and content revisions focused on privacy and security updates and annual mandatory education modules
- Established positive working relationships with internal customer base, business unit leaders, and stakeholders in order to promote cooperative systemwide efforts to reduce overall privacy risks

TRAINING AND DEVELOPMENT

- Facilitated training sessions to educate the workforce on strategic risk mitigation planning and system, state, and federal requirements
- Developed departmental guidance to refine specific protocols and procedures to ensure alignment with state and federal guidelines

(continued)

Figure E.3   Combination MSW Nontraditional Macro

Yvonne Salas

555-123-4567   YSalas@sampleemail.com

COMMUNITY ORGANIZING

- Developed and implemented plan to secure and donate toiletry items to children of incarcerated parents
- Coordinated with a local women's group and a school-based health program to secure and donate baby supplies for a community baby shower for teen moms
- Led annual adopt-a-family project to ensure that low-income families and families suffering hardships would have gifts for the holidays
- Planned monthly schoolwide efforts with Girl Scouts to provide toiletries to the local homeless population
- Organized a schoolwide sock drive to meet the needs of the student population who do not have access to transportation to and from school in winter months

INVESTIGATION

- Conducted face-to-face investigative interviews to gather information to assess possible HIPAA violations
- Developed policies and procedures in support of streamlining investigative processes for HIPAA violations

ADVOCACY

- Followed protocols and regulatory standards to maintain confidentiality of patients' protected health information
- Completed federal reporting requirements for reportable breaches to the Office of Civil Rights
- Mentored at-risk teen girls to empower them with tools to develop positive decision-making skills and encourage better life choices
- Championed various community service and team-building activities including co-leading staff retreats in order to promote teamwork and increase employee engagement

WORK EXPERIENCE

Michigan Medicine   March 2012 – April 2024
Privacy Specialist

- Investigated HIPAA violations, recommended corrective actions, facilitated compliance, and led risk mitigation efforts

City of Detroit Office of Targeted Business Development/Purchasing   June 2002 – Jan 2012
Project Coordinator

- Created process improvements for grant reviews and grant acquisition

VOLUNTEER EXPERIENCE

- Gleaners Food Bank Mobile Grocery Store – Volunteer (Detroit, MI)   2021–2022
- Bates Academy – Girl Scout Troop Community Service Lead (Detroit, MI)   2014–2016
- Unity Baptist Church – Self-Esteem Workshop Leader (Detroit, MI)   2001–2002
- Arbor Heights – Mentor (Ann Arbor, MI)   1998–1999

PROFESSIONAL MEMBERSHIPS

National Association of Social Workers – Member
National Association of Black Social Workers – Member

Sample provided by the University of Michigan School of Social Work Career Services

Figure E.3   Combination MSW Nontraditional Macro (*continued*)

Anthony Johnson, BSW Candidate
Ajohnson12345@gmail.com

EDUCATION

University of Wisconsin–Madison Madison, WI
Bachelor of Social Work Candidate May 2025
Minor: History

- Honors History Thesis: Social Services Utilized by Hmong Vietnam War Veterans in U.S.
- Dean's List 2024–2025

RELATED SKILLS

DIRECT SERVICES/CUSTOMER RELATIONS SKILLS

- Facilitated case management services to support women, children, and families
- Developed interpersonal skills by engaging with clients and customers in various settings
- Collaborated with residents, service providers, faith-based communities, and city government to promote neighborhood housing, green spaces, and safety

MANAGEMENT/LEADERSHIP SKILLS

- Facilitated training sessions for new staff members and volunteers
- Represented student body as an officer in student government, managed meetings
- Enrolled in a fundraising, grant-getting and contracting class focused on 501(c)(3) funding

COMPUTER TECHNOLOGY/SOCIAL MEDIA SKILLS

- Proficient in all Microsoft Office programs, Adobe, and WordPress publishing platform
- Created blog for nonprofit organization to better communicate with stakeholders
- Assisted nonprofit webmaster in website edits, improvement, and updates

WORK EXPERIENCE

Workers' Rights Center Madison, WI
Social Work Intern September 2024–Present

- Assisted women and their families with connection to services and advocated on their behalf when needed
- Collaborated with various stakeholders on projects related to housing and green spaces
- Served as a member of the communications committee to improve social media presence of the organization

Centro Hispano of Dane County Madison, WI
Room Attendant – Day Care Summers 2023–2024

- Assisted with the management of children and the room to create a fun and safe space
- Provided personal care for children in the center
- Communicated with parents regarding the needs of their children using various forms of technology

University of Wisconsin–Madison Housing Madison, WI
Residence Hall Desk Supervisor August 2022–May 2024

- Assisted with the hiring and training of new staff
- Managed student staff schedules
- Performed duties at the hall desk when needed

(continued)

Figure E.4 Combination BSW

Le Cafe — Madison, WI
Server/Host — August 2020–May 2023
- Welcomed and assisted customer check-in and assigned tables
- Took food orders and engaged with customers to provide positive customer service
- Addressed customer concerns in a timely manner

VOLUNTEER EXPERIENCE

Madison Food Pantry — May 2024–April 2025
President, University of Wisconsin–Madison SSW Student Government — August 2024–May 202025

AWARDS AND HONORS

NASW – WI BSW Student of the Year — April 2024

International Academic Programs Merit Scholarship — November 2023

Wisconsin Academic Excellence Scholarship — May 2022

LaTrese Malcolm, LICSW
LTMalcolm@gmail.com
617-987-6543

PROFESSIONAL SUMMARY

A lifelong member of the Boston community committed to a career serving those impacted by trauma, violence, and the criminal justice system. Demonstrated success in helping others navigate the culture of both Boston's streets and the large systems that serve its community members. Seven years of direct social work experience with forensic social work, children and families, trauma response, and, most recently, victim advocacy and policy.

EXPERIENCE

Deputy Director, Massachusetts Office of Violence Prevention (MOVA), Boston, MA   Jan. 2021–Present
- MOVA is an independent state agency governed by the Victim and Witness Assistance Board. MOVA strives to advance victim rights by ensuring all victims and survivors of crime across the Commonwealth are supported and empowered through access to high-quality services that are trauma-informed, culturally responsive, and reflective of diverse communities.
- Develop and maintain partnerships with key stakeholders including Massachusetts government offices; hospitals; nonprofits; local, county, and state police; and correctional facilities
- Chair committee that determines allocation of funding to support community agencies providing services to our vulnerable community members in a trauma-informed, culturally responsive way that reflects the diversity of our communities
- Oversee annual Victim Rights Awards & Ceremony

Adjunct Faculty, Boston College School of Social Work, Chestnut Hill, MA   Fall semesters 2018 and 2019
- Rethinking Diversity, Fall 2018
- Basic Skills in Clinical Social Work, Fall 2019

Mental Health Clinician, The Community Violence Response Team, Boston Medical Center, MA   July 2015–Dec. 2020
- Provided trauma-focused short- and long-term individual and family counseling services to survivors of violence and family members who have been impacted by violence, in both English and Haitian Creole
- Conducted crisis assessment and intervention for patients and their family members affected by violent crime or homicide
- Advocated and provided case management for impacted clients of all ages, maintained working relationship with collaterals including the court system, local police, medical providers, and community partners
- Supported family survivors of homicide victims with burial planning, ongoing support, and counseling

District-Based Clinical Social Worker, Youth Connect, Dorchester, MA   Aug 2013–June 2015
- Embedded with the local Boston police, worked collaboratively to support at-risk urban youth and their families through a 4-tier service model including referrals to community-based agencies, clinical case management, individual and family therapy, parental guidance and advocacy
- Conducted home visits, intakes and assessments, crisis intervention, and case conferences with families and providers
- Provided case management and linkage to community-based services
- Provided individual and family counseling in both English and Haitian Creole
- Developed and maintained relationships with community-based service providers and providers (Department of Children and Family, Department of Youth Services, schools, courts, churches)
- Attended community-based meetings pertinent to needs/issues of youth and their families
- Maintained accurate and timely case records via an electronic database
- Demonstrated ability to work across cultures, ethnic backgrounds, and socio-economic groups

(continued)

Social Work Intern, Boys and Girls Club of Boston (Orchard Gardens/Condon Clubs) Sept. 2012–May 2013
- Advocate for services, short-term goal-oriented individual and family ongoing support, crisis intervention, conflict resolution, and mediation
- Co-facilitated short-term psycho-educational small groups for members addressing issues/topics including substance use/abuse, sexuality, self-esteem, peer leadership, and health/fitness, including Girls Empowerment Program
- Helped identify at-risk members and their families for further interventions to help with healthy decision making
- Created process to collaborate/share ideas with staff from other BGCB clubhouses

School Social Work Intern, Cambridge Elementary School, Cambridge, MA Sept. 2011–June 2012
- Provided check-ins and individual meetings with students referred through their IEP due to behavioral and mental health challenges, worked with students in both English and Haitian Creole
- Facilitated weekly socialization groups, led social-emotional lessons in classrooms, and provided classroom support across grades K–5
- Attended IEP and 504 meetings and weekly support team meetings

COMMUNITY SERVICE/LEADERSHIP

Board Member/Membership Services Committee Co-chair, Urban League of Eastern Massachusetts, 2021–Present

Member 2017–2022; Vice President 2020–2022, Alumni Board, Boston College School of Social Work

Member, Criminal Justice Committee, NASW Massachusetts, 2012–2014

EDUCATION

Nonprofit Institute, Massachusetts College, Boston, MA
Certificate in Nonprofit Management, 2020

Boston College School of Social Work, Chestnut Hill, MA
MSW, Afrocentric Social Work, 2013

University of Massachusetts, Amherst, MA
BA, Criminal Justice, 2011

Figure E.5   MSW Macro/Clinical (Experienced) (*continued*)

Megan Smith, LMSW

10074 Hudson Street   Houston, Texas 70001   444-555-1234   LMSW@sample.com

A master's degree–level bilingual (Spanish/English) social work professional with expertise in geriatrics. Experienced in assessments, case management, community education, and referrals to community resources. Participates as a valued interdisciplinary team member in numerous geriatric care settings.

EDUCATION

May 2025	University of Houston, Houston, TX – **Master of Social Work** **Awarded Hartford Fellowship**
May 2021	University of New Mexico, Albuquerque, NM – **Bachelor of Social Work**

PROFESSIONAL EXPERIENCE

08/2025–Present   Vintner Hospice   Houston, TX
Social Worker
- Offer admission coordination, discharge planning, community contacts and referrals
- Facilitate community education about hospice care to families, patients, and staff
- Provide grief and bereavement counseling, crisis intervention, and family conference
- Serve as the social work member of interdisciplinary team

01/2025–05/2025   University of Texas–Houston   Houston, TX
Social Work Intern
- Provided geriatric care management in outpatient clinic setting
- Handled referrals and contacts for community resources
- Developed presentations on topics relating to geriatrics

01/2024–05/2024   Sheltering Arms Senior Services   Houston, TX
Social Work Intern
- Provided and documented case management services for seniors
- Handled outreach to the community and made home visits
- Made referrals and contacts with other agencies and resources
- Performed assessments and facilitated accessibility of services

09/2023–12/2023   New Hope Senior Housing of Houston   Houston, TX
Social Work Intern
- Performed outreach in the community; made referrals to needed resources
- Processed financial aid applications for subsidized renters; provided telephone support
- Attended organizational meetings related to geriatrics on behalf of the organization

07/2021–08/2023   Albuquerque Geriatric Center   Albuquerque, NM
Social Services Coordinator
- Served as a mediator between the facility, residents, and family members
- Participated in interdisciplinary team and care plan meetings
- Completed social histories, assessed residents' progress and provided documentation
- Developed and coordinated family council

AFFILIATIONS

National Association of Social Workers
Greater Houston Gerontology Association

Sample provided by University of Houston Graduate College of Social Work Center for Career & Professional Development

Figure E.6   Chronological MSW Micro

Mary Smith, MSW, LLMSW
555-123-4567 ~ MSmith@sampleemail.com ~ LinkedIn

EDUCATION

University of Michigan — Ann Arbor, MI
Master of Social Work — 05/2024
Interpersonal Practice and Mental Health

The University of Texas at Austin — Austin, TX
Bachelor of Arts in Psychology — 05/2023
Studied abroad in Nice, France, with the University of Texas at Austin

CLINICAL SOCIAL WORK EXPERIENCE

The Women's Center — Ann Arbor, MI
Personal Counseling Intern — 09/2024–12/2024
- Provided psychotherapy, which included utilizing relational, multicultural, and cognitive-behavioral therapy models, to people dealing with abusive relationships, trauma, divorce, depression, anxiety, eating disorders, grief, and aging.
- Assessed clients comprehensively, diagnosed clients using the DSM-IV-TR, and partnered with clients to create intervention plans for therapy.
- Facilitated two microskills counseling workshops and many discussions on domestic violence, feminism, person-of-the-therapist issues, and multicultural therapy.
- Participated in individual and group supervision meetings to evaluate current cases, share effective intervention strategies, and address therapist–client challenges.
- Promoted the center by working on the auction and marketing committees, and representing the center at fundraising events.

SafePlace — Ann Arbor, MI
Domestic Violence Response Team Volunteer — 05/2022–05/2024
- Reached out via phone or in-person visits to survivors at their homes, hospitals, and jails to provide on-call crisis support.
- Helped survivors identify and connect to needed emergency resources.
- Utilized non-judgmental, empathic, compassionate, empowering, and affirming communication and listening skills when interacting with survivors.
- Completed interaction summary reports, domestic violence survivor assessment summaries, and lethality assessment summaries after each interaction.

Youth Mental Health Center — Ypsilanti, MI
Social Work Intern — 01/2023–05/2023
- Provided clinical therapy to clients with intellectual impairments, suicidality, anxiety, aggression, relationship issues, and those at risk of psychosis.
- Utilized crisis intervention skills, empathy, and creative interventions, including play therapy and knitting, to engage clients in case management and psychotherapy.
- Completed comprehensive biopsychosocial assessments, mental status exams, person-centered plans, and progress notes in a timely manner.
- Co-facilitated Arts 'n' Minds Group and the Multi-Family Therapy Group.

ADDITIONAL RELATED EXPERIENCE

U.S. Census Bureau — Austin, TX
Enumerator — 01/2022
- Persuaded and interviewed roughly 150 people, including a few Spanish speakers, to complete their 2022 census questionnaires while at their doorsteps.
- Maintained strict confidentiality with personally identifiable census information.

(continued)

UT Learning Center Austin, TX
Administrative Assistant 09/2021–05/2023
- Assisted with Campus Outreach Program by developing curriculum, training peer educators, and monitoring the effectiveness of workshops.
- Contributed to in-house Diversity, Professional Development, and Communications committees; work resulted in publications, staff development, and creating an inclusive learning environment for students.

Austin Settlement Home Austin, TX
Individual Mentor Volunteer 01/2020–03/2022
- Mentored an 18-year-old woman with schizophrenia to prepare her for graduating and transitioning from the settlement home.
- Provided one-on-one supportive counseling utilizing a feminist framework.

UT Learning Center Austin, TX
Peer Academic Coach 09/2020–05/2022
- Coached three students weekly in their academic skills, such as effective note taking, time management, test preparation and anxiety, and making SMART goals.
- Connected students to campus resources, including the Wellness Center and Counseling Services.

PROFESSIONAL DEVELOPMENT

University of Michigan, Ann Arbor, MI
Midwest Bisexual Lesbian Gay Transgender Ally College Conference, 3/24

The Women's Center, Ann Arbor, MI
Morning of Mindfulness, 1/24
Divorce Dialogues, Legal & Financial Aspects of Divorce, 10/23

UT Learning Center, Austin, TX
LGBTQA Training, Mindfulness, & Business Writing, 8/22

HONORS AND AWARDS

University of Michigan, Ann Arbor, MI
School of Social Work Dean's Scholarship, Fall 2024
Eleanor Cranefield Scholarship, Fall 2023

University of Texas at Austin, Austin, TX
University of Texas at Austin College Scholar, Spring 2022
Outstanding Performance in Introductory French Class, 2021
Austin Area Texas Exes Scholarship Recipient, Fall 2020

Created by the University of Michigan School of Social Work Career Services

BRENDA HANSON, MSW
555-123-1234 • BrendaH@sampleemail.com • LinkedIn

EDUCATION

University of Michigan, Ann Arbor, MI December 2024
 Master of Social Work
 Concentration: Management of Human Services; Area: Communities and Social Systems
 Co-Editor in Chief of the *Michigan Journal of Social Work & Social Welfare*

Bryn Mawr College, Bryn Mawr, PA May 2020
 Bachelor of Arts
 Major: Sociology; Minor: Education

PROFESSIONAL EXPERIENCE

Community Service Center, University of Michigan Ann Arbor, MI
Master of Social Work Intern 09/2024–12/2024
- Performed research, data collection, and revision of the peer facilitator training program for Project Community, the Community Service Center's service learning program
- Developed a program evaluation plan and logic model for Project Community
- Facilitated a focus group of 10–15 undergraduates about the use of an online module on privilege, oppression, diversity, and social justice
- Performed data analysis using SPSS on surveys conducted in undergraduate sociology classes, including t tests, ANOVAs, and regression analyses

Housing Resource Center Ann Arbor, MI
Master of Social Work Intern 09/2023–5/2024
- Wrote, distributed, analyzed, and presented survey findings of formerly homeless tenants
- Completed a study of local rent levels in Ann Arbor to help set new rental rates for HRC's supportive housing units for single adults and families, comparing to national rental indexes
- Attended Washtenaw County Housing Alliance Board meetings with important community stakeholders, and Housing Resource Center staff meetings

Project H.O.M.E. Philadelphia, PA
Development Associate/Grant Writer 06/2020–07/2023
- Wrote grant applications **awarding over $2.7 million** to the agency
- Coordinated two major events celebrating the grand opening of St. Ivan's Recovery Residence, a housing facility for homeless men and veterans. Major supporters in attendance: singer Jon Bon Jovi; Mayor Michael Nutter; representatives from the U.S. Dept. of Veterans Affairs, U.S. Dept. of Housing and Urban Development, and more
- Managed in-kind donation program for entire organization (August 2021–July 2023)

Civic Engagement Office, Bryn Mawr College Bryn Mawr, PA
Program Assistant 05/2019–05/2020
- Provided administrative support to the undergraduate service learning program
- Updated database of student field placements for 2019–2020 school year
- Mentored and supported student recipients of a funded community service program

(continued)

PathWaysPA   Holmes, PA
Intern   01/2020–05/2020
- Interned with Family Economic Self-Sufficiency Department, the policy arm of a social services agency for low-income mothers, on grant funding from Bryn Mawr College
- Co-edited and updated the financial resources packet and an employment resource manual

Civic Engagement Office, Bryn Mawr College   Bryn Mawr, PA
Student Coordinator   01/2018–01/2020
- Coordinated and publicized volunteer events with community partners in Norristown, PA
- Helped recruit, interview, and train new student coordinators for the next academic year
- Recruited students to participate in Earned Income Tax Credit volunteer campaign

OTHER EXPERIENCE

Journal of Social Work & Social Welfare   Ann Arbor, MI
Co-Editor in Chief   09/2023–12/2024
- Supervised editorial board of 12 master's and doctoral students in a student-run, peer-reviewed academic journal within the UM School of Social Work
- Acted as lead liaison of the journal with UM administration, faculty, and alumni
- Oversaw and co-designed the production schedule and led staff monthly meetings
- Wrote feature story about the journal for publication in UM alumni magazine

University of Michigan, Development Department   Ann Arbor, MI
Class Gift Committee Member   09/2023–05/2023
- Co-planned and facilitated fundraising events benefitting the 2023 class gift
- Personally solicited donations from current UM students, staff, and faculty
- Assisted in the development and dissemination of marketing materials for class gift

RESEARCH EXPERIENCE

Bryn Mawr College Department of Sociology   Bryn Mawr, PA
Sociology Research Assistant   01/2020–05/2020
   "Immigration & Ethnicity" lab manager for Dr. Sheila Waldorff

PRESENTATION

Evanson, B., & Waldo, J. (2020). *Immigration at the Texas border: A critical analysis.* Poster session at the Sociological Research Conference, San Diego, CA

GRANTS AND AWARDS

   Summer Internship Funding, UM Nonprofit Management Center $1,500 (2024)
   Internship Funding, Pollack Fund, Department of Sociology, Bryn Mawr College (2019–2020)
   Internship Funding, Subra-Linden Fund, Department of Sociology, Bryn Mawr College (2020)

Sample provided by the University of Michigan School of Social Work Career Services

Figure E.8   Chronological MSW Macro (*continued*)

Eloise Strong

808 Montclair Drive Houston, TX 77000 555-123-4567 estrong@sampleemail.com

Licensed master's-level social worker with specialization in pediatric health care and childhood diseases. Experienced in working with patients and families afflicted with advanced kidney and liver diseases, issues surrounding transplants, and numerous other childhood illnesses. Expertise includes individual, group, and play therapies; family and crisis interventions; grief counseling; and resource referrals. Ongoing volunteer work displays commitment to children's health.

EDUCATION

University of Houston, Graduate College of Social Work   Houston, TX
  Master of Social Work, May 2025
  Dean's Advisory Council Scholarship

Tulane University   New Orleans, LA
  Bachelor of Arts in Psychology, 2023
  Presidential Scholarship, 2020

PROFESSIONAL EXPERIENCE

Pediatric Care Hospital of Houston, Houston, TX   05/2025–Present
Social Worker for Pediatric Transplant
- Screen patient charts, conduct patient consultations, perform psychosocial assessments, and evaluate children and families for transplant surgery
- Provide individual counseling and handle ongoing case management pre- and post-surgery
- Connect children and families to needed transplant resources
- Serve as social worker on multidisciplinary team and conduct case presentations post rounds

Pediatric Care Clinic of Houston, Houston, TX   09/2024–05/2025
Social Work Intern
- Provided assessment and treatment of children
- Screened patient charts, conducted patient consultations, performed psychosocial assessments and evaluations of both children and adults
- Provided individual counseling and assisted with discharge plans

Cystic Fibrosis Center, Houston, TX   09/2023–05/2024
Social Work Intern
- Conducted patient consultations and psychosocial assessments, and co-facilitated parent support group
- Served as a multidisciplinary team member and as a regional conference participant
- Provided program planning for Parents Empowering Parents support group and Camp Arrow summer camp

Psychological Health Lab, Tulane University   08/2022–05/2023
Research Assistant
- Assisted in research experiment to determine the effects of emotions on pain subjects and analyzed data

HONORS/AFFILIATIONS

Present   National Association of Social Workers   Tulane University
2022   Golden Key National Honor Society

Sample provided by University of Houston Graduate College of Social Work Center for Career & Professional Development

Figure E.9   Chronological MSW Micro (Recent Graduate)

Anthony Johnson, BSW Candidate
Ajohnson12345@gmail.com

EDUCATION

University of Wisconsin–Madison — Madison, WI
Bachelor of Social Work Candidate — May 2025
Minor: History

- Honors History Thesis: Social Services Utilized by Hmong Vietnam War Veterans in U.S.
- Dean's List 2024–2025

RELATED SKILLS

DIRECT SERVICES/CUSTOMER RELATIONS SKILLS

- Facilitated case management services to support women, children, and families
- Developed interpersonal skills by engaging with clients and customers in various settings
- Collaborated with residents, service providers, faith-based communities, and city government to promote neighborhood housing, green spaces, and safety

MANAGEMENT/LEADERSHIP SKILLS

- Facilitated training sessions for new staff members and volunteers
- Represented student body as an officer in student government; managed meetings
- Enrolled in a fundraising, grant-getting, and contracting class focused on 501(c)(3) funding

COMPUTER TECHNOLOGY/SOCIAL MEDIA SKILLS

- Proficient in all Microsoft Office programs, Adobe, and WordPress publishing platform
- Created blog for nonprofit organization to better communicate with stakeholders
- Assisted nonprofit webmaster in website edits, improvement, and updates

WORK EXPERIENCE

Workers' Rights Center — Madison, WI
Social Work Intern — September 2024–Present

Centro Hispano of Dane County — Madison, WI
Room Attendant, Day Care — Summers 2023–2024

University of Wisconsin–Madison Housing — Madison, WI
Residence Hall Desk Supervisor — August 2022–May 2024

Le Cafe — Madison, WI
Server/Host — August 2020–May 2023

VOLUNTEER EXPERIENCE

Madison Food Pantry — May 2024–April 2025
President, University of Wisconsin–Madison SSW Student Government — August 2024–May 2025

Figure E.10   Functional BSW

Suzie Socialworker, LMSW
functionalresume@gmail.com 2000 Valley Club Drive, Ann Arbor, MI 48104 · (123) 456-7890

EDUCATION

University of Michigan School of Social Work — Ann Arbor, MI
MSW, Community Organizing & Community and Social Systems;
Minor: Management of Human Services (August 2024)

University of Wisconsin–Madison — Madison, WI
Bachelor of Social Work; Minor: History (May 2023)
- Honors: Dean's List (Fall 2021–Spring 2023); International Academic Programs Merit Scholarship (Nov. 2022); Wisconsin Academic Excellence Scholarship (May 2022)

SKILLS

COMMUNITY ORGANIZING

- Developed educational recycling program in elementary school grounded in student participation
- Compiled an updated contact list of community block club leaders to improve resident communication
- Provided financial energy assistance information to community residents during winter months
- Collaborated with residents, service providers, faith-based communities, and city government to promote neighborhood housing, green spaces, and safety

MANAGEMENT

- Facilitated training sessions for new staff members and volunteers
- Planned, organized, and implemented resume workshops for summer youth program
- Completed graduate-level course on organizational change in the human services

FUNDRAISING AND BUDGETING

- Allocated food donations, awards, and gift certificates for annual volunteer appreciation dinner
- Managed budget of 10K for event planning and volunteer recognition
- Enrolled in a fundraising, grant-getting, and contracting class focused on 501(c)(3) funding

COMPUTER TECHNOLOGY AND SOCIAL MEDIA

- Proficient in all Microsoft Office programs, Adobe Premiere Pro, and WordPress publishing platform
- Created blog for nonprofit organization to better communicate with supporters and members
- Assisted nonprofit webmaster in website edits, improvement, and updates

WORK EXPERIENCE

Creekside Community Development Corporation — Detroit, MI
AmeriCorps Member and Social Work Intern — August 2024–Present

University of Michigan School of Social Work — Ann Arbor, MI
Graduate Student Staff Assistant, Office of Student Services — August 2023–Present

Workers' Rights Center — Madison, WI
Social Work Intern — September 2022–May 2023

Centro Hispano of Dane County — Madison, WI
Assistant Program Coordinator — September 2021–July 2022

University of Wisconsin–Madison Housing — Madison, WI
Residence Hall Desk Supervisor — August 2021–May 2023

(continued)

Figure E.11 Functional MSW Macro

Suzie Socialworker, LMSW

RESEARCH EXPERIENCE

Honors History Thesis: University of Wisconsin–Madison History Major Undergraduate, Completed May 2023
- Studied use of welfare and other social services utilized by Hmong Vietnam War veterans in U.S.
- Analyzed anti-immigration sentiment reflected in U.S. social policies in the 1990s
- Conducted independent research on the effects of 1996 welfare reform on legal immigrants

PROFESSIONAL DEVELOPMENT

Michigan's AmeriCorps Member Celebration — East Lansing, MI
Michigan Community Service Commission — November 2023
- Participated in social media for the nonprofit sector and grant-writing workshops

Advocacy in Multicultural Settings Field Seminar — Madison, WI
BSW Undergraduate Program, University of Wisconsin–Madison — September 2022–May 2023
- Studied work culture of various human service providers and developed professionalism skills

Juvenile Justice Conference — Madison, WI
Wisconsin Council on Children and Families — April 2023
- Organized and presented workshop on disconnected youth program to service providers

Created by the University of Michigan School of Social Work Career Services

Figure E.11 Functional MSW Macro (*continued*)

3031 COUGAR DRIVE   423-444-3344
HOUSTON, TEXAS 77021 tomjjones@gmail.com

THOMAS JONES, LCSW

A highly experienced licensed clinical social work professional with expertise in social services management and program development within the mental health arena. Bilingual in Spanish and English with progressive work accomplishments within social service agencies. A frequently requested conference presenter and a recognized author of numerous articles.

Highlights of Achievements

Program Design/Development

- Implemented Family Resource Center project at Houston Area Children's Center
- Created policy and procedures for Family Resource Center's Home Care Program
- Implemented countywide respite needs survey for the Houston area
- Designed supportive counseling groups for persons with mental health needs
- Developed training curricula for numerous programs serving those with mental illness
- Trained staff to implement programs

Management

- Supervised professional and support staff within agency
- Served as acting department director during absence of director
- Nominated for Supervisor of the Year 2026 for UH Social Work Practicum program
- Developed and monitored a $3 million program budget
- Maintained departmental statistical data for use in budget development and funding proposals

Clinical Practice

- Provided individual and family treatment and supportive counseling for those with mental illness
- Facilitated supportive counseling groups in Spanish for families and clients
- Prepared social histories and conducted psychosocial assessments
- Provided case management services to children and families with mental health problems
- Established community resource linkages for families and individuals in need

Professional Experience

Program Director	Houston Area Children's Center	Houston, TX	9/25–Present
Unit Director	Houston Area Children's Center	Houston, TX	6/22–9/25
Social Worker	Houston Area Children's Center	Houston, TX	1/20–5/22
Supervisor	Gulf Coast Service Center	Houston, TX	5/19–12/20
Caseworker	Salvation Army Family Center	Knoxville, TN	3/18–4/19

Education

Master of Social Work, University of Houston, Graduate College of Social Work, Houston TX, May 2025
Bachelor of Arts, University of Tennessee, Knoxville, TN, May 2021

Sample provided by University of Houston Graduate College of Social Work Center for Career & Professional Development

Figure E.12   Functional MSW Clinical (Experienced)

PAUL SANCHEZ
555-000-1234 | PAULSANCHEZ@EMAILSAMPLE.COM

EDUCATION

5/2024
MASTER OF SOCIAL WORK (MSW),
BROWN SCHOOL AT WASHINGTON UNIVERSITY IN ST. LOUIS

5/2021
BACHELOR OF SOCIAL WORK
TEXAS STATE UNIVERSITY
- Phi Alpha
- Texas State University Social Work Scholarship

LEADERSHIP EXPERIENCE

- **Treasurer,** Brown Association for Rural Needs, Washington University in St. Louis. 2023–2025
- **Co-Organizer,** Close The Workhouse Campaign, Washington University St. Louis. 2024–2025
- **Member,** NASW Missouri Chapter. 2024–2025

COMMUNITY DEVELOPMENT

- Created a mental health treatment center proposal for the **Meskwaki Nation.**
- Developed and implemented intercultural summer programming with **Albanian, Roma, and Ashkaeli youth.**

PROFESSIONAL SUMMARY

SKILLS

International experience
Community-Based System Dynamics
Demonstrated leadership skills
Program development and design
Program evaluation and assessment
Group facilitation
Youth development
Albanian language proficiency

EXPERIENCE

SPRING 2025
PRACTICUM STUDENT, STL YOUTH JOBS
- Conducting and implementing evaluation tools and strategies with youth and youth employment partners.
- Conducting focus groups, data collection, data analysis and synthesis. Creating measurement tools and long-term evaluation plans.
- Assisting in marketing and creating partner relationships.

FALL 2023–SPRING 2024
PRACTICUM STUDENT, CENTER FOR YOUTH ON THE RISE, ST LOUIS COUNTY YOUTH PROGRAMS
Designed a community service-learning program for the youth center. Assisted with implementing spring programming and developing and implementing summer programming, and with building partnerships with other community organizations.

FALL 2023–SPRING 2024
GRADUATE FELLOW, WASHINGTON UNIVERSITY VILLAGE RESIDENTIAL COMMUNITY
Managed BLOC (living-learning community) programs, provided training and support to BLOC leaders including leading one-on-one and group meetings, creating community-wide programming, acting as a member of the LLC working group for LLC improvement. Developed an LLC handbook; assisted with creating and implementing summer and winter RA and summer LLC training.

FALL 2021–SUMMER 2023
VOLUNTEER, PEACE CORPS KOSOVO
Co-taught elementary and middle school, conducted teacher training one-on-one, and developed curriculum and teaching aids. Coordinated teacher-training programs and youth leadership initiatives. Coordinated sustainable youth-lead summer school program. Promoted intercultural relationships among youth in a post-conflict zone.

SUMMER 2021
NATIVE SPEAKER ENGLISH TEACHER, GYEONGSANGNAMDO OFFICE OF ED.
Taught English language to middle school students in one urban and one rural middle school. Developed curriculum, textbook, and teaching aids. Conducted summer and winter language immersion camps.

Sample provided by Washington University in St. Louis Brown School Center for Career Engagement

Figure E.13   Chronological Modern MSW Macro

Danielle Martinez, LCSW
(512) 555-5555 | dmartinez@sampleemail.com

EDUCATION

05/2025   The University of Tennessee, Knoxville, TN
Doctor of Philosophy in Social Work
Dissertation title: The Implications of COVID-19 and Online Learning on School Social Work Practices
Dissertation Committee: Rene Howards, PhD (Chair), Tom Rodgers, PhD and Betsy Clark, PhD

04/2022   University of Southern California, Los Angeles, CA
Master of Social Work

04/2020   Texas State University, San Marcos, TX
Bachelor of Arts in Anthropology

RESEARCH INTERESTS
school social work; adolescents and mental health; health equity; children and families

TEACHING INTERESTS
Introduction to Social Work; Human Behavior and Social Environment, School Social Work, Social Justice, Communities and Organizations

RESEARCH EXPERIENCE

10/2020– Current   **Graduate Research Assistant**
Youth Services Collaborative
The University of Tennessee, Knoxville, TN
- Engages in scholarly inquiry to investigate the accessibility of community resources aimed at enhancing mental health outcomes within marginalized youth cohorts in Knoxville.
- Evaluates the efficacy of intervention programs within three distinct neighborhoods in Knoxville to discern impact on mental health outcomes.
- Collects datasets in adherence to state regulations and grant stipulations to ensure suitability for comprehensive analysis.
- Utilizes advanced methodological approaches including hierarchical linear modeling to interpret collected data.
- Synthesizes research findings to highlight programmatic achievements and for grant renewal endeavors.

(continued)

TEACHING EXPERIENCE

09/2021– Current
The University of Tennessee, Knoxville, TN
Assistant Instructor, Introduction to Social Work
- Instructs a cohort of 25 undergraduate students enrolled in an online course, emphasizing the fundamental principles of social work and social welfare within an academic framework.
- Develops a comprehensive syllabus, delivers lectures, devises assignments, and orchestrates class activities to facilitate student comprehension and critical engagement.
- Facilitates weekly office hours and lectures utilizing the Zoom platform to provide additional support and address inquiries from students.
- Leverages diverse online resources including discussion boards, interactive reading materials, polling utilities, and breakout rooms to enhance interactivity and foster collaborative learning environments within the virtual classroom setting.

FUNDING

08/2021
National Alliance for Mental Health
Role: Co-Investigator (PI: Jesus Mendez, PhD)
Evidence–Based Practices in School Mental Health Interventions for Youth Ages 12–18
$77,876

PUBLICATIONS

Peer-Reviewed Publications

Martinez, D. (2025). Utilizing solution focused therapy with high school students struggling with depression post COVID-19. *International Journal of School Social Work, 18*(1), 1–8. https://doi.org/11.11111/t.tttt.2025.100763

Under Review

Martinez, D., & Howards, R. (under review). Socio-economic status and remote learning during COVID-19: Implications for future learning experiences. *Journal of Social Work Research.*

Works in Progress

Martinez, D. (Manuscript in progress). School social workers as catalyst for change: Measuring the impact of school social workers pre and post COVID-19 in Tennessee Independent School District.

Book Chapters

Martinez, D. (2023). School-Based Solution Focused Therapy. *Encyclopedia of School Social Work* (pp. 23–45). NASW Press.

Opinion Editorials

Martinez, D. (2021). Schools should invest equally in student learning and mental health [Opinion editorial]. *Knoxville News.*

(continued)

Figure E.14 Curriculum Vitae *(continued)*

CONFERENCE PRESENTATIONS

Martinez, D. (2024, October). Solution focused from a distance: Strategies to engage elementary age students in online groupwork. National Association of Social Workers State Conference, Nashville, TN.

GUEST LECTURE

Martinez, D. (May 2024). *Engaging online learners – one computer at a time.* Guest lecture, Theories of School Social Work, The University of Tennessee, Knoxville, TN.

SCHOLARSHIPS AND AWARDS

03/2024	University Graduate Continuing Fellow 2023–2024, The University of Tennessee, Knoxville, TN
11/2023	University Finalist Three-Minute Thesis, The University of Tennessee, Knoxville, TN
08/2022	Certificate in Applied Statistical Modeling, The University of Tennessee, Knoxville, TN Department of Statistics
08/2017	W.B. Powers Endowed Presidential Scholarship, University of Southern California, LA

CLINICAL EXPERIENCE

08/2017–
08/2022

Los Angeles Children's Counseling Center, Los Angeles, CA
Clinical Social Worker
• Directed therapeutic sessions tailored to children ages 6 through 12, utilizing play therapy, solution-focused therapy, grief and loss counseling, and trauma-informed care.
• Conducted group therapy sessions spanning diverse age demographics, including children, adolescents, and young adults, addressing complex issues such as suicidal ideation, posttraumatic stress disorder, anxiety disorders, and depression.
• Evaluated therapy notes, diagnostic assessments, and treatment strategies authored by colleagues as part of annual performance evaluations within the therapeutic team.

(continued)

Figure E.14   Curriculum Vitae (*continued*)

UNIVERSITY SERVICE

01/2024	Council on Social Work Education Annual Program Meeting, Atlanta, GA
	Conference Student Volunteer
08/2020– 05/2024	PhD Committee at The University of Tennessee, Knoxville, TN
	Student Representative and Mentor

SERVICE TO THE PROFESSION

02/2020	Oceanside Fundraiser, Santa Monica, CA
	Volunteer
08/2017	Habitat for Humanity, San Marcos, TX
	Volunteer

PROFESSIONAL ASSOCIATIONS AND LICENSURE

American Association of School Social Workers, 2025
Society for Social Work and Research, 2020–2025
Council on Social Work Education, 2022–2025
ASWB Licensed Clinical Social Worker License #12738

Figure E.14   Curriculum Vitae (*continued*)

APPENDIX

F

Sample Cover Letters and Other Job Search Correspondence

Creating well-written and professional correspondence consistent with your professional brand is critical throughout your job search. Chapter 5 provides information and guidance to help your write cover letters, email requests for networking, and more. The samples shared here can be useful references to help you get started.

Sample Number	Correspondence Type	Specifics
1	Cover Letter	General LMSW (Experienced)
2	Cover Letter	Clinical MSW
3	Cover Letter	Macro MSW (Recent Graduate)
4	Cover Letter	Practicum
5	Cover Letter	BSW (Recent)
6	Cover Letter	LCSW (Experienced)
7	Cover Letter	Nontraditional MSW
8	Email	Resume and Cover Letter Attached
9	Email	Thank You Post Interview
10	Email	Request for Informational Interview
11	Email	Thank You for Informational Interview
12	Email	Request for Reference
13	Email	Thank You for Contact Referral
14	Letter of Acceptance	Following Job Offer
15	LinkedIn	Request for Connection
16	Letter of Recommendation	For a Former Employee

Michelle Smith, LMSW

Ann Arbor, MI, State • (314) 123-4567 • smithlmsw@sampleemail.com • LinkedIn

June 7, 2025

Shauna Jones, Director
Communities in Schools
125 Main Street
Ann Arbor, MI 48109

RE: Social Worker #4567

Dear Ms. Jones,

I am excited to express my interest in the social work position for Communities in Schools. I learned about this position through LinkedIn. I have a Master of Science degree in Clinical Mental Health Counseling, 4 years of counseling experience, and 6 years of management experience. I have enclosed a copy of my resume and references for your review.

The decision to attend graduate school is one that needs to be carefully evaluated and the payoff needs to be great. Students need to know what steps to take and how long it will take to accomplish their goals. My role as a career development professional is to give all students the tools they need to successfully complete their chosen educational programs and to see the manifestation of their career goals. I value the process of self-discovery and empowerment. I encourage my students to be decision makers and to take an active role in shaping their careers. I believe in exploring all the options and using every available resource to prepare students for success. In my current role as a career counselor, I see students of all majors and academic levels. I have had the pleasure of working with Public Health faculty to educate their students on proper resume writing techniques, graduate school application processes, job search strategies, and professionalism to increase their marketability. In all that I do, I want students to discover the best fit for their individual interests, skills, values, and personality.

Communities in Schools is dedicated to student success through providing world class education to its students with an outstanding reputation of diversity and empowering students to be catalysts for positive social change. Communities in Schools has paved the way for independent thinkers and responsible global citizens through cultivating educational and cultural awareness.

I look forward to meeting with you to discuss my qualifications for the position at the Communities in Schools in depth. I can be reached at any time to schedule an interview or to provide any additional information. Thank you for your time and consideration.

Sincerely,

Michelle Smith

Sample provided by the University Michigan School of Social Work Career Services

Figure F.1   Cover Letter, General LMSW (Experienced)

305 Cherry Hill Road, #3, Brighton, MA || 802-453-9856 || meiliang@yahoo.com

March 20, 2025

Human Resources Department
Optimum Senior Life
1200 Springfield Street
Boston, MA 02131

Dear Hiring Manager,

I would like to be considered for the position of resident services coordinator I found on the Optimum Senior Life website. Currently an MSW intern at the Rehab Center, I am very interested in continuing at OSL as a professional social worker. My experience in both long-term care and community settings allows me to understand the complex needs of clients and refer them to the needed support services available within the community or the agency they are residing at.

At the Rehab Center Long-Term Care Unit in Hyde Park, I provide both individual therapy and case management for residents and their families who have complex medical and psychosocial issues. I have gained both skills in psychosocial assessment and a sold knowledge of community supports and referrals. I have most enjoyed being a member of an interdisciplinary team in a hospital setting.

Previously, I interned at an adult day health program, working with both older adults and adults with disabilities. This required a flexibility in therapeutic approaches to enhance each client's psychosocial well-being from a strengths perspective. I was involved in the admission process for new clients and case management skills for individuals living in the community who attended the program. This allowed me to develop and expand my knowledge of community-based organizations.

I will earn my MSW from Boston College with a concentration in older adults and families. My coursework has been focused primarily on the mental and physical health of older adults, end of life issues, and family dynamics with elective classes in family therapy, narrative therapy, and death, dying, and bereavement.

My internship at Optimum has been amazing, with opportunities to hone my clinical skills while being trained and supported by caring and supportive experts in the field! I am very passionate about the agency's mission to respect and promote the dignity of elders. I look forward to contributing to this work as a resident services coordinator at the Rehab Center.

I look forward to meeting with you to further discuss this position.

Sincerely,

Mei Liang

Figure F.2   Cover Letter, General Clinical MSW

BERNICE EVANSON, MSW
123 Fort Montgomery Ave • New York, NY 10000 • (734) 855-4444 • b.evans@email.com

June 14, 2025

The Urban Center
302 Eleanor Rigby Way
New York, NY 20000

Dear Project Associate Hiring Committee:

I am writing to apply for the project associate position that I reviewed on The Urban Center website. I was encouraged to apply by fellow employee and Senior Project Manager Sandy Randle, who expressed that I was an ideal candidate for the position. I am excited by The Urban Center's mission and the work currently done to address several social justice issues in New York City.

Before graduate school, I was employed for three years as a grant writer at Project H.O.M.E., a nationally recognized nonprofit organization serving homeless individuals and families in Philadelphia. During my time there, I crafted grant applications and reports that awarded the organization roughly $1.7 million. I honed exceptional writing, editing, and research skills at Project H.O.M.E., working quickly and efficiently in a deadline-focused environment. I routinely handled multiple detail-oriented tasks simultaneously and developed strong project and time management skills. I also refined excellent oral and communication skills at Project H.O.M.E. by working with foundations, corporations, religious entities, and individuals to secure funding and while planning two high-profile donor recognition events.

This past year, I completed an MSW field internship at the Community Service Center, an on-campus community service office at the university. At the Community Service Center, I collected and analyzed student feedback from surveys, created an evaluation and assessment plan for the peer facilitator training program, and visited community partners in Detroit. I also performed data analyses of student surveys in SPSS and drafted a project poster that was presented at a national service learning conference at the university last May.

My experience working with SPSS, analyzing data, preparing for meetings, and developing presentations is directly translatable to the project associate's job duties, and would make me an excellent addition to your team!

Thank you for your consideration of my application. If you have any questions or need further information, please don't hesitate to contact me at b.evans@email.com or (734) 855-4444.

Sincerely,

Bernice Evanson

Sample provided by the University Michigan School of Social Work Career Services

---

Figure F.3   Cover Letter, Macro MSW (Recent Graduate)

Derrick White 132 Washington St, Springfield, MA   dhw@email.com

January 24, 2025

Madison Hitchcock
Director of Training
Child and Family Services
Springfield, MA

Dear Ms. Hitchcock,

I am writing to indicate my interest in the in-home therapy social work practicum offered at Child and Family Services. I will be a second-year MSW student at Springfield College eager to build on my experience supporting children and families dealing with the effects of trauma.

While pursuing my bachelor's degree in psychology at the University of Massachusetts, I worked at an after-school program at the YMCA. Although my job description involved running programs for kids, I realized early on that the role was so much more than playing gaga and overseeing homework. These were kids who were suffering from the effects of poverty and trauma and while I could help by being a mentor and trusted adult, I wanted to do more. After graduating I worked for two years as a milieu counselor at the Peabody residential program. Here I was a member of a multidisciplinary treatment team focused on the social, recreational, and behavioral needs of children with emotional and behavioral challenges. Through this role I learned about treatment plans and helped provide a therapeutic environment to implement children's treatment and individual support plans. I learned best practices for conflict resolution and crisis intervention. I participated in trainings on vicarious trauma and suicide prevention and decided to pursue my MSW at Springfield College.

My first-year practicum I remained at Peabody working as a social work intern in their therapeutic day school. Here I learned to help with family assessments, run social skills groups, and understand how classroom observations can inform therapeutic treatment plans. Through the family assessments I began to understand the impact of generational trauma and was eager to learn more.

I feel I would be a stronger clinician gaining in-home experience by having an opportunity to work with both the client and their family to understand the supports they need. I believe my prior experience in both residential and school settings will be beneficial in working in-home as clients sometimes transition between systems. I will be taking courses over the summer in family therapy and trauma and look forward to applying this new knowledge during my practicum experience.

I would appreciate the opportunity to talk with you further about this position and how I could contribute to the In-Home Therapy team at Child and Family Services.

Sincerely,

Derrick White

Figure F.4   Cover Letter, Practicum

Marian Riley, BSW
1234 Main Street
Austin, TX 78704 | MarianRiley@sampleemail.com
(555) 555-1234

November 17, 2025

Ms. Jane Jones
Director of Human Resources
Children and Family Services Center
3000 Hope Drive
Austin, TX 78702-2531

Dear Ms. Jones:

I am writing to express my interest in the patient navigator position advertised on LinkedIn. With a solid foundation in case management and specialized experience working with individuals grappling with substance use disorders, I am eager to offer my skills and expertise to your esteemed clinic.

During my tenure as an intern at Dell Medical Center, I played an integral role within a multidisciplinary team dedicated to facilitating patients' smooth transitions from hospitalization to outpatient care settings. In this capacity, I conducted comprehensive psychosocial evaluations; administered assessments; and coordinated referrals to various community resources, including local law enforcement agencies, psychiatric facilities, and chemical dependency outpatient services and support groups.

In addition to my social work experience, my leadership role as treasurer of the NASW student organization at Texas State School of Social Work has equipped me with strong leadership and communication skills. Through collaborating closely with faculty, staff, and peers, I have honed my ability to navigate complex organizational dynamics while advocating for the diverse needs of social work students. Furthermore, I am actively pursuing licensure and eagerly anticipate my upcoming examination. My fluency in both English and Spanish has enabled me to effectively engage with and support Spanish-speaking populations throughout my professional endeavors.

I hold a deep admiration for the impactful programs offered by the Children and Family Services Center and am drawn to the opportunity to contribute to an institution renowned for its commitment to excellence in patient care. I am enthusiastic about the prospect of discussing how my background, skills, and passion align with the mission and vision of your organization during an interview. Enclosed please find my resume, which provides further insight into my educational background and professional experience.

Thank you for considering my application. I look forward to the possibility of contributing to your esteemed team.

Sincerely,

Marian Riley, BSW

Figure F.5   Cover Letter, BSW (Recent)

Liz Norton, LCSW
1947 Jack's St.
Austin, TX 78704
liznorton@sampleemail.com
555-555-5555

May 28, 2025

Mind Works
1340 Lamont
Austin, TX 78712

Dear Hiring Manager,

I am writing to apply for the clinical director position at Mind Works, as advertised on Indeed. With my extensive experience in social services management and program development within the mental health arena, I believe that I possess the skills and qualifications necessary to lead and advance your organization's mission.

Throughout my career, I have consistently demonstrated a strong commitment to improving the lives of individuals and families affected by mental health challenges. As a highly experienced licensed clinical social work professional, I have developed and implemented various programs, including the Family Resource Center project at DePelchin Children's Center. I also played a key role in creating policies and procedures for the Family Resource Center's Home Care Program, which provided crucial support to families in need. Furthermore, I co-authored and implemented a county-wide respite needs survey for the Houston area, ensuring that services were tailored to meet the specific needs of the community.

In addition to program development, I have a proven track record in management and leadership. I have successfully supervised up to 15 professional and support staff within agencies, including acting as the department director during the absences of the director. My dedication and expertise were recognized when I was nominated for Supervisor of the Year 2026 for the UH Social Work Field Internship program. Furthermore, I have extensive experience in budget development and management, having overseen a $4 million program budget while maintaining accurate statistical data for funding proposals.

Direct treatment and client care are areas where I have excelled as well. I have provided individual and family treatment to adults with mental illness, facilitating supportive counseling groups in both English and Spanish. I am bilingual in Spanish and English, which has allowed me to effectively connect with diverse populations and ensure culturally sensitive care. Furthermore, my experience in conducting psychosocial assessments, preparing social histories,

(continued)

Figure F.6   Cover Letter, LCSW (Experienced)

and providing case management services to children and families has equipped me with a comprehensive understanding of the needs and challenges within the mental health field.

I am confident that my qualifications, along with my passion for improving mental health services, make me an ideal fit for the clinical director position at Mind Works. I am eager to bring my leadership skills, program development expertise, and commitment to quality care to your esteemed organization.

Thank you for considering my application. I would welcome the opportunity to discuss how my skills align with the vision and goals of Mind Works. Please feel free to contact me at your convenience to schedule an interview.

Thank you for your time and consideration.

Sincerely,

Liz Norton, LCSW

Sample provided by Jennifer Luna, MSSW, and OpenAI. (2021). GPT-3.5. [ChatGPT Version]. https://openai.com

Figure F.6   Cover Letter, LCSW (Experienced) (*continued*)

Ramon Garcia, LMSW

1111 Sample St. Santa Barbara, CA
RamonGarcia@Sampleemail.com 555-555-5555

March 20, 2025

Andrea Monroe
Amazon Corp
2024 Future Way
Santa Barbara, CA 11111

Dear Andrea Monroe,

I am writing to express my strong interest in the position of DEI director at Amazon Corp, as advertised on the Steer Your Career job portal. As a licensed MSW with a proven track record in social work and a deep passion for fostering diversity, equity, and inclusion in a variety of settings, including nonprofit organizations and government agencies, I am confident in my ability to drive positive change and make a substantial impact in this role.

Throughout my career as an LMSW, I have been dedicated to addressing social inequalities and advocating for underrepresented communities. In my role as engagement specialist, I have gained valuable experience in designing and implementing comprehensive DEI initiatives within the Los Angeles Independent School District. I collaborate with diverse teams and individuals, providing support and empowering them to overcome challenges related to discrimination, bias, and marginalization. I am adept at creating inclusive spaces where individuals feel heard, valued, and respected, and I believe this skill set will be instrumental in fostering an inclusive corporate culture at Amazon Corp. I am skilled in conducting diversity audits, developing diversity training programs, and implementing policies and procedures that promote equity and inclusion across all levels of the organization.

Additionally, my strong interpersonal and communication skills have allowed me to successfully collaborate with stakeholders from diverse backgrounds. I am skilled in building relationships with community organizations and fostering partnerships that drive meaningful change and expand access to opportunities for marginalized groups. I am skilled in analyzing data and utilizing metrics to assess the effectiveness of DEI initiatives, allowing for continuous improvement and accountability.

I am excited about the opportunity to contribute my expertise and collaborate with the talented team at Amazon Corp to develop and implement strategies that will create lasting change and ensure that diversity, equity, and inclusion are deeply embedded in the fabric of the organization. I would welcome the opportunity to discuss my qualifications further and how my skills align with Amazon's vision and values. Thank you for your consideration of my application.

Sincerely,

Ramon Garcia, LMSW

Sample provided by Jennifer Luna, MSSW, and OpenAI. (2021). GPT-3.5. [ChatGPT Version]. https://openai.com

Figure F.7   Cover Letter, Nontraditional MSW

Subject: Application for Social Work Position: Resume and Cover Letter Attached

Dear Mr. Vargas,

I hope this email finds you well. I am writing to express my strong interest in the social work position at Parkland Hospital and to submit my application materials for your review. Please find attached my resume and cover letter outlining my qualifications and experience.

As a dedicated and compassionate social worker with a strong commitment to making a positive impact on individuals' lives, I am excited about the opportunity to contribute to your organization's mission and work. With 2 years of experience in the field, I have developed a diverse skill set that allows me to effectively support and advocate for vulnerable populations.

I am particularly drawn to Parkland Hospital due to its excellent reputation in the field of health social work and its commitment to health equity of individuals and communities. I strongly believe that my qualifications, combined with my passion for social work, align well with your organization's values and goals.

Thank you for considering my application. I would welcome the opportunity to discuss my qualifications further and how I can contribute to the success of your organization. I am available for an interview at your earliest convenience.

Sincerely,

Dante Vega, LBSW
555-555-5555

Figure F.8 Email, Resume and Cover Letter Attached

Marcia Sellers, LMSW   msellers@sample.com   555-654-1234

March 30, 2026

Rosaria Smith
American Red Cross
123 Highland Avenue
Chicago, IL 12345

Mrs. Smith:

Thank you for setting aside the time this morning to discuss the psychiatric social worker supervisor position that is open at the American Red Cross on the Emergency Response Team. The position sounds very interesting to me and is right in line with my qualifications and experience.

My experience with Baker Ripley as a disaster relief social worker over the past three years has prepared me well for the Emergency Response Team's work with your agency. I am especially proud of the Employee of the Year Award I received in October for the work I have done as a member of the Disaster Relief Team. The team that I supervise responded to 250 crisis calls in August and received the highest ratings for excellence of any of the 35 teams within Baker Ripley. My supervisory skills, clinical expertise, and proven track record in teamwork effectiveness appear to exceed your requirements for the position.

I am very interested in the position, and I look forward to hearing back from you with a job offer to work for the American Red Cross. Please contact me with any additional questions you may have at msellers@gmail.com.

Sincerely,

Marcia Sellers, LMSW

Figure F.9   Email, Thank You Post Interview

Subject line: Request for Informational Interview; Referred by Cindy Snell @ BCSSW

Dear Ms. Garabedian,

I am graduating with my MSW from the Boston College School of Social Work in May 2024 and relocating to the Portland, Oregon, area. As I was talking with the director of career services, Cindy Snell, she gave me your name and contact information and suggested I reach out.

My area of interest is older adults and mental health, and I would love to connect with you to hear more about your experience as a social worker in Portland and any advice you might have as I explore my career options.

I will be visiting during winter break and would love to meet with you in person if possible but am certainly willing to connect remotely if that is more convenient. Is there a 20-minute time block during which you are available between January 1 and 17?

Feel free to reply via email or reach me by text at 617-234-5678.

Thank you and happy holidays.

Julia Linden

Figure F.10 Email, Request for Informational Interview

Subject line: Thank You for Meeting with Me for an Informational Interview January 12

Dear Minesha Garabedian,

I am so appreciative of the time you gave me to talk about social work careers in the Portland, Oregon, area. Your orientation to the scope of practice with an MSW license, major hiring agencies, and starting salaries is so helpful as I start my job search this semester.

I look forward to connecting with Mark Fulton at the Portland Mental Health Clinic, per your suggestion, and appreciate you making this connection.

All the best to you and hopefully we can reconnect once I move to Portland this summer!

Sincerely,

Julia Linden

Figure F.11 Email, Thank You for Informational Interview

Scott Brandon, MSW Candidate

555-123-4567 • sample@mail.com

June 16, 2025

Dear Professor Sanders,

I hope all is well. A lot has happened since our last meeting. I am graduating with my MSW this summer with a concentration in policy and evaluation. In addition, I have two job interviews scheduled within the next couple of weeks! I am writing to ask if you would serve as a reference for me?

I remember our conversations about my career path and how I was able to join your research team to build my research and analytical skills. That experience helped me to hone those skills in a real-world setting. Thank you!

The jobs that I am interviewing for are with consulting firms where I would be able to apply those skills developed while working on your research project. I hope that you will be able to speak about my advancement and preparation for this line of work. I have attached my updated resume for your reference.

Thank you in advance for your consideration.

Sincerely,

Scott Brandon

Figure F.12 Email, Request for Reference

BERNICE EVANSON, MSW
123 Fort Montgomery Avenue • New York, NY 10000 • (734) 855-4444 • b.evans@email.com

May 29, 2025

Hi Lauren,

I wanted to say thank you for the email introduction to Phil Brando regarding my job search in the Miami area. His insight into the job market there was crucial in determining agencies and organizations I should tailor my job search to. He informed me about which organizations are currently in need of social workers and what salaries to expect for these positions. He also provided me with key insight into licensure there and what questions to ask during interviews.

As you can see, our conversation was very productive. I will keep you posted on any updates.

Thank you again for being a support for me.

Sincerely,

Bernice Evanson

Sample provided by the University Michigan School of Social Work Career Services

Figure F.13 Email, Thank You for Contact Referral

BERNICE EVANSON, MSW
123 Fort Montgomery Ave • New York, NY 10000 • (734) 855-4444 • b.evans@email.com

May 29, 2025

The Urban Center
302 Eleanor Rigby Way
New York, NY 20000

Dear Sandra Brandon,

Thank you for offering me the project associate position in your organization. It is with great pleasure that I accept the offer of employment. As per our conversation, the starting salary is $68,000—full time—with salary and benefits. The signing bonus of $4,000 will greatly support my moving closer to Manhattan.

Thank you for giving me time to finish projects with my current employer and to move over the summer. I expect my start date to be July 5, 2025.

Let me know if you need any additional clarification regarding this matter. Please inform me of any next steps with securing my position and completing paperwork with the HR department.

I look forward to working at The Urban Center and as part of your team!

Sincerely,

Bernice Evanson

Sample provided by the University Michigan School of Social Work Career Services

Figure F.14 Letter of Acceptance Following Job Offer

Subject: Connecting with School Social Workers

Dear Jennifer:

I hope this message finds you well. As a fellow social worker, I am reaching out with great enthusiasm to connect and expand my professional network within the area of school social work.

Having come across your profile through a mutual connection, Dorothy Martinez, I couldn't help but notice the strong impact you have made in the area of community engagement in the Nashville Independent School District. Your commitment to empowering individuals, advocating for marginalized populations, and driving meaningful change is truly admirable.

With 2 years of experience as a school social worker, I have had the privilege of working in diverse settings, from community organizations to schools. I am considering moving to Tennessee next fall and I would love to learn about the landscape of school social work in your community.

I would be thrilled to learn more about your work, the organizations you partner with, and the challenges you have encountered along the way. Moreover, I am eager to share my own experiences and insights, discuss the latest advancements in our field, and explore potential avenues for collaboration or mutual support.

Thank you for considering my invitation. I look forward to connecting with you and embarking on this journey together.

Warm regards,

Michelle Farrah, LMSW
Michellefarrah@sampleemail.com

Sample provided by Jennifer Luna, MSSW, and OpenAI. (2021). GPT-3.5. [ChatGPT Version]. https://openai.com

Figure F.15   LinkedIn Request for Connection

October 31, 2025

Marian Cardone
Director of Clinical Services
Baybreeze Human Services
160 Lincoln Drive, Suite 456
Houston, TX 77000

Dear Marian Cardone,

I am writing to strongly recommend Mateo Alvarez for the social work position in the Teen Development Unit of Baybreeze Human Services.

Mateo has been a social work intern at my agency, Gentlebreeze Counseling, over the past academic year where he has demonstrated a willingness to learn, proper use of supervision, and an ability to apply the skills and knowledge he learned through his MSW program at the Hitchcock University School of Social Work. Mateo provided outreach and therapy for a cooperative program with the local middle school. Here Mateo was responsible for educational, preventative, and outreach programs for a diverse population of adolescents at this urban school. He utilized his own Latino background and bilingual skills in English and Spanish to create innovative programs that were well received by the middle schoolers.

Mateo also spent about half his time offering weekly individual counseling to students identified by the school as needing additional mental health support. Over the course of the year, Mateo became increasingly comfortable in this role and utilizing a variety of therapeutic modalities to meet the needs of his clients. During supervision he was open to feedback and working through the challenges he encountered with the students.

I am confident that Mateo Alvarez will be a contributing member to your therapeutic team. He is dedicated to providing trauma-informed care to adolescent populations and will continue to grow as a social worker.

Sincerely,

Jamal Henderson

Clinician, Gentlebreeze Counseling

Sample provided by University of Houston Graduate College of Social Work Center for Career & Professional Development

Figure F.16   Letter of Recommendation for a Former Employee

APPENDIX
G

Sample Questions to Evaluate Organizational Fit

A great predictor of how successful you will be in your new job is how well the organization's culture aligns with your values and goals. Chapter 7 discusses the importance of reviewing an organization's culture when making decisions about jobs and different methods to assess this information. The list of questions in this appendix can be used to take a deep dive into assessing workplace culture and explore an organization's diversity, equity, and inclusion (DEI) practices.

Organization Setup

- How is the space in the organization set up?
- Is the website updated?
- What is the onboarding process?
- Are there opportunities for remote or hybrid work schedules?

Communication

- How are staff meetings organized? How often do they occur?
- How is information communicated to staff?
- How does staff communicate with management? Each other?
- How are new ideas communicated?
- How is success celebrated?
- How is conflict handled within the organization?

Leadership

- How do leaders within the organization interact with others?
- How does management seek input?
- How transparent is leadership?

Community

- Are the employees part of a union?
- How do employees spend their lunch break?
- Are there staff events to create community?

Diversity, Equity, and Inclusion

- Is there a DEI office or formal DEI position (not just a volunteer group)?
- If there is a DEI office, do you have access to their report/plan?

Professional Growth

- What type of support is offered to employees for professional growth (training, conferences, certifications, education reimbursement)?
- What is the annual performance review process?
- Are there opportunities for advancement?
- Are there formal or informal opportunities for mentoring?

APPENDIX H

Determine Your Budget

Using the subcategories shown in Table H.1 (e.g., mortgage, cable, health insurance), make a spreadsheet of how much you spend each month. Review past bills, credit card statements, and bank statements for estimates. Once you have a complete list, add up all the dollar amounts and insert them into the table. This will give you an estimated budget for one month. If you multiply your monthly budget by 12, you will have an estimate of your yearly expenses. This should give you a good idea of what salary—minus taxes!—you need to maintain your current lifestyle. If you are planning to relocate for your new job, websites such as salaryexpert.com can assist you with estimating the cost of living for a geographic area. If you are anticipating big expenditures in the near future (e.g., new car, down payment on a house, medical expenses), be sure to budget for extra savings. Finally, be sure to understand if you will incur different expenses in your new job (train fare versus gas and parking), and include before and after estimates.

Table H.1 Suggested List of Budget Categories

Category	Estimated Expense
HOUSING	
Mortgage/rent	
Home/renters insurance	
Gas/heat	
Electricity	
Water	
Condo/association fees	
Cable/internet	
Maintenance (lawn/snow removal)	
Subtotal	
TRANSPORTATION	
Car payment	
Insurance	
Gas	
Public transportation	
Parking	
Car maintenance	
Subtotal	

Table H.1 Suggested List of Budget Categories (*continued*)

Category	Estimated Expense
INSURANCE	
Health	
Vision	
Dental	
Life	
Subtotal	
FOOD	
Groceries	
Eating out	
Subtotal	
CLOTHING	
Work	
Personal	
Subtotal	
CHILDCARE	
Daycare/school	
Clothing	
Subtotal	

Table H.1 Suggested List of Budget Categories (*continued*)

Category	Estimated Expense
EDUCATIONAL	
Professional fees (license, CEUs)	
Loans	
Subtotal	
ENTERTAINMENT	
Subtotal	
SAVINGS	
Subtotal	
MISC.	
Personal debt	
Subtotal	
Total Monthly	
Total Yearly (multiply monthly expense by 12)	

APPENDIX
I

Evaluate Job Offers

The grid shown in Table I.1 is designed to help you review job offers. List as much information as possible from your offer letter, including items that are important to you that were not offered and that you wish to negotiate. It is important to assess how well the position aligns with your career goals and financial needs when deciding to accept or reject a job offer.

Table I.1 Job Offer Evaluation Grid

	Job Offer 1	Job Offer 2 (if comparing)
Job Title and Agency		
Income		
Salary		
Bonus		
Potential for salary increases (yearly increase, increase when advanced license obtained, productivity bonus)		
Benefits		
Clinical supervision toward licensure		
Health insurance		
Dental insurance		
Vision insurance		
Life insurance		
Retirement		
Education/professional development/continuing education units		
Licenses/professional memberships/conference registrations		
Relocation		
Tuition repayment		
Discounts		
Maternity/paternity leave		
Career Goals		
Meets career objectives		
Opportunities for advancement		
Work/Life Balance		
Remote/hybrid options		
Work hours per week		
Time off (vacation, sick, personal)		
Culture		
Impression of organization: history/stability		
Communication with you through job process		
Team dynamics		
Management style		
Aligns with personal values		
Other Important Factors		
Start date		
Orientation/training		
Hires/sponsors international applicants		
Incidentals		
Car/mileage reimbursement		
Phone		

References

American Psychiatric Association. (2022). *Diagnostic and statistical manual of mental disorders: DSM-5-TR*. American Psychiatric Publishing. https://doi.org/10.1176/appi.books.9780890425787

American Psychological Association. (2020). *Publication manual of the American Psychological Association* (7th ed.). Author.

Conrad-Amlicke, G. (n.d.). *Understanding micro, mezzo and macro social work practice*. Retrieved May 20, 2022, from https://www.socialworkers.org/Careers/NASW-Career-Center/Explore-Social-Work/Understanding-Micro-Mezzo-and-Macro-Social-Work-Practice

Council on Social Work Education. (2022). *Educational policy and accreditation standards*. https://www.cswe.org/accreditation/policies-process/2022epas/

Escalante, D. C. (2023, January 27). *What is an agent of change?* London Spring. https://www.london-spring.org/what-is-an-agent-of-change/

Group for Advancement of Doctoral Education in Social Work. (2023). *2023 quality guidelines for PhD programs in social work*. https://www.gadesocialwork.org/Portals/0/docs/GADE%20PhD%20Program%20Quality%20Guidelines%202023%20Revised.pdf

Karls, J. M., & O'Keefe, M. E. (2009). Person-in-environment system. In A. A. Roberts (Ed.), *Social workers' desk reference* (2nd ed., pp. 371–375). Oxford University Press.

Luna, J., & Marks, A. (2014). *Using a professional development model to examine career-long learning with students*. Presentation at the Annual Program Meeting of the Council on Social Work Education, Tampa, FL.

Marston, W. M. (1928). *Emotions of normal people*. Harcourt Brace & Company. https://doi.org/10.1037/13390-000

National Association of Colleges and Employers. (2023, May 16). *Current benchmarks*. https://naceweb.org/job-market/compensation/current-benchmarks/

National Association of Social Workers. (2021). *Code of ethics of the National Association of Social Workers*. Author.

National Association of Social Workers Foundation. (n.d.). *NASW Social Work Pioneers*. Retrieved August 1, 2021, from https://www.naswfoundation.org/Our-Work/NASW-Social-Work-Pioneers

Rath, T. (2007). *StrengthsFinder 2.0*. Gallup Press.

Tarr-Whelan, C. (2009). *Lifting while we climb: Empowerment, organizing, and mobilization in the women's movement*. Feminist Press.

Index

In this index, *t* denotes table.

360-degree assessment, 136

A

acceptance letters, 221
administration/development skills and sample job title, 8–9
advanced education, 150
advanced social work skills, 165–167
　See also experienced social workers
affiliations. *See* professional associations; professional licenses, certifications, and affiliations
agent of change career tips, 134–153
annual performance evaluation, 139, 143
annual salary, 123
artificial intelligence (AI), 65–66
assistant dean of students job description, 17–18
attire, for interviews, 98, 106–107
audience, for bio statements, 57
audience, for communication skills, 147, 148
award nominations, 152
awards. *See* funding, grants, and awards, in CV

B

base salary, 123
behavior interview questions, 111–112
benefits packages, 124, 126–127
bio statements, 54–57
blogs, 146, 149
board memberships, 149–150
branding. *See* professional brand, creation of

BSW versus MSW, 25
budgets, 121, 227–230
Bureau of Labor Statistics, 122
business cards, 82, 83, 85

C

calling, finding your, 24–25
capabilities, in resumes, 70–71
career change professional summary example, 72
career coaches, 136
career contributions, 149–150, 151
career development. *See* professional brand, creation of; Professional Development Cycle of Social Workers (PDCSW)
career options, researching, 45–48
career planning, 21–32
career-defining moments, 52–53, 75–76, 179–180
case study presentations, 110, 111
certifications. *See* professional licenses, certifications, and affiliations
CEUs, 46
　See also continuing education
change. *See* agent of change career tips
chronological resumes, 191–196, 201
CliftonStrengths assessment, 134, 136
clinical experience. *See* practice and clinical experience, in CV
clinical social work
　about, 6–8
　cover letters, 209
　job search tips, 96
　knowledge areas and skills, 6–7, 156–157

professional summary examples, 71–72
sample job title, 6
sample resumes, 182, 189–190, 192–193, 200
specific interview questions, 109–110
colleague support, 152–153
combination (or targeted) resumes, 68–69, 182–190
communication skills, 147–148
See also blogs; elevator pitches; presentations and publications; social media presence
community, professional, and university service, in CV, 79–80
community engagement officer job description, 11–12
community organizing skills and sample job title, 9–10
community service, service learning, and volunteer experience, 74–75
compensation, evaluating, 121–128
context, for bio statements, 57
continuing education, 144–145, 150
See also presentations and publications
counteroffers, 128
cover letters, 80–82, 84, 208–215
curriculum vitae (CV), 77–80, 202–205

D

Davis, L., 120
development jobs. *See* administration/development skills and sample job title
DiSC assessment, 136
doctoral degrees, 150
dress for success, 98, 106–107

E

education, in CV, 77
education, in resumes, 72
education, pursuit of, 25–26, 150
See also continuing education
education and youth employment project officer job description, 15
elevator pitches, 57–59
email samples, 216, 217, 218, 219, 220
emotional intelligence assessment tools, 136
endorsements. *See* references; skills and endorsements, in LinkedIn profile
entry-level to mid-level social work
about, 28–29
cover letter samples, 209–210, 212, 215
resume samples, 182–188, 191–199, 201

experience highlights, in resumes, 73
See also community service, service learning, and volunteer experience
experienced social workers
cover letter samples, 208, 213–214
professional summary example, 72
resume samples, 189–190, 200
See also advanced social work skills
experiences, reflecting on, 34, 35
See also power words
expert witnesses, 150
expertise, demonstration of, 29–31
extrinsic values, 38, 40

F

facilitators, 150
field placements, 26–28
flexible spending accounts, 126
follow-ups
after interviews, 115–117
thank-you communication, 47, 152, 217, 218, 220
functional resumes, 68, 197–200
funding, grants, and awards, in CV, 79

G

generalist social work, 3–6, 71, 155–156

H

headers, resume, 69–70
headshots, 60–61
health insurance, 126
health savings accounts, 126
hiring bonus, 127
holiday time, 126
honors, in CV, 79

I

image. *See* professional brand, creation of
Indeed.com, 98
informational interviews, 46–47, 99, 122, 218
international social work, 13–15, 97, 160–161
internships. *See* volunteering, temporary work, and internships
interview attire, 98, 106–107
interview follow-up, 115–117
interview prep sheet, 115*t*
interview rehearsals, 107
interview tracking sheets, 115–116

interviewing, 105–115, 177–178
  See also informational interviews
intrinsic values, 38

J

job applications, 103–105
job boards, 98
job descriptions, matching skills to, 83*t*
job descriptions, sample, 5, 7, 11–12, 17–18
job fairs, 98
job offers
  dilemmas with, 129–131
  evaluating and negotiating, 119–131, 231–232
  sample letter of acceptance, 221
  sample offer letters, 124–125
job postings, 45–46
  See also job descriptions, sample
job search key words, 93–95
job search materials, 63–90
job search plan
  interview follow-up, 115–117
  interviewing, 105–115
  job applications, 103–105
  opportunities, finding, 92–103
job search spreadsheets, 104*t*
job titles
  as key words, 94
  power words and, 59
  samples, 4, 6, 9–10, 13, 15, 16

K

Karls, J., 2
key words, for job search, 93–95
knowledge, in self-assessments, 36, 38
knowledge areas and skills
  administration/development jobs, 9
  clinical social work jobs, 6–7
  community organizing jobs, 10
  comprehensive list of, 155–167
  generalist social work jobs, 3, 4
  international social work jobs, 14
  as key words, 94
  macro social work jobs, 9, 10
  nontraditional social work jobs, 16–17
  policy/evaluation/research jobs, 10

L

leadership roles, in resumes, 75
leadership skills, 134–138
learning opportunities. *See* continuing education; professional development

legacy mapping, 133–153
letters
  acceptance, 221
  cover, 80–82, 84, 208–215
  job offer, 124–125
  recommendation, 223
  See also email samples; thank-you communication
liability/malpractice insurance, 127
licensure
  clinical social work, 8
  generalist social work, 4
  international social work, 14
  macro social work, 12
  negotiating payment of, 127
  nontraditional social work, 18
  See also professional licenses, certifications, and affiliations
life insurance, 126
limitations or weakness, addressing, 107, 108–109
LinkedIn connections, 116, 145, 146, 222
LinkedIn profile, 86–89
Luna, J., 22

M

macro social work
  about, 3, 8–13
  continuing education, 144–145
  cover letters, 210
  job search key words, 94
  job search tips, 96–97
  knowledge areas and skills, 9, 10, 158–160
  professional summary examples, 71
  sample job title, 9–10
  sample resumes, 183–186, 189–190, 194–195, 198–199, 201
  specific interview questions, 111
  writing skills, 148
malpractice insurance, 127
marketing. *See* job search materials; professional brand, creation of
Marks, A., 22
medical social worker job description, 5
memberships. *See* board memberships; professional associations
mentorships, 152–153
mezzo practice, about, 3
micro practice, about, 3
  See also generalist social work
micro practice sample resumes, 191, 196
mid-level social work. *See* entry-level to mid-level social work

mileage reimbursement, 127
MSW versus BSW, 25

N

NASW *Code of Ethics*, 2, 25, 27
NASW Social Work Pioneers, 30, 151
National Association of Colleges and Employers (NACE), 121
negotiations. *See* job offers, evaluating and negotiating
net salary, 124
networking, 46–47, 99–103, 104, 116
    See also LinkedIn connections; LinkedIn profile
networking spreadsheets, 102t
nontraditional social work
    about, 15–19
    cover letters, 215
    job search tips, 97–98
    knowledge areas and skills, 16–17, 161–162
    sample job descriptions, 17–18
    sample job title, 16
    sample resume, 185–186

O

O'Keefe, M., 2
onboarding, 130–131
organizational fit, evaluating, 120, 225–226

P

paid time off, 126
paraprofessional social work, 26–28
PDCSW. *See* Professional Development Cycle of Social Workers (PDCSW)
performance evaluation, annual, 139, 143
personal days, 126
person-in-environment framework, 2
policy/evaluation/research jobs, 10
power words, 59–60, 144
practice and clinical experience, in CV, 78–79
preparation, 64–65
    See also interview rehearsals; questions and answers, for interviews
presentations and publications, 75, 79, 147–148, 152
priorities. *See* values and priorities, in self-assessments
professional associations, 27, 145
professional brand, creation of, 51–62
    See also job search materials
professional brand, reassessment of, 138–139, 140–142
professional contributions, 149–150, 151
    See also presentations and publications
professional development, 75, 127
    See also continuing education
Professional Development Cycle of Social Workers (PDCSW), 22–31, 44, 135, 169–175
professional headshots, 60–61
professional licenses, certifications, and affiliations, 73–74
professional summaries, in resumes, 71–72
    See also bio statements
professorships, 149
publications. *See* presentations and publications; writing skills
purpose, for bio statements, 57

Q

questions and answers, for interviews, 105–106, 108–110, 111–112, 177–178

R

raises, 130
recommendation letters, 223
recruiters, 98, 104–105
references, 85–86, 116, 219
    See also recommendation letters
relocation costs, 127
research, of organizations, 106
    See also informational interviews; work culture, evaluating
research experience and interests. *See* policy/evaluation/research jobs; teaching and research experience and interests, in CV
researching career options, 45–48
resumes
    content and formatting, 66–69
    headers, 69–70
    informational interviews and, 47
    interviews and, 114
    samples, 182–201
    sections and suggested headings, 69–76
retirement plans, 126
reverse chronological resumes, 68

S

salary discussions, 114, 115
    See also compensation, evaluating

salary history, 123
salary negotiation lingo, 123–124
salary requirements, 123
salary research, 122–123
school social worker networking strategies, 100–101
scopes of practice, 3
second interviews, 107
self-assessments, 33–49
   See also annual performance evaluation; knowledge areas and skills
Seneca, 65
service learning. *See* community service, service learning, and volunteer experience
sick/personal days, 126
skills and abilities, in self-assessments, 34, 35–36, 37
   See also knowledge areas and skills; power words
skills and endorsements, in LinkedIn profile, 88–89
social media presence, 86–89, 145–147
   See also LinkedIn connections; LinkedIn profile
social work education, 25–26, 150
social work educators, 149
Social Workers' Desk Reference (Karls & O'Keefe), 2
social work–specific knowledge and skills, 36, 38
   See also knowledge areas and skills
social work–specific values, 40–41
STAR method, 112–113
start date, negotiating, 127
subject matter expert, 30–31
supervisors, defining ideal, 41, 43

T

take-home pay, 124
targeted resumes. *See* combination (or targeted) resumes
teaching and research experience and interests, in CV, 77, 78
temporary work. *See* volunteering, temporary work, and internships
thank-you communication, 47, 116, 152, 217, 218, 220
themes and patterns. *See* bio statements; career-defining moments
thought leaders, 136–137
360-degree assessment, 136
trainers, 150
transferable skills, 34, 35–36, 162–165
tuition reimbursement, 127

U

university service. *See* community, professional, and university service, in CV

V

vacation, planned, 127
vacation time, 126
values, social work–specific, 40–41
values and priorities, in self-assessments, 38, 40, 42
volunteer experience. *See* community service, service learning, and volunteer experience
volunteering, temporary work, and internships, 98

W

weaknesses. *See* limitations or weakness, addressing
work culture, evaluating, 120, 225–226
work experience. *See* experience highlights, in resumes
work qualities, in self-assessments, 38, 39–40
writing skills, 89, 148–149
   See also blogs; presentations and publications

Y

youth employment project officer job description, 15

Acknowledgments

For nearly two decades, we have worked collaboratively and met annually at the conference of the Consortium of Career Development in Social Work Education (CCDSWE). It was at this conference, which is uniquely tailored toward career services professionals in social work education, that we had the opportunity to talk shop about the joys and challenges of providing career assistance to students and alumni. Here we met Carol Nesslein Doelling, then director of career services at the Brown School of Social Work, Washington University in St. Louis, and author of *Social Work Career Development: A Handbook for Job Hunting and Career Planning* (2nd edition, NASW Press). Carol was the first career development professional to work with students in a university-based social work career services program. For many of us new to this field, this book was our foundation of knowledge in launching career services for social workers. It has been over 15 years since the publication of the second edition of her book, and there have been many new developments in the field of social work, the job search, and the job market. When we decided to write this book, we contacted Carol about our idea, and she generously offered support and encouragement. Her professional wisdom provided the foundation for many of our career service offices and was an inspiration for this book. Our interactions with her were invaluable in our own professional development.

Working for decades in career services for social work students has been a uniquely fulfilling experience. We did not anticipate dedicating our careers to this field, but we are grateful for the opportunity to make a difference in the lives of thousands of social work professionals. This would not have been possible without the camaraderie of our professional colleagues from the CCDSWE. Many of the strategies, tips, and examples shared in this book are a testament to the collective wisdom and collaboration of our colleagues in the consortium.

We collectively extend our deepest gratitude to the support and encouragement provided by our home institutions: Boston College School of Social Work; Steve Hicks School of Social Work, University of Texas at Austin; and the University of Michigan School of Social Work, including special thanks to Dr. Luis Zayas, whose support and encouragement were pivotal to the launch of this project's success. We are also grateful for the help of Dr. Sam Allan, Marian Concepcion, Mackenzie

Denofio, and Betsy Williams, who contributed to the editing and valuable student prospective that strengthened the book. Andi Armstrong and Jonathan Sherchand kept us on track and helped to facilitate our weekly meetings amid our challenging schedules across various time zones. We are also indebted to the support of our coworkers and social work colleagues who provided moral support, advice, and reassurance throughout the process.

Cowriting a book is harder and took longer than we had imagined. We learned the strengths each of us brought to the process. Combining our different writing styles, personalities, and experiences created a book that speaks to a broader range of readers than any one of us could reach individually. Through this process, we each grew professionally and personally. A team of people provided helpful hints, encouragement, expertise, opinions, and time, and allowed us to persevere. A key member of this team was Rachel Meyers, acquisitions editor at NASW Press, who was committed, encouraging, insightful, dedicated, and motivating.

CINDY SNELL

I am so grateful for the experience of cowriting this book. Jennifer Luna was the originator of the idea, and I feel honored to have been invited to be a coauthor. Integrating our shared life and professional experience into the content of this book was what made it most rewarding for me both personally and professionally. I gained so much in going through the process of articulating my thoughts in a way that was most helpful to the reader, and learning from the feedback from Rachel and my coauthors, students, and family. A heartfelt thanks to my family of Martin, Alex, and Owen—my cheerleaders, readers, and editors.

JENNIFER LUNA

The late Andrew T. Marks profoundly shaped my career and served as the catalyst for the creation of this book. Throughout the late 1990s, as we contemplated the state of social work career development, we realized the absence of a clear career trajectory for professionals in our field. However, from these discussions emerged the Professional Development Cycle of Social Workers (PDCSW). Andrew's intellect, humor, and dedication to the advancement of social work professionals left an indelible mark on countless individuals, including me. Even today, I encounter social workers whose paths were influenced by Andrew's insight and passion. I am eternally grateful for his leadership in establishing the PDCSW and for inspiring the writing of this book.

The success of this book is largely attributable to the expertise, skills, and dedication of my coauthors, Cindy Snell and Michelle Woods. Cindy's strong career development knowledge, outstanding organizational abilities, and efficient management ensured we maintained momentum throughout the project. Meanwhile, Michelle's recognized expertise in social work, coupled with her acumen in macro social work and salary negotiation, has significantly contributed to the depth and quality of our work. Our deep friendship and mutual respect have been the foundation on which the book was written. I am profoundly grateful for their contributions and their friendship, which made this project as rewarding as its completion.

To my sons, Eli, Elvis, and James Iduñate, I extend my heartfelt acknowledgment. Your curiosity, keen intelligence, and sharp wit are a constant source of inspiration in my life. It is your spirit that sparks my ambition and sustained my passion for writing. Finally, I would like to thank my friend and colleague Liz Nowicki for her expertise in social work professional development, friendship, and boundless encouragement. Thank you all for lighting up my world and for giving me a multitude of reasons to strive for excellence.

MICHELLE WOODS

When Tim Colenback hired me at the University of Michigan years ago, I never would have dreamed that I would work in career services, let alone contribute to a book on the subject. Thank you for being a champion, mentor, and most of all, great friend. I cannot thank my other University of Michigan family enough for their encouragement, love, and laughter—Dr. Lorraine Gutierrez, Erin Zimmer, Betsy Williams, and Lauren Davis. Go Blue! Jennifer and Cindy are the best colleagues—smart, gracious, witty, and extremely patient with first-time writers like me. With gratitude and love to Delores, Vanessa, Arnetta, Diane, Michael, and Shawn—my family and source of support through it all. Thank you to the many students who shared their career aspirations and journey with us! You are indeed the next generation of change agents!

About the Authors

Jennifer Luna, MSSW, is a passionate and accomplished social work career coach, administrator, author, speaker, and trainer. She is the owner of Jennifer Luna Consulting, LLC, and serves as the program coordinator for the Network for Social Work Management. She has over 25 years of experience in presenting and training on career development topics specific to the profession of social work at the local, state, and national levels. She is also a certified Gallup CliftonStrengths coach and a certified John C. Maxwell coach, teacher, trainer, and speaker, helping social workers identify and leverage their strengths, skills, and leadership potential.

As the former director of the DiNitto Center for Career Services at University of Texas at Austin School of Social Work, she founded and oversaw the daily operations of the first named social work career center in the country. She collaborates with other schools of social work, the National Association of Social Workers, and the Council on Social Work Education on career development issues, including licensure, labor market, and professional identity. She also writes a column for *The New Social Worker* magazine and hosts a YouTube series called *Conversations on Social Work Careers*. She has published and spoken on topics such as personal branding, academic job search, and resiliency. Jennifer's mission is to empower social workers to achieve their career goals and make a positive impact in the world.

Cindy Snell, MEd, is the director of career services and alumni relations at the Boston College School of Social Work (BCSSW), providing strategic leadership and direction for the past two decades. She has applied her strong creativity, resourcefulness, and program management skills to establish comprehensive career services offices for graduate students and alumni at BCSSW and previously at the Heller School for Social Policy and Management at Brandeis University. As a member of a one-person office, she has a strong understanding of all aspects of the career development process and the importance of forging collaborative relationships with key stakeholders inside the university and with outside constituencies such as alumni and employers. Cindy has reveled in the opportunity to support a diverse group of students and alumni committed to careers in social justice. With a long-standing commitment to higher education and student and alumni services, Cindy continues to be inspired by supporting others in reaching their goals.

Michelle Woods, LMSW Clinical and Macro Practice, is the director of career services at the University of Michigan School of Social Work. She has over 30 years of social work experience. She oversees an office that provides professional development for students and alumni, recruitment services for employees, and the collection of alumni employment data for the school. She completed her BA in political science and her MSW at the University of Michigan. For several years, she worked for the Michigan Department of Human Services in child welfare and adult services before returning to the University of Michigan School of Social Work Office of Student Services. As a part of the Office of Student Services, she assisted with the recruitment, admission, and financial aid distribution for MSW students. She is a member of the Career Development in Social Work Education Group and the National Association of Social Workers and served as past president of the Huron Valley Association of Black Social Workers. Her professional interests include career advising for students, resume and cover letter writing, and advocating for better salaries for social work graduates.